American Talmud

SUNY series in Modern Jewish Literature and Culture

Sarah Blacher Cohen, editor

American Talmud

The Cultural Work of Jewish American Fiction

Ezra Cappell

State University
of New York
Press

Published by
State University of New York Press, Albany

© 2007 State University of New York

All rights reserved

Printed in the United States of America

Cover art: Orah, 1987, acrylic on wood, 79 3/4 x 23 in., by Tobi Kahn.

An early version of chapter 2 was published in *Modern Jewish Studies*. I am grateful to the editor, Professor Joseph Landis, for granting me permission to reproduce this article. Sections of chapters 4 and 5 appeared in *Holocaust Literature*. I thank the editors for granting me permission to reproduce this material.

For information, address State University of New York Press,
194 Washington Avenue, Suite 305, Albany, NY 12210-2384

Production by Susan Geraghty
Marketing by Fran Keneston

Library of Congress Cataloging-in-Publication Data

Cappell, Ezra, 1971–
   American talmud : the cultural work of Jewish American fiction / Ezra Cappell.
      p. cm. — (SUNY series on modern Jewish literature and culture)
   Includes bibliographical references and index.
   ISBN-13: 978-0-7914-7123-4 (hardcover : alk. paper)
   ISBN-13: 978-0-7914-7124-1 (pbk. : alk. paper)
   1. American fiction—Jewish authors—History and criticism. 2. Jewish fiction—United States—History and criticism. 3. American fiction—20th century—History and criticism. 4. Jews—United States—Intellectual life. I. Title.

PS153.J4C37 2006
813'.5093896—dc22

                                                                              2006023732

10   9   8   7   6   5   4   3   2   1

To my wife, Ilisa, who always believes.

To the memory of Charles Cappell:
Zionist, survivor, grandfather.

CONTENTS

ACKNOWLEDGMENTS

It is a great pleasure to acknowledge my family, friends, and colleagues who have supported me throughout the writing of this book. I would especially like to thank David Ruiter, Director of Literature at the University of Texas at El Paso, who tirelessly read numerous drafts of this book. His friendship, insight, and generosity inspire all who are fortunate enough to know him. I would also like to acknowledge the wisdom and friendship of Cyrus Patell, who has encouraged and guided me for many years. A very special thanks goes out to Sarah Blacher Cohen who has been a source of support and laughter throughout the writing of this book. Sarah is the perfect embodiment of her biblical namesake: "God has brought me laughter; everyone who hears will laugh with me" (Genesis 21.6).

I am grateful to my colleagues in the Department of English at the University of Texas at El Paso and to Howard Daudistel, Dean of the College of Liberal Arts at the University of Texas at El Paso, for their encouragement and support. I was fortunate to have the opportunity to discuss with them many aspects of this book. I would like to thank Tony Stafford and Evelyn Posey, the former and current chair of the Department of English at the University of Texas at El Paso, who have created a fertile environment for scholarship and who offered me their generosity and support in the writing of this book. I would like to thank Morris Dickstein, the ultimate "Double Agent": scholar and *mentch*. Morris's wisdom has been guiding me since the moment I first picked up *Gates of Eden*. Alan Berger, theologian and friend, whose support I could not do without. Mark Mirsky whose brilliance and affection encourages all my writing.

A special thanks goes to Cynthia Ozick my fellow late-night discussant on Jewish American fiction; her work inspires this book. I would also like to thank the following people: Rebecca Goldstein for her generosity in granting me an interview; Thane Rosenbaum for his post-Holocaust trilogy and whose warmth and concern have meant so much to me throughout this project. Most especially I owe a debt of gratitude to all my current and former students at New York University, City College, and the University of Texas at El Paso whom (to paraphrase Bernard Malamud) I have hopefully taught to teach me, and from whom I have benefited enormously.

I wish to thank Susan Blond for her generous hospitality and enthusiastic support of this book. Of the many friends who have helped me during the writing of this book, I would especially like to mention Natalie Stiene; I am grateful for her insightful comments, wisdom, and thorough reading of the manuscript.

I would like to thank Tobi Kahn and Nessa Rapoport for many wonderful *shabbos* meals and discussions on art, literature, and Judaism. I am also grateful to Tobi Kahn for granting me permission to reproduce "Orah," on the cover of this book. "Orah," as both a work of art and a fully-functioning ritual object (a portable Torah ark), is the perfect representation of *American Talmud*. Kahn has taken an ancient Jewish object and recreated it within a contemporary Jewish American context.

I am grateful to all my family and friends for their unceasing support. My father Raoul Cappell, my mother Francine Cappell, my grandfather Rabbi Nathan Taragin, my first Talmud and Bible rebbe, and my grandmother Beatrice Taragin have always been my role models in Jewish dedication and perseverance. I would also like to recall the memory of my grandparents Charles and Paula Cappell—their history has motivated my work in Jewish American literature. I would like to thank my family members: Selena, Yosef, Arielle, Yoni, Rachel, and Danit; Shani, Adam, and Hannah; Jimmy, Linh, Olivia, and Isabella; Marvin, Gail, and Adam. I would (even) like to thank Jeffrey Rubenstein. His brilliant writing on Talmudic stories informs each chapter of this book.

I would like to thank James Peltz and the entire staff at SUNY press for their unwavering support and encouragement throughout the writing of this book.

Last, I would like to thank my wife, Ilisa; this book is dedicated to her.

INTRODUCTION

You don't have to be Jewish to be a compulsive interpreter, but, of course, it helps.

—Harold Bloom

PARADISE REGAINED?

The Babylonian Talmud[1] contains two distinct parts: *Halacha and Aggadah*. *Halacha* refers to any legal issues and their discussion, while *Aggadah* comprises anything outside the legal sphere. *Aggadah* encompasses roughly one quarter of the Talmud as a whole and generally consists of stories and homilies, advice on ethics, biographies of wise men, and *midrashim* or interpretations of important, as well as confusing and troubling, biblical passages. The following *aggadic* passage, taken from Tractate *Menachot*, is a typical example of the genre:

> Rabbi Judah said in the name of Rab: When Moses ascended on high (to receive the Torah) he found the Holy One, blessed be He, engaged in affixing *taggin* (crown-like flourishes) to the letters. Moses said: "Lord of the Universe, who stays Thy hand?" He replied: "There will arise a man at the end of many generations Akiba ben Joseph by name, who will expound, upon each little letter, heaps and heaps of the laws." "Lord of the Universe," said Moses, "permit me to see him." He replied: "Turn thee around."
>
> Moses went (into the academy of Rabbi Akiba) and sat down behind eight rows of Akiba's disciples). Not being able to follow their arguments he was ill at ease, but when they came to a certain subject and the disciples said to the master "Whence do you know it?" and the latter replied, "It is a law given to Moses at Sinai," he was comforted. (Talmud Bavli: *Menahot* 29b)

This *aggadic* short story[2] might seem peculiar to those not regularly engaged in the study of the Talmud. Although the Talmud is often perceived as being a rigid book comprised of legal maneuverings designed

1

to codify the intricate Mosaic laws, it might more accurately be thought of as a blueprint for modern and postmodern fictional play. Far from being a dry legal document, the Babylonian Talmud, particularly its *aggadic* sections, revels in the fantastical and the ambiguous. Not merely capable of tolerating dissent, the Talmud (once again, especially its *aggadic* sections) honors and celebrates a difference of opinion; time and again the Talmud honors radical rethinking, even about its foundational concepts. In the previous passage, for example, the Talmud tells a seemingly heretical story in which Moses, the greatest leader of the Jewish people, cannot follow the basic logic of even a simple Talmudic argument.

This foregoing *aggadic* passage reveals the storytelling aspects, the cultural work performed by the Babylonian Talmud: through its literary passages the Talmud reinterprets the Torah anew for its own generation. This open-endedness, this celebration of multiple perspectives, is not only a characteristic of the Babylonian Talmud; it is also a hallmark of twentieth-century and contemporary Jewish American fiction. There are so many analogues between the two that Jewish American fiction writers embracing modern and postmodern life are often mistakenly perceived as radically breaking with their traditional past. Yet they are one more link in the great chain of rabbinic thought conveyed to us through the centuries as a means of interpretation designed to ensure that scripture will remain vital and new for each generation.

By arguing that twentieth- and twenty-first-century Jewish American fiction writers have been codifying a new Talmud, an American Talmud, I am making a value judgment: I am forcefully suggesting that the literary production of Jews in America be seen as one more stage of rabbinic commentary on the scriptural inheritance of the Jewish people. The defining hallmark of rabbinic literature is its ongoing interpretation of history. Yosef Hayim Yerushalmi notes that the rabbis "did not set out to write a history of the biblical period; they already possessed that. Instead they were engrossed in an ongoing exploration of the meaning of the history bequeathed to them, striving to interpret it in living terms for their own and future generations" (*Zakhor* 20). Although Yerushalmi is speaking about the redactors of the Talmud, I cannot think of a more exact definition for the role of Jewish American fiction writers and the work they have produced.

Yet before we get carried away with simplistic comparisons between rabbinic thought patterns and Jewish American literature, there are those who would surely say that while the two literary modes share certain characteristics which structure their flights of fancy (all writing must share something in common), the two part company over a crucial difference. Anyone schooled in even the basics of Talmudic argument (surely the thirteen years of Talmud lectures I endured in Yeshiva are not necessary to make this point) would say that Jewish American fiction and rabbinic literature diverge over the centering element of all rabbinic imaginative writing: scripture. Rabbinic *aggadah* and storytelling always return to the dominant force of scriptural text. It is the Old Testament that so comforted Moses in the *aggadic* Talmudic passage quoted above. To paraphrase Robert Frost: without scripture, *aggadic* literature might be parallel to writing free verse: "playing tennis with the net down."

But this line of thought begs the question of just how free form is Jewish American literature? Do Jewish American writers also in fact have a holy scripture that they return to after each new variation on fictional form? Furthermore, what would Jewish American fiction writers place in their American Holy Ark: *Goodbye Columbus, The Rise of David Levinsky, Call It Sleep?*

The very belatedness of Jewish American writers forces them to return time and again, whether consciously or not, to a centering text in their work, and yes, they too, much like the rabbinic writers of old, are centered by scripture. Jewish American writers also, perhaps less slavishly than their Babylonian counterparts, often refer to scripture, sometimes doing so without full awareness of being under scriptural sway. I do not mean to suggest that Jewish American writers are born with an innate feel for Jewish texts, but the writers I have chosen to discuss in this book all contribute to what I would call an *American Talmud.* Each writer in this study responds to the belatedness of being a twentieth- or twenty-first-century Jew with his or her particular literary style, yet however far they may stray from Jewish tradition, these writers often return to the centering force of Judaism: scripture and the Holy Books. Although there are numerous writers who might meaningfully contribute toward the formation of an American Talmud—Philip Roth and Cynthia Ozick immediately spring to mind— I have chosen the writers studied in this book not as an exclusive set, but as representative of a particularly diverse and interconnected sample of Jewish American fiction writing. Henry Roth's gloss on Lurianic Kabbalah, Bernard Malamud's attempt at Holocaust representation, Saul Bellow's ongoing engagement with Jewish history and memory (whose work might collectively be viewed as a late twentieth-century *midrash*), Allegra Goodman's satire on the misuse of the Haggadah in contemporary Passover services, Thane Rosenbaum's critique of contemporary Jewish ritual, Rebecca Goldstein's formulation of an ethical aesthetic for Holocaust representation: all these writers are creating a new chapter to Jewish tradition and postrabbinic thought. In a postmodern, postfaith world, these writers are no longer attempting to "Justify the ways of (an increasingly absent) God to man." What they are attempting through their strong agonistic interpretive and imaginative powers, is in the words of Harold Bloom, to "open up the Bible to [their] own suffering" (*Zakhor* xxiii). In doing so they recreate, in postwar America, the vital link to a covenantal relationship, a relationship brutally damaged in the Holocaust, while they concurrently interpret Jewish history in vivid fictional color for their own and for future generations. Indeed, if Yerushalmi insists that for nineteenth-century Jews "history becomes what it had never been before—the faith of fallen Jews" (86), then I would maintain that literature, or more specifically Jewish American fiction, becomes the faith for fallen contemporary Jews searching for an artistic validation by which to understand and account for the horrific history of the twentieth century.

When thinking of the numerous parallels between Jewish American fiction and traditional Jewish texts and culture, it is important to be reminded of Rabbi Adin Steinsalz's remarks on the Babylonian Talmud: "Although its main objective is to interpret and comment on a book of law, it is, simultaneously, a work of art that goes beyond legislation and its practical application. And although the Talmud is, to this day, the primary source of Jewish law, it cannot be cited as an authority for purposes of ruling" (4). Perhaps we owe the Talmud's continued relevance for Jews in America as much to its entertainment value, as for its legal and religious purposes. *Daf yomi* (lit: a page a day) classes during which a double-sided page of Talmud is discussed in about an hour, usually after morning prayers, have proliferated across America. The *daf yomi* format has kept pace with modern and postmodern technological advancements. At first, lectures were available on audiotape; now, however, people follow Talmud classes on CD-Rom, over the internet, or most conveniently on special iPods called DafPods. To underscore the popularity of this practice, there is even a dedicated *daf yomi* car on the Long Island Rail Road for commuters to join in with on their way to work in Manhattan. The recent *siyum hashas*, a party celebrating the completion of the entire 2,711 double-sided pages of the Talmud, a process which takes seven-and-a-half years to complete, drew twenty thousand people to a sold-out Madison Square Garden.[3] Additionally, more than one hundred thousand people participated in concurrent parties held across North America, arguably the largest single book party in American literary history.

This renaissance or return to traditional Jewish texts and modes of study has much relevance to *American Talmud*. This is especially true when we consider the primary "objectives" of Jewish American fiction, which while not being didactic, perhaps inadvertently become a primary centering force in the lives of American Jews and has assumed a larger role in the return to traditional Jewish identification in America than has previously been realized.[4]

ANXIOUS INTERPRETERS

Harold Bloom has said that "You don't have to be Jewish to be a compulsive interpreter, but, of course, it helps" (*Zakhor* xxiii). This obviously applies to Bloom himself, as much as it attaches to the only two modern writers he believes write a genuinely "Jewish" literature: Freud and Kafka. Bloom goes on to suggest that what Jewish writing attempts to interpret is the Bible, or more specifically all Jewish literature worthy of the moniker implicitly asks the difficult question, "How to open the Bible to one's own suffering?" (xxiii).

Bloom's negative formulation would seem to fit rather well with my conception of a theological Jewish literature. Despite the seemingly limited role the Bible and biblical themes would have within the wider scope of twentieth-century literature written in America, biblical themes do in fact animate much of *Jewish* American fiction, certainly in the Bloomian sense of opening the Bible to one's own personal afflictions. As Bloom suggests "What holds together modern Jewish writing, whether it be in Hebrew or Yiddish, in German or in American English, is the Jewish Bible" (xxv).

Traditionally the term "Jewish writing" referred to liturgical or holy books, not works of entertainment or diversion, what we might consider as fiction writing. In fact, despite the prevalent belief to the contrary, Jews have traditionally not been interested in writing history either. To show the low esteem that medieval Jewry had for historical works, Yosef Hayim Yerushalmi quotes the preface to the 1554 edition of *Dibrey ha-yamim*, to which the following lines were appended:

When the author's nephew, Zerahiah Halevi,
saw the glory of this book, and the nectar of its honeycombed words,
the Lord lifted his spirit and he began to speak.
So he opened his mouth with song and hymn, and declared:
Let anyone who delights in a time that was before ours
take this chronicle and read it when his sleep wanders. (67)

In his discussion of this passage Yerushalmi makes obvious
Zehariah's allusion to the Book of Esther in which King Ahashveros's
book of days is brought to him when "his sleep wanders" (67). We may
conclude that by as late a date as 1554, historical works were still
largely considered *bitul z'man*, a waste of valuable time which could
instead be devoted to studying the sacred works of the Torah. Had the
rabbis been aware of novels, how much greater a waste of time might
they have found fictional works, books whose raison d'etre is for pure
entertainment without any didactic purpose at all?

A highly unlikely source, Cynthia Ozick, recently makes just such
a case. Given that Ozick is one of the most prominent and highly
regarded Jewish American novelists, her recent characterization of the
Jewish American novel as a specious concept would seem shocking. Yet
when one considers Ozick's long-stated antipathy to being labeled a
Jewish American writer, her dismissal of Jewish American writing
seems less a radical departure and more a reworking of her previous
claims that writers must be unfettered in their creation of art. In a
splashy article on the front page of the Arts section titled "What's a
Jewish Book?" *The Forward* commissioned responses from two leading
Jewish American intellectuals to argue the case. Ozick's response
appeared side by side with noted Yiddishist Ruth Wisse's article on the
same subject. Ozick begins: "What is a Jewish book? A narrow definition—but also conceptually the widest—would chiefly include the
Torah and the Talmud (the Hebrew Bible and the other texts that
strive to un-riddle the Job-like vagaries of the human heart while urging it toward the moral life" (B1). Fair enough. But in the very next
paragraph Ozick begins to show her hand: "A Jewish book is didactic.
It is dedicated to the promotion of virtue attained through study" (B1).
Once Ozick has set up her straw-man definition of a Jewish book, it is
not much of a reach toward her dismissal of the very concept of a Jewish American novel. What sound-minded reader would read a novel
for didactic purposes? Or as Ozick says: "If a novel's salient aim is
virtue, I want to throw it against the wall" (B1). Perhaps Oscar Wilde

put it best in his preface to *The Picture of Dorian Gray*: "The moral life of man forms part of the subject-matter of the artist, but the morality of art consists in the perfect use of an imperfect medium. No artist desires to prove anything" (3).

Similarly, answering the same question about just what is Jewish American literature, Ruth Wisse bitterly complains about the paucity of Jewish content within contemporary Jewish American novels. Wisse traces this "insufficiency" not necessarily to the novelist (although that has previously often been the problem) but to the Jewish American public who are largely ignorant of things Jewish. Wisse writes: "Our present anxiety about Jewish literature derives not from a slump in contemporary Jewish writing but from the insufficiencies of American Jewish life" (B1).

To whom is the "our" in the above passage referring: Wisse and Ozick, or other Jewish American literary critics? I happen to be optimistic about the current Jewish American literary scene. Not only do I completely disagree with Wisse's "anxiety" about Jewish American literature, but Ozick's and Wisse's remarks beg the question of whether or not the only two alternatives for Jewish literature are either as a didactic guide for the promotion of moral virtue or as a license to indulge in the demonic freedom of a Norman Mailer novel. Are novels ever only one extreme or the other? Taking this logic one step further, do Ozick's own novels pass her literary litmus test? If they do not, might we consider, for example, *The Messiah of Stockholm* and *Levitation*, as well as her latest *Heir to the Glimmering World* quintessentially Jewish in nature?

Momentarily putting aside Ozick's and Wisse's complaints, and despite the *halachic* (Jewish law) proscription of *bitul z'man or bitul torah*, I believe that, far from being a waste of time otherwise devoted to Torah study, the fiction discussed in this study serves a cultural purpose similar to the role provided by ancient holy texts, and would thus not necessarily be dismissed by the rabbis and redactors of the Talmud. From my literary perspective, the reading of Jewish novels might be seen as an act of Jewish renewal, and it deserves to be analyzed in light of the obvious (and well-documented) vitality of postwar Jewish life in America.

ENLIGHTENED JEWISH AMERICAN WRITERS?

More than ten years ago Mark Shechner could confidently proclaim that Jewish American literature may only be understood in light of its internal history, a history Shechner proclaims has a dialectical framework and which can be traced back to the *Haskalah* (the Enlightenment that swept through Eastern Europe in the eighteenth century). Shechner sees all of Jewish American literature as an extension of the *Haskalah*'s challenge to a traditional mode of life, the *halachah*, or Jewish law. All of Jewish American fiction may be placed beneath Shechner's rubric of "secular fiction, story-telling without liturgical intent" (84).

It is precisely the dissolution of a coherent Jewish community which is the hallmark of the *Haskalah*, an age Shechner maintains we are still within. Shechner argues: "the one enduring subject of all Jewish writing from Mendele to Philip Roth has been the end of Judea as a unified moral community" (85). Shechner suggests that if the hallmark of pre-Enlightenment Jewish literature was communal and liturgical in nature, Jewish literature in America bears the marks of Emersonian individualism and self-fulfillment—precisely the antithesis of a liturgical literature.[5]

Is Shechner's argument still relevant today? Is the Enlightenment the *mesorah* (lit: the tradition) that Jewish writers have inherited from the European masters Sholem Aleichem, Mendele Mocher Seforim, and I. L. Peretz? Did Bruno Schulz, sitting alone in his decrepit Drogobych studio, gain inspiration from the Enlightenment? Can Isaac Babel's unique contribution to world literature be reduced to a *drash* (sermon) upon Emersonian individualism? Or, in vastly different and idiosyncratic ways, have both writers (Babel and Schulz) returned to the older and more stable tradition encoded in Jewish texts, the Babylonian Talmud, and Scripture? Babel and Schulz are the progenitors of genuine Jewish American literature in America; they have indelibly stamped their style onto contemporary Jewish American literature even more so than have I. L. Peretz and Shalom Aleichem (Tevya notwithstanding).[6]

THE HISTORICAL JEWISH RESPONSE TO TRAGEDY

In the aftermath of assimilation, by the late 1960s many of America's foremost literary critics had predicted the demise of Jewish literature. Famously, Irving Howe spoke of an attenuating of material due to the loss of Yiddish in America. What Howe, Leslie Fiedler, and other literary critics failed to account for in their formulations was the traditional Jewish literary response to tragedy. Had these critics been schooled in Jewish foundational texts—biblical, Talmudic, Kabbalistic—they would never have made their dire predictions. If Howe had understood the vast Jewish literary tradition, instead of introducing his collection, *Jewish-American Stories*, in 1977 with a dour obituary, he might have celebrated the obvious renewal of Jewish literature in America, a renewal that corresponded to a newfound Jewish identification in the diaspora after the Yom Kippur War of 1973. These critics would have laced their commentaries with pointed questions for what would become a post-Holocaust and postbiblical, but not necessarily postassimilational Jewish American literature at the close of the twentieth century. Much like Bloom, these literary critics might have asked "How does one accommodate a fresh and vital religious impulse, in a precarious and even catastrophic time of troubles, when one inherits a religious tradition already so rich and coherent that it allows very little room for fresh speculations?" (Bloom, *Kabbalah and Criticism* 33). While I disagree with Bloom's intuiting of a closed theological system, I agree with his mode of inquiry. Such a line of inquiry would have led Howe and Fiedler to understand along with Louis Ginzberg, who while introducing the Babylonian Talmud stated that "postbiblical Jewish Literature was predominately interpretive and commentative" (qtd. in Bloom 33), that far from ending Jewish literature, assimilation was just one more theme within the ongoing drama of Jewish literary production in America.

In other words, throughout Jewish history just when Jewish literature seems to have run its course, Jewish writers set about belatedly (to borrow a Bloomian concept) reinventing themselves. This becomes obvious to even a casual student of Jewish literature through the ages. After great turmoil, instead of laying down in darkness Jews have traditionally reinvented themselves through texts. This was true in Yavneh after the destruction of the Second Temple, it was true after the expulsion from Spain in the Middle Ages that led to Lurianic Kabbalah,[7] and it was true in Eastern Europe in the rise of Hasidism and Hasidic literature as a counterbalance to the ravages of the *Haskalah*, the Enlightenment. It is no less true in a post-Holocaust (and postassimilation) America. Jewish American writers have for some time now been contributing to a radical reworking and a radical reimagining of Jewish texts in the new world. In this study I hope to begin an explication of some of those belated, but no less strong, attempts at theological and imaginative refashioning.

JEWISH FICTION OVER JEWISH HISTORY?

In a postfaith world, contemporary Jewish American writing is essentially revisionist in nature and is, therefore, open to numerous interpretive modes and meanings. As a result of its inherent rootlessness and its perpetual state of exile and reinvention, Jewish literature might be perceived, I argue, as paradigmatic of the postmodern condition. In *Framing the Margins*, Phillip Brian Harper has noted "postmodernist theory suggests that our sense of the individual psyche as an integrated whole is a necessary misconception, and that various technological, economic, and philosophical developments of the late twentieth century demonstrate to us the psyche's fundamentally incoherent and fragmentary, or 'decentered' nature" (3). In his study Harper attempts to analyze "key sociopolitical factors" which have traditionally led to marginal groups being "decentered" in America (3). Harper critiques Frederic Jameson's juxtaposition of the historicist versus the poststructuralist "position." The historicist perspective assumes that a centered subject once existed, but as a result of the fragmented state of postmodern culture such a state no longer exists. By questioning the comparable effects a "decentered subject" has had on "socially marginalized and politically disenfranchised" (3) groups in postmodern America, Harper reveals the inadequacy of postmodern theory's accounting for marginalized cultures in America. While following through the logic of his argument, Harper makes a startling observation: "Granting the historicist claim for 'a once existing centered subject,' it must also be acknowledged that, for certain groups in the United States—people of African descent, for instance—the historical status of such a subjectivity is precisely that of *never having existed*, due to the historical distribution of the power to conceive of oneself as a centered, whole entity" (11). In *American Talmud* I make a similar argument concerning the historically transplanted and perpetually exiled state of the Jewish people. My argument helps account for the redactors of the Talmud having shied away from historical narratives in favor of *aggadic* "fictional" flights of fancy. Not only were the redactors of the Babylonian Talmud firm believers in the divinity of scripture—Bloom has noted they "kept the line clear between text and commentary" (53)—they were also master fictionists.

Much like their Kabbalistic predecessors, the postmodern audience for Jewish American literature, as well as postmodern and contemporary writers, privilege both text (scripture) and commentary (interpretation and invention). This is certainly true for Henry Roth, who, despite painful and debilitating rheumatoid arthritis continued working on his monumental last novel *Mercy of a Rude Stream*.[8] Furthermore, the case of Henry Roth highlights the continued relevance of commentary and interpretation by the diasporic Jewish community in America. If not for several astute Jewish American literary critics, Fiedler and Howe among them, Roth might have remained a forgotten writer. Had *Call It Sleep* not been reissued, what eventually became a sixty-year-long writer's block might be remembered as a lifelong silence; Roth probably would never have attempted his second masterpiece, the postrabbinic *Mercy of a Rude Stream*.[9] Thus, in contemporary Jewish American fiction, we can trace the traditional dialectic between text and commentary. The paradigmatic component of both biblical and Talmudic texts remains intact, flourishing on the shores of the new world.

In a post-Holocaust diasporic world, most American Jews would prefer the salve of myth to the reality of history. This preference is in keeping with generations of Jews who, in the aftermath of the Spanish inquisition and expulsion, turned in great numbers to mysticism and Lurianic Kabbalah for spiritual sustenance. But for postmodern Jews, myths will no longer suffice. To fill the void left by Jewish history, particularly in the aftermath of the destruction of European Jewry, what postmodern Jews need now are novels. As Yerushalmi states "it is hard to escape the feeling that the Jewish people after the Holocaust stands today at a juncture not without analogy to that of the generations following the cataclysm of the Spanish Expulsion" (99).

In *American Talmud* I hope to better understand the choice that American Jews have made time and again in the difficult years after the cataclysm of the Holocaust. Jewish American society has an insatiable need for novels, and not just any novels, but fictional works that purport to explain the historical situation Jews throughout the diaspora find themselves in, works that dramatize their bifurcated identities, split between their yearning for the stability of tradition while embracing the lures of modernity—identifying what it means to be a covenantal Jew in the postmodern world.

CANONICITY IN *AMERICAN TALMUD*

In ancient Greece, an author worthy of study was called *kanonikos*, "one who comes up to the standard" (Alter, *Canon and Creativity* 1). Since the modern era, canon formation has become a lens by which to study those who have traditionally been excluded from study, perhaps as a result of ethnicity or religious persuasion. Canon formation is also used as a critical device to reevaluate those chosen as having met the standard.

Werner Sollors speaks of the ways in which the concept of ethnicity, often perceived as an ancient construct, is in reality an invention of the modern period. Sollors says, "The invention of nationalisms and ethnicities must have been peaking in the eighteenth and nineteenth centuries, in a period of very dramatic changes" (*The Invention of Ethnicity* xi). Following Benedict Anderson's logic, Sollors says that in the wake of the French and American revolutions, bourgeois systems developed "which relied on the more *imaginary* ways of connectedness" (xii). Sollors goes on to say that chief among these imaginary means of connection was a national or ethnic literature (xii).

While I would not question the legitimacy of Sollors's argument in relation to most ethnic literatures produced in America, his formulation is misleading in relation to Jewish culture. In perpetual exile since ancient times, for thousands of years (and not just since the modern period), Jews have relied upon *imaginary* texts and words (literature) to sustain a national (ethnic) identity in the diaspora. What are the Babylonian Talmud, and the Bible, if not compilations of the stories that have been deemed central to the history of the Jewish people, the stories worth preserving?

According to Gershom Scholem the primary determining factor for a text's canonicity was precisely its inherent need for analysis and exegesis (Alter, *Canon and Creativity* 16). In a Jewish context, analysis refers to the systematic taking apart of a text, not for the semantic game of de(con)struction, but to translate the beauty of a text into a new critical medium.[10]

In attempting to codify an American Talmud, a canon of secular books which merit inclusion, I take my cues from the original canon: the Old Testament. Robert Alter has convincingly argued that the Hebrew Bible, by which he means *Tanach*,[11] didn't include a book merely because it represented a prevailing political movement; rather each book was chosen as a consequence of its literary excellence. According to Alter, the canon makers of the Hebrew Bible were conscious of the necessity of "dialectic elements of autocritique" (29). More importantly for our purposes, Alter believes that the canon makers were more interested in forging a national literature based upon high literary merit. Thus Alter maintains "that the bible in Hebrew speaks resonantly, even to the most pious readers, as a collection of great works of literature" (32). How else, Alter asks, to explain the inclusion of the carnivalesque *Book of Esther*, or the erotic *Song of Songs*?

Seen in the glaring light of contemporary biblical scholarship, my critical study of Jewish American fiction (in which I argue for a new American Talmud) seems less revolutionary and more "old school," following the very traditions it would seem, by its secularity, to violate or threaten to supplant. The writers I have chosen for my study all perform this "binocular vision": in an age which for most American Jews is postfaith based and assimilated, these writers are both highly literary and dedicated to helping shape a communal conception of a shared historical moment if not a shared history. Thus these postbiblical Jewish American writers included in this study constitute the latest link in the great chain of Jewish *mesorah* or tradition stretching back thousands of years.

MULTICULTURAL JEWISH?

Recently, several authors have asserted that a reductive multiculturalist ethos is to blame[12] for contemporary Jewish American literature's obscurity and seeming irrelevance to the late twentieth- and early twenty-first century burgeoning multicultural scene. For example, Andrew Furman has argued that Jewish American literature has been excluded from the "canon of victimization." Yet I believe the seeming irrelevance of Jewish American fiction is not the fault of multiculturalist theory, but rather is a consequence of contemporary Jewish American literary critics who often lack the cultural and linguistic tools to interpret diasporic Jewish culture in America.

In popular media Jewish American culture has often been reduced to a "Bagels and Lox," or Woody Allen *shtick* caricature (think of *Seinfeld* and *Friends*), a perspective which is not at all representative of the varied and vibrant contemporary Jewish American cultural scene. Yet there have not been many critics capable of interpreting and decoding that which is most authentically Jewish about Jewish American culture, particularly its literary production. There has yet to appear a group of critics who might counterbalance this misconception of Jewish American culture, perpetuated by popular culture. The end result has been that the vast majority of Jewish American writers have for the large part (with the exception of a "crossover" best-selling success like

Allegra Goodman) toiled in relative, and in some cases complete, obscurity. How many contemporary literary scholars have heard of dazzling Jewish American writers like Steve Stern,[13] Mark Mirsky, and Hugh Nissenson? Forget about entering the mainstream of literary studies, many of these writers would be happy just to see their novels back in print. Previously, part of the problem with creating a sustained theoretical approach to the Jewish nature of Jewish American fiction is that such an approach requires not just fluency with traditional Jewish texts and culture, but a real expertise in the traditional texts many Jewish American writers make reference to in their fiction, as well as an understanding of the Jewish rituals and praxis which has become more and more prevalent in contemporary Jewish American fiction. Lacking these basic Jewish literary "tools" it has been nearly impossible to interpret Jewish American fiction's content, let alone appreciate (and disseminate) its high literary art and merit.

In *The Art of Biblical Narrative*, Robert Alter claims that the Bible is novelistic. Saying that the Bible employs many of the same literary techniques as prose fiction, Alter points to the Bible's "artful use of language, the shifting play of ideas, conventions, tone, sound, imagery, syntax, narrative viewpoint, compositional units, and much else" (11). What Alter finds true of the Bible is even more paradigmatic of the Talmud, a book that reads like a gigantic epic novel, a romp through hundreds of years of Jewish diasporic culture. This study hopes to elucidate the Buberistic "I-thou encounter" between Jewish American writers and their readers. To interpret this encounter, I have found traditional biblical and Talmudic analytic tools to be most helpful. The literary "play" which this study undertakes replicates Jewish tradition without supplanting it. Having sojourned with Marx and Freud, Derrida and Foucault, I have belatedly returned to the analytic tools that haunted my Yeshiva training, PaRDeS:

1. **Peshat**—the literal (simple) explanation
2. **Remez**—using allusion to explain a passage
3. **Derash**—to "search" for deeper meanings, to interpret
4. **Sod**—that which is hidden.

In *American Talmud* my main analytic method will be *derash*, literally a "searching out" for the hidden meanings within Jewish American fiction. This is fitting because Jewish literature itself remains hidden and overlooked not just by literary critics and the academy but by an increasingly uncomprehending secular American reading public. Such a readership fairly shouts: give us Uris, not Ozick! However, as more and more Jewish Americans become fluent in traditional Jewish texts, we will see a wider audience for those Jewish American writers either already conversant with or genuinely steeped in traditional Jewish culture. Despite this hope for the future, one need not have even a cursory understanding of Jewish traditional texts to enjoy the late novels of Philip Roth or Cynthia Ozick; however many of the deeper meanings will remain elusive. For example, while one might enjoy Ozick's *The Messiah of Stockholm* without ever having heard of Bruno Schulz or having read his marvelous stories or been captivated by his disturbing paintings, one might not fully grasp all that Ozick, as the consummate artist, has encoded in her short, dazzling novel, one that I will here interpret as a *drash* on the nature of Jewish mesorah, the bequeathing of tradition. Without an understanding of Jewish history and Jewish texts, without the proper analytic tools (PaRDeS), a reader will never "get" all there is to comprehend in *The Messiah of Stockholm*, leaving the complete picture elusive. To paraphrase Harold Bloom, "it doesn't hurt" to have an understanding of traditional Jewish texts when reading Jewish American fiction, particularly contemporary Jewish American fiction. Given the proper interpretive mode, Jewish literature might be more widely understood by a multiethnic American readership. *American Talmud* hopes to fill this interpretive gap and thereby secure a wider, more appreciative audience for Jewish American fiction.

To play upon Buber's conception of an I-thou relationship, Jewish American fiction is the interpretation that the people of Israel gave to the I-thou encounter between diasporic, immigrant Jews and the new world. Today, after more than a century of sustained immigration, that relationship is revealed in the fiction Jewish writers have produced in America.

RELIGION AND LITERATURE:
THE DARK AND BLOODY CROSSROAD

From the center of the twentieth century, in his classic *The Liberal Imagination*, Lionel Trilling spoke reverently and dramatically of "the dark and bloody crossroads where literature and politics meet." As a literary critic, Trilling saw himself as operating primarily within the public sphere. More recently the critic Morris Dickstein identified Trilling's great contribution with his way of "connecting the act of writing to the life of the community" (*Double Agent* ix). If the road between politics and literature seemed bloody at mid-century, what might Trilling have thought of the early twenty-first-century super-highway where literature and mass communications meet? Better yet, what about the conflict between religion and literature?

Dickstein uses the term "double agent" for the critic who searches for a higher calling beyond that of specialist, beyond the rarified world of literary theory. The "double agent" is someone capable of "combining a deep feeling for art with a powerful sense of its changing place within society" (xiv). More than fifty years after Trilling published *The Liberal Imagination* and long after Derrida's famous claim that "there is no outside-the-text," when I began to work on this study the very notion of a religious impulse in literature seemed downright absurd or, more charitably, quaint. Yet I believe that today's postmodern society is in desperate need of what Morris Dickstein (after Matthew Arnold) calls "a secular instrument of salvation" (11). In the aftermath of the culture wars of the late eighties and early nineties, postmodern society may in fact be demanding a critical endeavor not unlike the cultural study of literature that *American Talmud* undertakes.

This study posits the idea that what is missing in Jewish American literature is a mediator able to transmit Jewish American fiction, often steeped in esoteric cultural praxis and ritual, to a wider audience. That mediating role of the literary critic hearkens back to an earlier age of criticism where a critic lucidly wrote for the people at large not a jargon-laden prose for a few in-the-know academics and French intellectuals. For example, what cultural significance is heralded by the presentation of a frozen gefilte fish served in the midst of a Passover seder in Allegra Goodman's brilliant short story "The Four Questions," collected in *The Family Markowitz*? Without an understanding of the myriad cultural markers sprinkled on every page of Goodman's redolently Jewish prose, a reader would surely miss the larger implications of her nuanced (if barbed) social satire. In other words, it takes an affiliated reader to cook Goodman's ethnic markers, to understand the social nuance being revealed in these small, but by no means unimportant, cultural signs.

THE TALMUD AND THE INTERNET?

In *The Talmud and the Internet* Jonathan Rosen suggests that the Baby-lonian Talmud finds its contemporary analogue in the amorphous world of the Internet. Despite Rosen's thesis being equally provocative and brilliant, his analogy between the Talmud and the Internet is not only false, but patently dangerous as well. The Talmud was created out of a moral imperative; it ranges seemingly freely on every conceivable medieval topic, but at its definitive center stands the Torah, the *halachah*, the law. Despite their numerous supernatural stories and their frequent migrations into myth, the redactors of the Talmud were squarely focused on codifying Jewish law and Jewish morality. The Internet by its very nature is amoral; it is largely focused on nothing more than instant gratification. The "community" sustained by the Internet is mostly a virtual one, whereas the Talmud has sustained a very real, dispersed, and persecuted community for two millennia.

That being the case, are there any analogues in the modern or postmodern world to the ancient Talmud of the Babylonian exile? The modern-day equivalent of the Babylonia Talmud is not the Internet; the central force arguing and perpetuating Jewish continuity today is the same as it has always been: Jewish literature. It is the argument of this book that twentieth-century and contemporary Jewish American fiction has been redacting a new Talmud, an American Talmud, for itself all along. Jewish American fiction has served as a moral center in the lives of not just American Jews, but for non-Jews as well for the past century. From Abraham Cahan's David Levinsky who taught a generation of "Greenhorns" of the false promise of American materialism, to Philip Roth's Swede Levov who taught us all not only of the inherent dangers of assimilation, but who also dramatized the blistered underside of the American dream itself. These two and countless other Jewish American fiction writers have successfully fulfilled the Old Testament *mitzvah* of being a "[literary] light unto the nations."

I realize that in substituting one contemporary phenomenon, Jewish American fiction, for another, the Internet, I am venturing onto treacherous ground; nonetheless, permit me to state the case. The Talmud and Jewish American fiction are actually quite similar in both aim and scope: both attempt to improve humanity by allowing their readers to temporarily see the world through another character's eyes. As Rabbi Akiva summarized: "That which is hateful to your neighbor do not do. All the rest is commentary. Go and study it."

Akiva's aphorism is often quoted, although interestingly, the last line, arguably the most important part of Akiva's construction, the studying part, is often excluded. After the destruction of the Temple in Jerusalem all sacrificial work ceased to exist for the Jewish people as a means of serving their God. In the exilic state of the diaspora the only remaining means of serving God is through the "work" of reading and studying the Torah. Through the process of reading and studying not only is God served, but also a community is created. All that is required is one rabbi and one student: within this dialectical *mesoraic* relationship, Jewish values and morality flourish. Similarly, a reader and writer, met together on the filled fictional page, together engage in just such a dialectical argument, the reading and writing process engenders a discussion that ensures the vitality and continuity of Jewish culture in the diaspora.

THE NATURE OF THE TALMUD

For all the Talmudist's concern with oxen being gored, at its heart, the Talmud primarily deals with the nature of man and a moral code by which to act. For all of Jewish American fiction writers' concern with the particularity of the Jewish experience on America's shores, the overwhelming question they ponder is not the nature of the Jew, but rather the nature of humanity. Despite being separated by sixteen centuries and numerous continents, the Talmudic redactors and Jewish American writers share a continuity of moral design and purpose.

An aspect of Akiva's dictum is the concern for one's neighbor; there is no distinguishing between Jew or non-Jew, only between neighbor and neighbor—fellow human beings. This idea of concern for all people and cultures, what post-Enlightenment cultures call Humanism, is a running theme throughout *halachah*, or Jewish law. The laws of a country which a Jew resides in are as important, sometimes even more so, than the Jewish law contained in the Torah. It is a moral imperative, a *mitzvah*, for every Jew that *dinah d-malchoto dinah* meaning "the law of the (gentile) land is your (Jewish) law." Jewish culture, always viewed as an outside presence in a strange land, was perpetually involved in a balancing act between two often-opposing cultures; it sought to mediate a homeland between the two within the confines of *halachah* (Jewish law) and whichever *shtetl* or ghetto settlement the Jewish community found themselves confined to. Yet by the time the *Haskalah* was overwhelming European *shtetlach* in the eighteenth century, waves of Jews were no longer attempting to balance modern life with Jewish tradition, *halachah*. Many Jews, given the choice of emancipation and its false promise of acceptance, gave up their Jewish culture in favor of conversion.

By the mid-nineteenth century something had to be done to stem the tide of assimilation; Rav Samson Raphael Hirsch developed the concept of *Torah im Derekh Eretz*,[14] which Hirsch explained as adherence to the commandments of the Torah combined with a full engagement with Western culture. As far as Hirsch was concerned Jews no longer had to make a choice between secular and religious cultures and lifestyles. Rather than seeing the secular world as being in opposition to Judaism, the Hirschian *weltanschwaang* proposed the idea that Judaism and modernity (secularity) complement each other. In other words, God wants his chosen people to be Torah true Jews while being within and part of the modern world. In fact, according to Hirschian philosophy (which has had a profound and lasting influence on American Jewish culture) one could not truly be a "Torah Jew" without being in the midst of the world. One of the basic tenets of Judaism states that Jews need to become a "light into the nations." Hirsch's philosophy asks, how can Jews be a light unto the nations while cloistered away in a ghetto shining brightly only among themselves?

In the aftermath of the Holocaust Hirsch's theories have been successfully integrated into mainstream American Orthodoxy. More importantly, for our purposes in this study, Hirsch's ideas, which have given birth to a varied and fascinating Orthodox community, have more recently become the focus of Jewish American fiction writers. Writers from Chaim Potok to Allegra Goodman have seized upon the complex mediation required of Orthodox Jewish life in America. These and numerous other writers, such as Steve Stern, Melvin Bukiet, Rebecca Goldstein, Thane Rosenbaum, Myla Goldberg, and Tova Mirvis, have exploited this duality (Orthodoxy/modernity), a state of being which leads to an array of interesting and complex fictional characters.

In his introduction to *American Jewish Orthodoxy in Historical Perspective*, Jeffrey Gurock explains that it is "The freedom America has always granted its Jews, through the legal separation of Church and State, to either practice their religion or to voluntarily abandon connections with their faith [which] has posed unparalleled challenges to the continuity of Judaism in this country" (xiii). Or, as Sorella more memorably states the case in Saul Bellow's *The Bellarosa Connection*: "The Jews could survive everything that Europe threw at them. I mean the lucky remnant. But now comes the next test—America. Can they hold their ground, or will the U.S.A. be too much for them?" (65).

As Gurock correctly expresses, the vast majority of scholarship on American Orthodoxy has focused on "the rabbis and lay leaders who attempted to find ways to accommodate Judaism to the powers of the American environment" (xiii). Understanding the ways that Jews have managed to preserve ancient traditions in the face of an increasingly secular American culture, or the ways those ancient traditions have been modified to accommodate the changing condition of American Jews, has been "the underlying theme of all serious historical research that has examined Jewish religious activity in the United States" (xiii).

Yet what has never entered into the equation are forces proven to be as powerful as any ancient voice written in stone and thunder: that of American popular culture and mass media. Fictional stories of big-city ways written by Sholom Aleichem and I. L. Peretz held great sway in the European *shtetlach*, and had a great effect on those leaving behind the constraints of small-town Jewish life in favor of the wonders of Warsaw and beyond toward the *Goldena Medina*, the golden streets of the new world. Surely Jewish American writing has exerted as strong and powerful an influence on not just the religious faith and practice of American Jews but on their Americanization as well. *American Talmud* attempts to understand not necessarily the world that Jews found in America, but perhaps more importantly the world they created within their minds, the transportable homeland which is Jewish American fiction and which has always encompassed Jewish textual history.

In postwar America, Rabbi Joseph Soloveitchik further tailored Hirsch's ideas for an increasingly mainstreamed Jewish American *kehillah* (community). His theories are more saliently glimpsed in the thousands of American Orthodox rabbis he trained for over half a century at the Rabbi Issac Elchanan Seminary of Yeshiva University in New York, than in the thin corpus of rabbinical writings he left behind. His influence has been enormous and will be helpful in understanding the nuanced views of American Orthodoxy being written today. In his classic study on the nature of evil in this world, *Kol Dodi Dofek* (the voice of my beloved knocketh), taken from *The Song of Songs* and translated from Hebrew as *Fate and Destiny*, in the aftermath of the Holocaust the Rav rejects theodicy and instead turns his attention to a proactive agenda, repeatedly asking: "What obligation does suffering impose on man?" (8). The Rav answers that the responsibility of a Torah Jew, a Jewish person committed to a traditional Jewish lifestyle, must "transform fate into destiny" (6).

> Man is born like an object, dies like an object, but possesses the ability to live as a subject. . . . Man's task in the world, according to Judaism, is to transform fate into destiny; a passive existence into an

active existence; an existence of compulsion, perplexity and muteness into an existence replete with a powerful will, with resourcefulness, daring, and imagination. (6)

The Rav's theorem for leading a Torah-true Jewish life has as its corollary the life of the Jewish American writer. Is not the Rav's credo for a Torah-true Jew the selfsame aim of the fiction writer? To turn passivity into action and imagination? To transform readers from muteness and confusion toward daring and imaginative leaps with an "other," an invention on the page, a fictional character?

ORTHODOXY AND THE
HOLOCAUST IN *AMERICAN TALMUD*

On March 17, 2002, the art exhibit "Mirroring Evil" opened in New York City. Yet even before the show's opening the exhibit stirred as much controversy as any recent art exhibit in America. The controversy centers on the show's numerous exploitations of Holocaust images that often become conflated with images from contemporary popular culture. For example, one of the "artists" in the show takes a famous photo of emaciated Buchenwald inmates and superimposes an image of himself standing among the Nazi victims, in his hand he holds a can of diet Coke. *The New York Times* chatted with another of the artists from the show, Tom Sachs. When the *Times* asked Sachs to explain his piece titled "Prada Deathcamp," included in "Mirroring Evil," this is what he had to say: "It's a pop-up death camp. It's a sort of best-of-all-worlds composite, with the famous Gate of Death and Crematorium IV from Auschwitz. I made it entirely from a Prada hatbox" (Solomon 19). When asked what possible connection his "art" has to do with the Holocaust, Sachs elucidates: "I'm using the iconography of the Holocaust to bring attention to fashion. Fashion, like fascism, is about loss of identity. Fashion is good when it helps you to look sexy, but its bad when it makes you feel stupid or fat because you don't have a Gucci dog bowl and your best friend has one" (Solomon 19).

One might expect to find this work being exhibited at some underground neo-Nazi museum, yet what might surprise readers is that this show was exhibited at the Jewish Museum in New York City. *American Talmud*, through tracing the dissolution of Holocaust images in twentieth-century and contemporary Jewish American fiction, attempts to understand how and why the Jewish cultural establishment

promotes an assimilated Jewish artist like Tom Sachs who inter-
changeably uses the term "Holocaust" to describe the destruction of
European Jewry as well as the "pressures" associated with postmodern
fashion. How has a mainstream artist like Sachs been able to make use
of the Holocaust to make frivolous claims about the role of fashion in
postmodern culture, when just a generation or two ago barely anyone
(least of all survivors) was even talking about the Holocaust at all?
American Talmud, through analyzing the ways in which Holocaust
images have been represented and misrepresented, used and misused,
by writers and artists of other media since the end of the Holocaust,
attempts to understand the aesthetical dilemmas associated with Holocaust representation. Even in the case of a writer or artist with the best
of intentions, attempting to represent the Holocaust is fraught with
aesthetic and therefore moral danger. For example, in chapter 3 of this
study, through the use of Bernard Malamud's work, I analyze the ways
images have dissolved over the course of four generations of writers
and artists to become, in the hands of artists like Sachs, a dangerous
simulacra.

NOVICK VERSUS YERUSHALMI

The two main objects of inquiry in *American Talmud* are Holocaust
representation and the concomitant return to Orthodoxy and tradition
that has transformed the American diaspora in the postwar years; my
study analyzes the aesthetic representation of the Holocaust and
Orthodox ritual and praxis within Jewish American fiction.

One of the most influential fin de siecle studies concerning American Jewry has been Peter Novick's award-winning diatribe *The Holocaust in American Life*. As he explains in his introduction, Novick set
out to understand the "inexplicable" reason "why in 1990s America—
fifty years after the fact and thousands of miles from its site—the
Holocaust has come to loom so large in our culture" (1). Novick's stated
aims, far from a usual cool, dispassionate historical endeavor, are loaded
from the start, and his opening question is disingenuous. How can the
Holocaust not be a central facet of what it means to be a Jew today?
No affiliated Jew would suggest that the destruction of the Temple in
Jerusalem in the year 70 C.E. is an event merely encapsulated in the
historical past. Indeed, world Jewry, thousands of years removed from
the tragic events of the Second Temple period, and even more geo-

graphically distant than Europe is to America, solemnly proclaim with the psalmist: "If I forget you, Jerusalem, / may my right hand wither away; / let my tongue cling to the roof of my mouth / if I do not remember you, / If I do not set Jerusalem / above my chief joy" (Psalm 137, *The Oxford Study Bible* 644).

What Novick's study reveals is his conceptual ignorance of Jewish memory. As a disaffiliated Jew, Novick can assuredly claim that the Holocaust is the only historical landmark upon which to stake a Jewish American identity. Concurrently, being far removed from any Jewish identification, Novick also maintains a stunned amazement at the centrality of the Holocaust in contemporary American life. As both a scholar of Jewish American culture and a grandson of Holocaust survivors, I find Novick's book deeply offensive.

Novick asks in his introduction: "On what grounds can a distinctive Jewish identity in the United States be based?" (7). Novick goes on to systematically (and supposedly dispassionately) dismiss Jewish religious beliefs, cultural traits (whatever these look like?), and Zionism. As Novick tells it, the only idea uniting American Jewry is "the knowledge that but for their parents' or (more often) grandparents' immigration, they would have shared the fate of European Jewry" (7).

Novick disregards the tremendous resurgence of Jewish identification in America, an identification that is based more on Jewish practice and ritual than "mere" Holocaust rumination as Novick suggests. Indeed, Andrew Furman, in his recent study *Contemporary Jewish American Writers and the Multicultural Dilemma*, discusses the "revitalization" of Jewish American culture. In his introduction Furman quotes a study undertaken by Bershtel and Graubard who suggest that this resurgence goes beyond a mere "re-identification" with traditional Judaism. Rather, according to Furman, they suggest that Jews in America have reinterpreted and "transformed" their Jewish identification (18). It is this transformation in diasporic Jewish American culture, so clearly expressed in Jewish American fiction, that I encounter in this study.

When comparing Peter Novick's study *The Holocaust in American Life*, a book which presupposes the absence of any meaningful Jewish identification in America, with Yosef Hayim Yerushalmi's *Zakhor*, a book which takes as its raison d'etre the long arc of Jewish history and identification in order to understand the Jewish response to tragedy and the nature of Jewish memory, the necessity of placing the relatively recent developments of the American Jewish community within the larger context of the lengthy Jewish diaspora becomes apparent. This great need is not only manifest in recent scholarship. The work of an earlier generation of Jewish American literary critics, again notably Howe and Fiedler, is also marked by a disengagement from genuinely Jewish concerns. One concludes that earlier generations of literary critics believed that the only way to understand Jewish literature is by ignoring its Jewish content while focusing instead on what makes the literature universal.

My hope for readers of *American Talmud* is that they will recognize that it is impossible to speak of a Jewish literature outside of Judaism; to do so is both absurd and pointless. Just as it takes a Yerushalmi to understand contemporary Jewish history and memory, it takes someone well grounded in traditional Jewish texts to understand Jewish American fiction. It is with this long tradition in mind that I have termed Jewish American fiction "postrabbinic."

In "The Fiction Writer and His Country" Flannery O'Connor sought to refute the regional label under which all Southern Literature languished. She began by attempting to define the word "country," a term with much resonance in her own work. She says: "It [country] suggests everything from the actual countryside that the novelist describes on, to, and through the peculiar characteristics of his region and his nation, and on, through, and under all of these to his true country, which the writer with Christian convictions will consider to be what is eternal and absolute" (*Collected Works* 801). Thirty years before the "invention of ethnicity" O'Connor both creates and explodes the very idea of an ethnic fiction. Although she probably never had this in mind, the aims O'Connor identities for "a writer of Christian convictions" might help us shed light upon the ambitions of "writers of Jewish convictions" in America as well.

When one thinks of Orthodox Judaism one thinks of an unyielding resistance to the forces of assimilation and Americanization. The stereotype of Orthodoxy in America as being opposed to modernity and all other forms of Judaism (Reform, Reconstructionist, and Conservative) was given credence not only by many exhaustive but skewed studies, but this idea came prepackaged with an image as well, in the scolding, unyielding figure of Rabbi Jacob Joseph, the immovable and antiassimilation and American acculturation Orthodox rabbinic figure. In recent scholarship a more nuanced portrait has begun to emerge. For example, while researching chapter 7 of this study I came across an article on the early nineteenth-century Jewish community in Harlem.[15] In this article Jeffrey Gurock explains "Orthodoxy, had in the pre-1920 period, a vibrant accomodationist strain" (xx). Gurock calls this brand of Judaism "American Orthodoxy." This brand of Judaism was clearly distinct from the conservative movement but was not, Gurock maintains, unyieldingly toward Americanization and other movements in American Jewry.

PaRDeS (PARADISE) REGAINED?

Jewish tradition expounds two separate myths concerning the nature of God. One posits a transcendent God, above and separate from our world, a God who created our world but is now totally removed from his handiwork. This is the fearful God of Judgment who created the world and, if he so chooses, can destroy it as well. The alternate view presents a God who is immanent, a God who is accessible and who created humanity in his own image and endowed us with his divine characteristics. These two conceptions of God have coexisted throughout Jewish history. Sometimes, in times of stress, one took precedence over the other, but Jewish belief is founded on these two seemingly incongruous beliefs. As David S. Ariel says: "All of Jewish belief is commentary on the two, interrelated sacred myths of God" (16). The redactors of the Talmud alleviated this divide by emphasizing the dual nature of the One God of Israel.

American Talmud argues that twentieth-century and contemporary Jewish American writers have unwittingly become the theologians of contemporary Jewish American culture. There is an ancient Jewish tradition that states every Jew is required to write a Torah scroll during their lifetime. The rabbinic commentators debate whether a literal or figurative interpretation of this tradition should take precedence. One rabbi argues that hiring a *halachicaly* trained scribe to write a Torah scroll fulfills this *mitzvah*. I would argue for an even less literal interpretation. The tradition relates that each Jew must literally "write" the Torah, through an act of interpretation a Jew symbolically inscribes a new Torah scroll. It is in this spirit that I have attempted to add to and interpret the continued Jewish diaspora in *American Talmud*. In accord with Deuteronomy 30:12 and Rabbi Joshua, I state "*Lo beshamayim hi*," the Torah is not in heaven. It is alive and well and being written in the American diaspora as it has been for over a hundred years of sustained literary production of undoubtedly high merit. But do not take my word for it. Following Rabbi Akiva, for those who want to know just what is inside the American ark of the covenant, on one foot I say to you: *Nu?* Go and study!

CHAPTER 1

Henry Roth's First Novel:
Call It Jewish?

INTRODUCTION

Recently, at the Modern Language Association's annual meeting, I helped organize a panel on contemporary Jewish American writing. We decided on the topic of "New Voices," and as part of that panel I discussed the work of Henry Roth, a writer usually associated with the modernist movement in literature—hardly a "new voice" that the panel seemed to call for. Indeed, numerous conference participants thought Roth a strange choice for a panel dealing with fresh and new literary voices. However, with the publication of all four volumes of *Mercy of a Rude Stream*, we are now in a position to more fully understand all of Henry Roth's voices: the old and the new, the modern novelist alongside the postmodern memoirist. Therefore, Henry Roth might well be the perfect choice to begin this study.

JEWISH AMERICAN LITERARY RENAISSANCE

In *Major Trends in Jewish Mysticism*, Gershom Scholem quotes Thomas Aquinas's definition of mystics as people who follow the psalmist: "Oh taste and see that the Lord is good" (Psalm 34:9). Henry Roth's *Call It Sleep* might stand as the antithesis to this maxim. Roth repeatedly asks his readers to taste and see the slums of turn-of-the-century Lower East Side of New York City. Roth posits a more naturalistic motto, perhaps along the lines of "Oh taste and see that the Lord is both evil and absent." Jewish culture, as indeed any culture, is about continuity and the passing on of tradition. Roth as a modernist wrote a first novel of assimilation, of the end of Jewishness; I would go so far as to label *Call It Sleep* a novel of anti-Jewishness and self-loathing. As late as 1963, nearly thirty years after he wrote *Call It Sleep*, Roth was still advocating the disappearance of both Jews and their culture. In a mid-1960s interview, Roth said: "I feel that to the great boon Jews have already conferred upon humanity, Jews in America might add this last and greatest one: of orienting themselves toward ceasing to be Jews" (*Shifting Landscape* 114). Yet in an act that seemingly defies comprehension, twenty-five years after he gave this interview—at this point he was a man in his late eighties—Roth was once again going to *cheder*; this time not on the Lower East Side but in his New Mexico mobile home. In the late 1980s Roth began relearning Hebrew in hopes of making *aliyah* to Israel. These facts beg the question of just how are students of Jewish American literature able to make sense of the confusing, disjointed trajectory of Henry Roth's writing career.

Recently, numerous literary critics have identified a renaissance in Jewish American fiction. Casting off the gloomy prognostications of an earlier generation of critics who sounded the death knell for Jewish American fiction in the 1960s, these critics have, in my view correctly, pointed to a reidentification with traditional Jewish culture as a hallmark of this new wave of Jewish literature. Andrew Furman has recently argued as such in the pages of *Tikkun* as well as in his *Contemporary Jewish American Writers and the Multicultural Dilemma*. Furman locates in the revitalization of Jewish life in America "a concomitant renaissance in Jewish American fiction" (18). This new fiction is marked by what critic Morris Dickstein, in his survey of the field, calls "the return, or the homecoming" ("The Complex Fate of the Jewish American Writer" 384) of Jewish American writers. No longer content to give their characters Jewish names and sprinkle a few Hebrew and Yiddish incantations over the course of a novel, current Jewish American writers often engage in a far deeper examination of Jewish American mores and culture. Writers like Cynthia Ozick, Steve Stern, Rebecca Goldstein, and Allegra Goodman have moved beyond creating Jewish characters as symbols and have developed fully realized Orthodox characters, characters who abundantly exhibit Rabbi Samson Raphael Hirsch's mid-nineteenth-century doctrine of *Torah Umaadah*—of being a Torah-true Jew while concurrently being a full participant in the modern world. That the vast majority of these writers are women should not surprise even the casual observer of the significant changes undergone by Modern Orthodox communities in America. One striking example of Orthodox women's newfound leadership roles within their communities is the numerous women's *tefillah* (prayer) and study groups that have recently proliferated across the country.

HENRY ROTH'S TIKKUN: IN SEARCH OF LOST MERCY

Momentarily moving away from the current renaissance of Jewish American fiction, I'd like to go back a bit in time to the dark years of the depression when Henry Roth was completing his first novel. *Call It Sleep* is a book almost universally hailed as the "quintessential Jewish American novel," so much so that it even appeared on Ruth Wisse's Jewish American Canon—a high mark indeed.[1] Yet I would suggest that Roth's first novel is less a Jewish novel than an *anti*-Jewish novel. While recent Jewish American fiction, through a reacquaintance with Jewish texts, has been marked by an embracing of traditional Jewish law and culture, I believe Roth's first novel stands as a pillar of opposition to that continuity; it is precisely these Jewish texts that are parodied and mocked throughout *Call It Sleep*. If a culture must be about continuity and must be text centered, then Roth's first novel fails on both scores. Modernism embraces discontinuity, rupture, the turning of one's artistic back on a culture, all in the hope of reinventing a new culture from new artistic materials.

If *Call It Sleep* represented not only the beginning but the end of Henry Roth's career, he would hardly have merited inclusion in my *American Talmud* canon. However, still unbeknownst to many, *Call It Sleep* was in fact only a beginning in Roth's long tortuous career as a Jewish American writer. In his late seventies Roth began writing again and he did not cease until his very last days in 1995. The four volumes of *Mercy of a Rude Stream* that have already been published stand in repudiation of all that Roth had done in his youth.

While I do not view *Call It Sleep* as a Jewish novel, I do view Roth's career in classically Jewish terms. While many critics have pointed to Roth's fascination with Freud and the Oedipus complex as the driving symbolic structure for Roth's first novel, a variant reading of *Call It Sleep* is in order, a reading which superimposes a different symbolic system for understanding Roth's first novel, and more importantly for understanding the difficult arc of Roth's career: a Lurianic Kabbalistic reading.

THE THREE STAGES OF LURIANIC KABBALAH: ZIMZUM, SHEVIRAH, AND TIKKUN

In Lurianic Kabbalah, *Adam Kadmon*, defined as "man as he should be," is engaged in an endless battle of light versus light. This light emanates out of his head and creates fresh vessels of creation through writing. In Isaac Luria's conception of *Adam Kadmon*, this light represents God's name, a word that contains too much light, a word too strong for this world; when it is spoken it leads to the breaking of the vessels created to contain it. Harold Bloom has interpreted this process to be one of displacement, of substitution "in which an original pattern yielded to a more chaotic one that nonetheless remained pattern" (*Kabbalah and Criticism* 41). Henry Roth's penultimate chapter in *Call It Sleep* is a masterful reworking of *shevirah* of this breaking of the vessels which sends off sparks of creation worthy of ingathering and which just might, given the proper interpretation, eventually lead to a *tikkun olam*, or healing of the world. This *tikkun olam* through the ingathering of these sparks does not occur all at once. In Roth's case it took over sixty years for those sparks, first glimpsed in *Call It Sleep*, to once again give light in *Mercy of a Rude Stream*.

The Jewish mystical tradition, far from being a continuation of rabbinic Judaism, is in many ways a radical reworking of the creation story told in *Tanach*.[2] Instead of the process of *Tikkun olam*, of healing the world through the Jewish people becoming "a light unto the nations," Kabbalah reimagines *Tikkun olam* as a personal process of *Tikkun aztmi*, a healing of the self. After the expulsion of the Jews from Spain in 1492, the Jewish people entered yet another difficult exile within an exile. The spiritual force was turned inward. Rabbi Michael Lerner retells the basic Kabbalistic creation story like this: "God contracted to create space for the universe to come into existence and filled that space with Divine Light. But the vessels built to contain the Light were overwhelmed and shattered, and the world is now filled with fragments of Divine Light, shards of holiness that are broken and need repair. Our human task is to raise and reunite those shards, releasing divine sparks, and through *tikkun*, bring God's presence (the Holy Shekhinah) back into the world" (xvi).

Roth's first novel *Call It Sleep*, although far from being the quintessential Jewish American novel as it is often portrayed, is in reality a novel which dramatizes the *shevirah* stage of Lurianic Kabbalah, the breaking of the vessels. The central theme of *Call It Sleep* is one of disrupting Jewish tradition, the overthrowing and dissolution of Judaism.

In Lurianic Kabbalah some of the sparks cast off from the breaking of the vessels return to God, while the sparks that are left become the *kelliffot* or evil forces in the universe. Far from signaling a return to the mother's womb or regeneration after David's trolley-track explosion (as several critics have maintained), the sparks that descend upon the streets of the Lower East Side, viewed through a Lurianic prism, enter this world as evil forces. Thus the explosion at the end of the novel signals David Schearl's physical and mental maturation. This evil, adult force will bedevil Roth for over sixty years and will signal his turn from six-year-old David Schearl as an *Adam Kadmon* substitute in *Call It Sleep*, to an incestuous predator named Ira Stigman in the *Mercy* cycle, where Roth will unsparingly document the post *Call It Sleep* years, a time filled with sexual and personal debasement.

The first two Lurianic stages of *Zimzum* and *Shevirah* undoubtedly take place in *Call It Sleep*; the third stage, that of *Tikkun*, the most important in Lurianic Kabbalah, is glimpsed within the whole of Roth's second novel. Roth would struggle with this last stage for over sixty years before approaching the mercy of *Tikkun* in his last novel. In New Mexico Roth would have to undergo a second personal exile from the Lower East Side before he could create Ira Stigman, a doubly exiled youth. Ira, in a Joycean portrait of the artist, eventually becomes a writer; through his individual act of creativity, his *Tikkun atzmi*, Ira enables the sparks of creation, which had become *kelliffot* or evil inclinations in the world, to become liberated from the broken shards and assume a beautiful form. This promise was fulfilled in the writing of *Mercy of a Rude Stream*. Yet Roth's last act of creativity was predicated upon an act of destructive violence; in order to once again create, to break the block that set in after the *shevirah* in the conclusion to *Call It Sleep*, Roth had to reveal the long-held secret of his real-life incestuous relationships. Roth fictionalizes this reality in *Mercy of a Rude Stream* through Ira's incestuous relationships with his sister Minny and his cousin Stella. Here too Roth followed a Lurianic path. According to Gershom Scholem, Isaac Luria believed that man "could create only by catastrophe" (41).

In Lurianic symbolism the breaking of the vessels corresponds to the world's inability to hold all of God's power and light. In Roth's symbolic world, the breaking of the vessels might be understood as the breaking of the novelistic vessel, the form of the naturalistic novel which begins to disintegrate as a vehicle able to convey all of young David Schearl's multifaceted experience, thought patterns, and most of all the traumatic rupturing of David's psyche. David's fractured psyche will not easily mend; long after his charred foot has healed, young David will be nursing the numerous psychological wounds that *Call It Sleep* dramatizes. This fracture in his identity will never entirely heal, and Roth will be consumed by this split for the rest of his life through his always-changing occupations, religious disaffections, and political affiliations. Through all these shifting landscapes, Roth is perpetually haunted by a split sense of self, a ruptured identity.

Early in *A Star Shines over Mt. Morris Park*, the first volume of *Mercy of a Rude Stream*, Roth discusses the shattered vessel of his psyche, dating the split in self to the moment the Stigman family (clearly the Schearls from *Call It Sleep*) abandoned East Ninth Street in their move uptown to a non-Jewish block near Mt. Morris Park in Harlem. Roth suggests that "it was then and there the desolate breach opened between himself and himself that was never to close" (18). Roth's project in writing *Mercy* is an attempt in old age to confess and give testimony to the horrors of his formative years and in so doing reconcile with himself. Although Roth maintains that the "void was never to close," it is through the writing of his narrative and the working through of his difficult narrative structure that he is reconciled and made whole.

ALL ABOARD: CHAPTER 21 OF "THE RAIL"

For all Kabbalists, as well as for young David Schearl, the "question of [the] immanence of God's presence permeating the world, is a matter of central importance" (Hallamish 184). The famous scene in chapter 21 of *Call It Sleep*, when David's milk dipper finally catches fire, is an almost exact replica of the scene of *shevirah* as described in Lurianic Kabbalah:

> Power
> Power! Power like a paw, titanic power
> Ripped through the earth and shackled him
> Where he stood. Power! Incredible,
> Barbaric power! A blast, a siren of light
> Within him, rending, quaking, fusing his
> Brain and blood to a fountain of flame,
> Vast rockets in a searing spray! Power!
> The hawk of radiance raking him with
> Talons of fire, battering his skull with
> A beak of fire, braying his body with
> Pinions of intolerable light. (Roth 419)

This scene is as close an approximation of the *shevirah* or story of creation as told in Lurianic Kabbalah as we are likely to find anywhere in American literature. David sends sparks flying out from the Lower East Side trolley tracks when he sticks his father's milk dipper into them. These sparks signal his growth and rebirth into maturity and his overcoming of the oedipal conflict. However, David's maturity also signals his sexual awakening, an awareness which will very shortly lead to ultimate evil, and not just the usual devilments which the Lower East Side boys experiment with throughout *Call It Sleep*, sticking a "*petzel* in a knish" as the act is memorably called in Roth's first novel. Once the family moves to non-Jewish Harlem in *Mercy of a Rude Stream*, David's nascent sexuality will seek out incestuous predatory couplings with both his sister Minnie and his cousin Stella. Thus, despite the last chapter of the novel having been interpreted by numerous critics as representing a reconciliation of the family unit, of David's being uneasily welcomed back into the family, these last scenes might in Kabbalistic terms more truthfully represent, through the sparks which emanate from the trolley tracks, the birth of the *kelliffot* or evil inclination being brought into this world.

The concluding paragraph of *Call It Sleep* draws attention to the unfinished business that Roth must strive to complete through the long course of his writing career, a career that spanned most of the twentieth century. Roth ends the novel with the words "One might as well call it sleep," suggesting that David finally possesses "strangest triumph" (441). Yet the novel ends less upon a condition of triumph as in a "trancelike state" of indeterminacy as Hana Wirth-Nesher suggests. Roth and his *Adam Kadmon* creation David are in a state of suspended animation, waiting for the elusive third stage in Lurianic Kabbalah, the long journey of Tikkun which looms ahead as a perpetual state of indeterminacy for the young Jewish American writer.

Although the critics have disagreed over the ultimate meaning of David's electrocution in chapter 21 of "The Rail," most tend to read this chapter as a rebirthing scene in which David reaffirms his Judaism. At the conclusion of the novel David has finally given up the fiction of his *goyish* parentage, a fallacy which forms a recurring subplot within *Call It Sleep*. Other critics interpet this scene as a classic rebirth-into-manhood tale. Caught up in myth, none of these interpretations seem to be troubled that the ending doesn't easily lend itself to even a remotely positive view, a positive ending which would have subverted the modernism and realism Roth had expended so much linguistic effort in establishing leading up to the pyrotechnics of the electrocution scene. Why would Roth engage in such a radical departure at the conclusion of *Call It Sleep*?

ROTH'S OEDIPUS COMPLEX

Numerous critics have commented on Roth's strict adherence in *Call It Sleep* to Freudian psychology, particularly Freud's doctrine of the Oedipus complex that sets in motion the plot and love triangle of *Call It Sleep*.[3] Allen Guttmann in his 1971 book, *The Jewish Writer in America*, even hyperbolically said *Call It Sleep* was "the most Freudian of the great American novels" (Guttmann 50). Roth himself dismissed such notions, suggesting on numerous occasions that he had never seriously read Freud. In a 1965 letter, Roth wrote: "I don't know much about Freud and I never did." In 1972 he told William Freedman, "Of course, I knew about Freud, but I only had a smattering of it" (qtd. in Sollors, *Beyond Ethnicity* 165). We need not belabor this point to determine whether Roth did or did not read Freud. Roth was nothing if not consistently inconsistent throughout his long career. There is however a far more Jewish text which truthfully corresponds to the arc of Roth's enigmatic career as a writer, yet to my knowledge, no one has made the obvious connection of Roth's novel to an even older Jewish tradition than Freud's psychoanalytic theory: Lurianic Kabbalah. Harold Bloom has remarked on the many ways in which Freud's secular scientific religion of psychoanalysis borrows from traditional Kabbalah. Bloom maintains, "As a psychology of belatedness, Kabbalah manifests many prefigurations of Freudian doctrine" (*Kabbalah and Criticism* 43).

Roth shared one more connection with Isaac Luria as well. Most of Luria's work was codified and written by his students. In fact when asked why he didn't commit more of his thoughts to book form, Luria replied: "It is impossible, because all things are interrelated. I can hardly open my mouth to speak without feeling as though the sea burst its dams and overflowed. How then shall I express what my soul has received, and how can I put it down in a book?" (*Scholem* 254). Henry Roth, itinerant chicken slaughterer and tool-gauge maker, from the midst of his fifty-year writer's block, might just as easily have spoken these words. Indeed how could he begin to write again, while he denied the very reality of his own experience, the subject of his life's work?

MERCY WITHOUT END (*EYN SOF*)

In *Major Trends in Jewish Mysticism*, Gershom Scholem links Sabbatianism to other revolutionary movements in Jewish history such as the reform movement, the *Haskalah* or Enlightenment, even, according to Robert Alter, "Jewish participants in the French Revolution" (*The Art of Biblical Narrative* xx). To this already extensive list I would add, in Henry Roth's case, literary modernism and communism, before in the second phase of his career, with what I call his "New Voice," Roth finally embraces Zionism as the reigning "ism" of his political and religious ideology.

Despite his intention to make everything new, his desire to break the vessels of art and culture, from our vantage point we can see the dialectical aspect inherent in the modernist work of Roth's youth. Perhaps more importantly, we can see the transformation of his thought from anti-Jewish and the breaking of the vessel, the novelistic form at the conclusion of *Call It Sleep*, to the approaching redemption, the *tikkun atzmi* and *tikkun olam* glimpsed in *Mercy of a Rude Stream*.

To the charge that Roth had little conception of Jewish mysticism and thus my reading of the arc of his career is yet one more symbolic system artificially grafted onto his novel, I would recall Genya's (David's mother in *Call It Sleep*) definition of God at the center of the novel. She gives a classic Lurianic explanation, tinged with the mocking accent of a disbeliever, an attitude resonant throughout the text. Genya quotes an old woman in Veljish who says: "that He [God] was brighter than the day is brighter than the night. You understand?" (241). This definition of an Almighty is dependent upon the irreducibility of God; God is everywhere and cannot be quantified. Or as David, with his six-year-old mind, reasons: "How can he look in every dark, if He's light?" (240).

Genya and David's conception of God is in opposition to the personal nature of God glimpsed in both biblical and Talmudic stories. It is, however, reminiscent of the Kabbalistic conception of a transcendent God as *eyn sof* defined by Gershom Scholem as "that which is infinite" (12). It is not coincidental that Roth ends this scene with David's mother repeating the old woman's sardonic twist on the Kabbalistic idea of the *shechinah*'s light. Still speaking of the old woman from Veljish, Genya appends to her story: "But she always used to add if darkest midnight were bright enough to see whether a black hair were straight or curly" (241).

Here in his first novel we glimpse Roth's rejection of any sort of Jewish mystical conception of a transcendent God. By quantifying this *eyn sof* of God, the old woman's second part of her definition comprises a sardonic twist at God himself; the ironic humor negates the first part of the definition. Not only is God *not* without end, but also he is quantified and severely limited. God is only as bright as the difference between the lightest night and the regular light of day. This playful definition of God through light foreshadows the penultimate scene of the novel and the *shevirot*, or manifestations of evilness, the sparks of evil that will enter the world during David's trolley-track explosion.

CONCLUSION

After David has become the unwitting accomplice to the sexual misadventures between his cousin Esther and his newfound *goyish* friend Leo, David flees Aunt Bertha's candy store, the scene of the sexual crime. The narrator ominously reports: "He must hold gnashing memory at bay. He must! He must! He'd scream if he didn't forget!" (359).

Much like David Schearl, Roth also could not hold "gnashing memory" completely at bay; he too was unable to forget the truth of his sordid immigrant past. Long after the sparks of light that showered the Lower East Side had dimmed, the persistent voice of Roth's battered memory churned on. Only after completing *Mercy of a Rude Stream* did Roth achieve the *tikkun atzmi* that had eluded him in *Call It Sleep*. In true Lurianic style, within the act of reading Roth's definitively Jewish work, *Mercy of a Rude Stream*, his personal *tikkun atzmi* becomes transformed into a communal *tikkun olam*. In his second novel Roth collected all the sparks he could recall, those spots of light that remained after the *shevirah*. Just as the conclusion of *Call It Sleep* represents the *shevirah* and the entrance of evil into the world, through his monumental effort at creating a new voice in *Mercy of a Rude Stream*, Roth's second career and second novel signal a measure of mercy and the bringing of the *shekhinah* back into this world.

CHAPTER 2

Reflecting the World:
Bernard Malamud's Post-Holocaust Judaism

INTRODUCTION

Unlike Henry Roth with his extraordinarily complex career trajectory, Bernard Malamud, even now twenty years after his death, is still frequently portrayed as the archetypal Jewish American writer. Malamud is credited with the literary invention of "Yinglish," the affecting mixture of Yiddish cadences and subject-verb reversal within the English dialogue of the first-generation Eastern European Jewish immigrants who populate his fiction. However, beyond his pitch-perfect ear for Jewish immigrant speech patterns there is little genuine Jewishness in Malamud's prose. In fact, as this chapter will illustrate, Malamud's representations of Judaism rely more upon Christian iconography than any classically Jewish sources. Malamud's Judaism is steeped in an ethos of Christian suffering rather than a conception of messianic Jewish redemption.

While one can choose any work from Malamud's oeuvre to prove this point, Malamud's lack of Jewish content is perhaps best glimpsed in those stories where Malamud actually attempted to deal with a particular Jewish theme or when his work was inspired by actual Jewish history. Thus, in this chapter I analyze Malamud's two attempts at such fiction, both stories which purport to deal with the Holocaust.

HOLOCAUST REPRESENTATION

As Warsaw falls to the Nazis in September 1939, Martin Goldberg, the first-person narrator of Bernard Malamud's "The German Refugee," sits in New York's Institute for Public Studies listening to the perfect English pronunciation of his student Oskar Gassner who is lecturing on Walt Whitman to a packed house. The young Goldberg has spent an arduous summer tutoring English to Gassner, an eminent

German Jewish literary critic displaced in the aftermath of Kristall-nacht. As Goldberg listens to Gassner's lecture he thinks to himself: "How easy it is to hide the deepest wounds, and how proud I was at the job I had done" (*The Complete Stories* 367).

Martin Goldberg accurately assesses Gassner's ability to hide his terror at speaking English; his thought also reflects Malamud's reluctance to grapple with the deepest wounds of the Holocaust in his fiction. The deepest wounds Malamud does address are casualties of aesthetics and representation, not the barbarism normally associated with the Holocaust. By abandoning a limited omniscient third-person narrator in favor of an inarticulate, first-person storyteller, Malamud—through indirectly addressing the Holocaust—directly addresses the difficulty of creating art out of the ashes of the Holocaust.

For a humanist, the deepest wound is comprised of the millions of victims of Nazi genocide; for a writer attempting to create art out of destruction, the deepest wound and cruelest irony is the inability to write effectively concerning the monumental loss sustained not only by European Jewry but also by twentieth-century history as well. Malamud's post-Holocaust dilemma might be seen in terms of contrasting questions, one humanistic and the other aesthetic: how is a good person to live, and how might a good writer best represent the cataclysm of the Holocaust?

Malamud once said: "The suffering of the Jews is a distinct thing for me. I for one believe that not enough has been made of the tragedy of the destruction of six million Jews. Somebody has to cry—even if it's a writer, twenty years later" (Rothstein 26). In interviews Malamud often asserted that the advent of World War II and the Holocaust first convinced him to become a writer. If this quote helps answer the question of Malamud's thematic interest in World War II—if not as text, then certainly as subtext—for much of his fiction, it also raises another equally troubling problem: Just what sort of Jewish identity has he become aware of, and how will he represent that newfound Jewish identification in his fiction?

In an often-quoted interview, Malamud remarked: "All men are Jews, though few of them know it." This comment has widely been interpreted as Malamud's thesis, which underscores the universality of his suffering heroes. As Malamud says in *The Assistant*: "The world suffers" (5), and it is the responsibility of his good and ethical characters to empathize with this suffering. Consequently, Malamud's characters are judged based on their ability to learn "what it means [to be] human" from their suffering. This universal conception of suffering piety creates a Jewish identity that is more symbolic than actual. Malamud's symbolic system of Judaism is generally effective in gaining a reader's empathy when he writes novels and stories not set in a particular historic framework, as is the case with his allegorical short stories and his fables, or when he resorts to supernatural and fantastic elements in his work. However, this symbolic Judaism is less effective, indeed it becomes deeply problematic, when Malamud attempts to invest his symbolic Jews, identified with traditional Judaism in name and speech only, with the concrete reality of history,[1] particularly the awesome legacy of the Holocaust. When he makes such an attempt in two short stories, "The Lady of the Lake" and "The German Refugee," his marginally identified and always assimilated, paper-thin Jews are unable to shoulder the awesome historical weight they are forced to bear.

COVENANTAL JUDAISM

In his book *Crisis and Covenant: The Holocaust in American Jewish Fiction*, Alan L. Berger argues that in attempting to distinguish between what he calls "genuine from spurious Holocaust literature" one may focus on a writer's covenantal awareness or orientation. By *covenant*, Berger refers to the traditional relationship between God and his chosen people, a relationship distinguished by two qualities: "the people's witness and divine protection." Jewish history has traditionally been viewed through this relationship. As Berger notes: "Various crises in Jewish national existence were measured against the norms of divine promise and divine judgment" (1). The covenant promised future salvation and created a spiritual reading of history—a means of accounting for historical trauma as divine judgment.[2]

In pre–World War II Jewish American fiction, Orthodoxy had a marginal role, serving as a point of departure for many protagonists as they pushed away from the old world and all it represented. Orthodoxy was disparagingly treated, usually in the form of the stereotypically crafted rabbi in the fiction of Abraham Cahan or Henry Roth. The rituals and traditions associated with Orthodoxy were used as a contrasting device to differentiate between the old world and the new.

Within the post–World War II push for suburban assimilation, the Orthodox camp seemed like an easy target, a group of "unmeltable" people not willing to make any concessions towards Americanization. They thus opened themselves up to ridicule and disdain and were thought of as a people with limited fluency in English, with one foot still *shlepping* in the nineteenth-century *shtetl*. As a result, Orthodoxy, with its strict adherence to tradition and continuity, came to represent the antithesis of the aspirations of the Jewish American writer. Ironically, in the post-Holocaust second half of the twentieth century, many Jewish American writers found themselves in the uneasy, some would say untenable, position of filling the hollow identity carved out by many assimilated American Jews, the types of Americanized Jews who populated much postwar Jewish American fiction. Berger goes so far as to suggest, "many American Jews depend on novels, rightly or not, for their knowledge about fundamental Jewish issues. Increasingly it is the case that American Jewish novelists, whether grudgingly or willingly, have assumed the role of theologians of Jewish culture" (37).

SURVIVOR TESTIMONY

Primo Levi also spoke of the theological dimensions of Holocaust testimony. Midway through his memoir *Survival in Auschwitz*, Levi is assigned a new bunkmate. On the march to work they exchange a few words:

> He told me his story, and today I have forgotten it, but it was certainly a sorrowful, cruel and moving story; because so are all our stories, hundreds of thousands of stories, all different and all full of tragic, disturbing necessity. We tell them to each other in the evening, and they take place in Norway, Italy, Algeria, the Ukraine, and are simple and incomprehensible like the stories in the Bible. But are they not themselves stories of a new Bible? (65–66)

Berger's conception of the theological role played by Jewish American novelists, when coupled with Primo Levi's insistence that survivor testimony represents the holy book of a new theology, presumes a significant responsibility for Jewish American writers, while concurrently presenting them with the dilemma of what to place in the covenantal Ark of this new religion. Bernard Malamud attempted to solve this quandary in 1958 in "The Lady of the Lake," before strenuously revising his narrative technique when dealing with the Holocaust in 1963 when he published "The German Refugee."

While much of Malamud's fiction seems to be haunted by the Holocaust—one can point toward *The Fixer* and *The Assistant* as Holo-

caust parables, because both deal with Jewish persecution, and both
Morris Bober and Yakov Bok seem afflicted by the unnamed Holocaust—many of his short stories feature immigrant survivors suffering
their meager fates, it is these two stories, "The Lady of the Lake" and
"The German Refugee," which many critics have pointed to as representing Malamud's most direct concern with the Holocaust. What
critics have yet to discuss is Malamud's self-conscious reappraisal of his
own use of the Holocaust within these stories. In writing "The German Refugee," Malamud is attempting to grapple not with the Holocaust itself, but with the difficulties of aesthetic production not only in
the aftermath of World War II, but particularly with art which
attempts to either directly or indirectly address the Holocaust, an event
which in the words of Shoshana Felman "is the watershed of our
times . . . and which is not an event encapsulated in the past . . . [but]
whose traumatic consequences are still actively *evolving*" (xiv).

Once awakened to the fictional uses of Jewish history in the aftermath of the Holocaust, Malamud is forced to contend with the trou-
blesome issue of Jewish identity. But if it took the Holocaust to awaken
Malamud to his neglected Jewish history, then will his Jewish identification be largely based upon a legacy of persecution and destruction?
Furthermore, how are the two separate issues of the destruction of the
Jewish people and the representation of the surviving remnants of that
lost world dealt with in Malamud's fiction?

Theodore Solotaroff suggests that Malamud's Jewishness, despite
his Yiddish-drenched inflections, is in fact pure image—a useful representation of a moral life easily applicable to any religious or ethnic
affiliation. Solotaroff says, "Malamud's Jewishness is a type of
metaphor—for anyone's life—both for the tragic dimension of anyone's life and for a code of personal morality and salvation that is more
psychological than religious" (199). Solotaroff correctly explains that
Malamud's Jews become symbols "fashioned to the service of an
abstraction" (199). In essence, Malamud uses Judaism as a moral tem-
plate upon which to judge a character's process of *mentchification*
through suffering.

METAPHORICAL JUDAISM

His theoretical representations of a moral code serve Malamud well in
much of his fiction, but such abstractions might be emblematic of why

Malamud generally eschewed writing Holocaust fiction. Malamud's symbolic Jews cannot sustain the awesome responsibility of bearing witness to the Holocaust—the actual (and not symbolic) watershed event of the twentieth century. Put another way: how to represent the reality of Nazism without its paling in light of his metaphorical and symbolic Jews when, as Robert Alter has claimed, Malamud's Jewish milieu is nothing more than a "shadow of a vestige of a specter" ("Jewishness as Metaphor" 31)?

In creating a metaphor out of the image of a Jew (all men are Jews),[3] Malamud has severed ethnicity from religion, hoping to render it universal and all encompassing. The twinning of an ethnic culture within a religious system ensured the survival of the Jewish people through their history of persecution and destruction. Ironically, in an effort aimed at universalizing the Jewish experience, Malamud separated ethnicity from religion, thereby insuring his inability to create an effective Holocaust story—one that may properly bear witness to the destruction of European Jewry.

Dorothy Bilik suggests that Malamud's ethics are a modern version of the famous aphorism attributed to the ancient scholar Hillel who was challenged to explain the wisdom of the Torah while standing on one foot. He reportedly said: "That which is hurtful to thee do not do to thy neighbors! This is the entire Torah; all the rest is commentary. Go and study it" (56).

While Malamud's suffering heroes clearly demonstrate the first tenet of Hillel's saying, they certainly don't spend much time with the studying part. Consequently, Malamud portrays a hollow version of traditional Judaism, a reductive ethics that leads to caricatured representations of Jewish Orthodoxy and tradition. Malamud himself pokes fun at this unadorned spirituality in *The Assistant*: after Morris Bober has explained to his clerk Frank Alpine that the Jewish law is comprised of "to do what is right, to be honest, to be good. This means to other people. . . . We ain't animals," Morris's non-Jewish clerk answers, "I think other religions have those ideas too" (150). The ironic humor in this exchange is obvious, but beyond the humor and irony Malamud suggests that this simple and universal humanism is precisely what is needed to ensure a better world.

Malamud's symbolic Judaism isn't based in any religious system dealing with covenantal (traditional) values, but rather with his own ethical system which, while humanistic, is ahistorical. Through suffering, each new Malamud *schlemiel* must reinvent this social code. It is difficult to find fault with Malamud's ethics, as voiced simply yet with dignity, by Malamud's long-suffering Morris Bober. However, once Malamud's characters step out of their small, decrepit grocery stores, or run-down shoe repair shops, and assume their parts on the stage of world history, such simple pieties lose their efficacy—they become overwhelmed within the larger implications and need for particularity when confronting the Holocaust through fiction. In Malamud's two attempts at a Holocaust fiction, we glimpse the shortcomings of his abstract and universal moral system, and perhaps understand why he felt compelled to turn to fable and allegory in later apocalyptic works.

A FIRST ATTEMPT

In "The Lady of the Lake," Malamud's first attempt at a Holocaust fiction, published in 1958, he tells a story as simple as any biblical tale: a New York Jew named Henry Levin changes his name to Henry R. Freeman and travels to Europe to find a woman "worth marrying." After meeting and falling in love with Isabella, Freeman proposes to this beautiful Italian woman. On several occasions in the story, Isabella (who also hides her Jewishness until the story's conclusion) asks Freeman if by chance he might be a Jew. Upon his third vehement denial of his heritage, Isabella slowly unbuttons her shirt, thoroughly confusing the aroused Freeman. The omniscient narrator observes: "When she revealed her breasts—he could have wept at their beauty—to his horror he discerned tattooed on the soft and tender flesh a bluish line of distorted numbers" (240).

The story concludes with Isabella explaining her reasons for rejecting Freeman's marriage proposal. "Buchenwald, when I was a little girl. The Fascists sent us there. The Nazis did it." She continues: "I can't marry you. We are Jews. My past is meaningful to me. I treasure what I suffered for" (240). Isabella flees from Freeman, who attempts to reverse his denials, but it is too late, and he ends the story enveloped in the veiled mist rising from the lake as he embraces moonlit stone instead of his lover.

In 1958 Malamud takes it on faith that this image of suffering and unspeakable horror will create a lasting impression on the reader. I would argue that Malamud's misuse of this Holocaust image has the opposite effect on his readers: instead of sensitizing them to the destruction of Nazi totalitarianism, such misuse of Holocaust imagery anesthetizes readers. I use the word *misuse* as a result of the utility in which Malamud uses Isabella's tattoo. In Malamud's hands, Isabella's tattoo becomes not a symbol of Nazi dehumanization, but instead is used as a cudgel in which to beat the self-hating Freeman into a realization of the folly of rejecting his Jewish past. Additionally, in moving the tattoo from Isabella's arm to her sexualized breast, Malamud has distorted one of the most potent Holocaust images and turned it into an object of prurience. Is this really the appropriate lesson to be gleaned from the horrors of the Holocaust, or is Malamud relying upon an easy plot device to neatly tie up his story? Malamud's simple narratorial moralizing concerning Freeman hypocritically glosses Isabella's duplicity. Despite her survivor status, Isabella attempts to trick Freeman into believing that her father is a del Dango and owner of the palace, instead of a poor caretaker named della Seta; Isabella thus disavows not only her religion, but her social position as well.

It would be easy to comment on the irony of this story and the moral heft by which Freeman-Levin is reprimanded for rejecting his past and for his mistaken belief that he can take part in the American tradition of remaking himself through the simple act of changing his name.[4] Less apparent is just what Malamud's beautiful creation Isabella values so highly. Isabella rebuffs Freeman because her past is meaningful to her, and therefore she must marry a Jew. Her next line spoken to Freeman reveals just what constitutes that past: suffering. Isabella's treasured past is not oriented around any covenantal or traditional value which has sustained the Jewish people for thousands of years, and which before the Holocaust constituted a communal history. Instead Isabella, like many of Malamud's characters, treasures the reminders of her immediate past of suffering and anti-Semitism. Malamud would place in the Holy Ark not a living parchment representation of the divine law, but the scarred breast of a survivor—a tattooed representation of genocide.

As stated previously, Malamud's characters are typically marginal, assimilated Jews, and the characters in "The Lady of the Lake" are no exception—seeming to have little Jewish orientation or conception of a meaningful Jewish past. Isabella's one reference to traditional law and culture of Judaism is to suggest that the mountains of Italy remind her of a *menorah*, although she quickly changes her mind, calling them a seven-pronged candelabra, ostensibly to cover for Freeman, but perhaps, like Freeman, also to hide her discomfort at being seen as a Jew by a gentile. She is just as duplicitous as Freeman in hiding a traditional past and culture.

Thus, Isabella's treasured past, with which she, and by extension Malamud himself, hypocritically rebukes Freeman, seems as hollow and fake as the Titians and Tintorettos that hang in the halls of the tourist trap her father oversees as caretaker. In Malamud's system, Italian Jews are just as symbolic and assimilated as their American counterparts. Consequently, Isabella's suffering becomes divorced from Judaism itself, rendering her rejection of Freeman on the grounds of a Jewish identity contrived and hypocritical. Through Isabella's conjuring of her treasured past, Malamud has begun to dissolve and distort Holocaust images, and thereby mask and denature the profound historical reality of the Nazi era.

HOLOCAUST SIMULACRA?

Famously Theodor Adorno suggests that aesthetics after Auschwitz is barbaric and that "language itself had been damaged, possibly beyond creative repair, by the politics of mass terror and mass murder" (qtd. in Berger, *Crisis and Covenant* 30). As the Nazi concentration camps were being liberated across Europe, George Orwell, in his essay "Politics and the English Language," spoke of the dangers of imprecise language and the dissolution of language's capacity to represent experience through bureaucratic double-speak and totalitarian terror. In his book *Simulacra and Simulation*, Jean Baudrillard explains the process of imagistic change and rebirth that Orwell decried. His theory on the decomposition of images might help us understand Malamud's use of Holocaust images, and perhaps explain how Isabella's Jewish identity becomes transformed.

According to Baudrillard, an image passes through the following four stages of representation:

1. it is the reflection of a profound reality
2. it masks and denatures a profound reality
3. it masks the absence of a profound reality
4. it has no relation to any reality whatsoever: it is its own pure simulacrum.[5]

Novelists, particularly Jewish American novelists, creating art out of the destruction of the Holocaust, are thus faced with a perplexing conundrum: they must balance their moral imperative to acknowledge their history, while hoping that their attempt at representation will not weaken language's capacity to represent their legacy. In "The Lady of the Lake," Malamud has failed to balance these two competing imperatives. His evocative image, a tattooed breast of a Buchenwald survivor, instead of spurring the reader's condemnation of Freeman's rejection of his Jewish heritage, ultimately denatures the profound reality of this particular image from the Holocaust.[6] By his misuse of this image, Malamud has begun to turn Isabella's tattoo into what Baudrillard calls a simulacrum, one which over time may be used in unusual and less than appropriate contexts—often by contemporary Jewish American novelists.[7]

In the years after the publication of "The Lady of the Lake," Malamud was not entirely oblivious to the dissolution of Holocaust imagery. In fact, his second attempt at writing a Holocaust fiction might be read as a conscious effort at making up for his first unmasking and denaturing of Holocaust imagery. We should thus understand Malamud's writing "The German Refugee" as an attempt to turn back the clock on language's power to represent—an effort which ultimately fails, but which might serve as a warning to future generations of writers attempting to represent the Holocaust in their fiction.

REVISED WITNESSING: A SECOND ATTEMPT

This shift in Malamud's perspective on writing about the Holocaust might best be viewed in his shift from a limited omniscient third-person narrator, and the relative assurance of such a narrative voice in "The Lady of the Lake," to the halting and uncertain voice of a first-person limited consciousness of an unsophisticated American narrator, Martin Goldberg, in "The German Refugee." Goldberg begins the story as an older man looking back on his youthful experiences. As a young college student in the summer of 1939, he worked as an English tutor for intellectual German refugees. He tells the story of his friendship with one such refugee, the critic Oskar Gassner who has fled Germany in the aftermath of Kristallnacht. Once resettled in New York City, Gassner has been hired as a college lecturer, and by summer's end he must prepare, in English, a speech on Walt Whitman's poetry. Gassner is in desperate fear of his heavy German accent, and Goldberg, a novitiate in the ways of suffering, a quester in need of understanding to go with his American exuberance, has a long and hot summer of work before him. He says at the outset of the story: "Here I was panting to get going, and across the ocean Adolph Hitler, in black boots and a square mustache, was tearing up and spitting at all the flowers" (357). These lines reveal the narrator's naiveté with what was to come; here focused on surface physical characteristics, Goldberg misses the deeper story and truth—as did Malamud in 1958 in his earlier attempt at a Holocaust fiction. Had the story been set in 1939 in the present tense one could accept Goldberg's simplicity. But the narrator is writing years after the war is over with the full knowledge of the atrocities of the Holocaust, yet this reality never impinges on the consciousness of the narrator. It is as if the events of the summer of 1939 were happening in real time—the illusion of which is given further solidity with periodic radio broadcasts of the advancing European war. There is no hint of irony in the narrator's voice.

This switch in narrative perspective corresponds to Malamud's newfound Holocaustal voice and his delving into the narratological difficulties associated with representing the Holocaust. Malamud recognized the tawdriness of his use of the Holocaust tattoo on the naked breast of his beautiful Italian survivor and was determined to make amends in "The German Refugee." We see this contriteness in Goldberg the narrator—who might just as easily be speaking for Malamud—when he says: "I was in those days a poor student and would brashly attempt to teach anybody anything for a buck an hour, although I have since learned better" (357).

In this story rather than contribute to the dissolution of Holocaust imagery as he had in "The Lady of the Lake," Malamud has Goldberg go about his task in an incidental way; by setting the story in 1939, the Holocaust looms on the horizon as a great historical reality which will soon envelope the world that Oskar Gassner has left behind. Consequently, in "The German Refugee" Malamud attempts to represent the Holocaust without its numbing imagery. A typical sentence from the story—one in which Goldberg is fleshing in the particulars of Gassner's flight from Germany—reveals Malamud's newfound anxiety with approaching the Holocaust: "He had come a month before Kristallnacht, when the Nazis shattered Jewish store windows and burnt all the synagogues, to see if he could find a job for himself" (358).

The ease with which Goldberg relates this information—Kristallnacht becomes a dependent clause in a sentence describing Gassner's American prospects—goes beyond irony and forces the reader to confront Goldberg's and Malamud's evasiveness. Surely Malamud doesn't share the ingenuousness of the young Goldberg who says after hearing Gassner's story about his anti-Semitic mother-in-law and gentile wife, "I asked no questions. Gentile is gentile, Germany is Germany" (358). As established earlier, if Malamud felt so strongly about "not enough being made of the Holocaust" then why has he narrated "The German Refugee," perhaps his most important story, with the voice of the unsophisticated Martin Goldberg?

Reading with an eye toward the complexities of representation, Malamud's intentions soon reveal themselves. Goldberg speaks in generalized terms about the difficulties intellectual German refugees had in acculturating to New York society. He says: "To many of these people, articulate as they were, the great loss was the loss of language—that they could not say what was in them to say" (360).

REPRESENTING THE UNREPRESENTABLE

Now we can begin to see what Malamud's problem, first evidenced in his unsubtle conclusion to "The Lady of the Lake," truly is—the insufficient nature of language to represent the watershed event of the Holocaust. He had tried back in 1958 and had to revert to melodrama and a sensationalized image in his story's conclusion. How could the results have been any different? As Goldberg says of the German refugees—in essence all Jewish intellectuals, Malamud included—attempting to make not only sense but art out of the ashes of Auschwitz, "You have some subtle thought and it comes out like a piece of broken bottle" (360). In search of aesthetic beauty, Malamud was left sorting through the detritus of Kristallnacht.

Malamud's thematic dilemma of representing the Holocaust without its imagery is compounded in "The German Refugee" by characterizing both his narrator and protagonist as marginal and assimilated (symbolic) Jews. Gassner, in particular—as contributor to the influential German journal *Acht Uhr Abendblatt*—represents the quintessence of the assimilated pre-War German Jew. Unlike in "The Lady of the Lake" in which Malamud sprung the Holocaust on both Freeman and his readers as a deus ex machina on the last page, now in "The German Refugee" Malamud is faced not only with the problem of representing the Holocaust, but with representing the victims of the Holocaust as well. The results are that Malamud's ahistoric symbolic Jews are not capable of bearing true witness to the historical event of the Holocaust.

Martin Goldberg's quip aimed at Gassner seems to be an apt summation for Malamud: "He would attempt to say something and then stop, as though it could not possibly be said" (358).

Malamud attempts to rectify this problem through one more misstep: he reasons that if his symbolic Jews are not capable of representing the Holocaust, perhaps they can represent all humanity. Thus in "The Lady of the Lake" Malamud has misused Holocaust imagery, and in "The German Refugee" he distorts history.[8] Malamud's conclusion to "The German Refugee" underscores the shortcomings of his symbolic and universal system of Judaism, while highlighting his own difficulties with traditional Judaism. The final paragraph of "The German Refugee" might stand as the fictional accompaniment to his remark that all men are Jews.

After his successful speech on Whitman, Gassner commits suicide by gassing himself in his apartment. He leaves all his possessions to Martin Goldberg, his young tutor. In attempting to piece together the events leading to Gassner's death, Goldberg stumbles upon a letter from Gassner's mother-in-law. The final paragraph follows:

> She writes in a tight script and it takes me hours to decipher that her daughter, after Oskar abandons her, against her own mother's fervent pleas and anguish, is converted to Judaism by a vengeful rabbi. One night the Brown Shirts appear, and though the mother wildly waves her bronze crucifix in their faces, they drag Frau Gassner, together with the other Jews, out of the apartment house and transport them in lorries to a small border town in conquered Poland. There, it is rumored, she is shot in the head and topples into an open ditch with the naked Jewish men, their wives and children, some Polish soldiers, and a handful of Gypsies. (368)

What is striking about this paragraph is its shift in tone and tense from Martin Goldberg's earlier narration, characterized by an uncertain, wavering voice. Lawrence Lasher notes that the unsophisticated Martin Goldberg has been supplanted by "the mature Martin Goldberg, the narrator who will impose a larger meaning on the story as the events are penetrated by the omniscient eye of the artist" (79). In Lasher's conception of the final paragraph, the words do not belong to Gassner's mother-in-law, a confirmed anti-Semite, but rather to Martin Goldberg and his newly acquired artist's vision. Consequently, in this paragraph the blatant scapegoating of the rabbi cannot be excused as only the ranting of Gassner's anti-Semitic mother-in-law, but rather the mature artist Goldberg—Malamud's doppelganger—must also share in the responsibility.

The text reads that Gassner's wife "is converted to Judaism by a vengeful rabbi." Malamud's text suggests that if not for this rabbi who converted Frau Gassner, she wouldn't have been deported and murdered, and Gassner would not have committed suicide. In Goldberg's interpretation of the letter, Frau Gassner does not actively seek to be converted—the text makes her the passive recipient of a vengeful Judaism. In Malamud's symbolic Judaism the rabbi becomes the active agent of destruction.[9]

These lines also signal a final switch from Martin Goldberg's limited omniscient, past-tense perspective to a more comprehensively omniscient and present-tense narrating of the final dramatic lines. This final paragraph of omniscience signals Martin Goldberg's development from a naive and "poor student" to a mature artist who can actively interpret and shape Gassner's story.

This lapse from a limited first-person perspective is signaled in the opening line of the story: "Oskar Gassner sits in his cotton-mesh undershirt and summer bathrobe at the window of his stuffy, hot, dark hotel room on West Tenth Street as I cautiously knock" (357). Malamud submerges this level of narratorial knowledge and vision for the remainder of the story until Goldberg's concluding omniscience brings the story full circle as he sits in the very same armchair Gassner wearily rises from at the story's outset, translating and interpreting the letters left behind.

The concluding lines of "The German Refugee" once again show the shallowness of Malamud's symbolic Judaism. After being shot, Frau Gassner's body "topples into an open ditch with the naked Jewish men, their wives and children, some Polish soldiers, and a handful of gypsies" (368). Here we can witness the strain on Malamud's symbolism desperately attempting, through irony, to echo Whitman's promise of universal brotherhood in death rather than life. Malamud himself admitted, "I feel that indeed I try to represent in my fiction the Jew as universal man . . . and I suppose that what I hope by saying that is that recognition of this drama should ally human beings to one another" (Cheuse and Delbanco, *Talking Horse* 137). By drama, Malamud refers to a Jewish history of exile and dispersion. Just such an attempt at universalism through an omniscient voice at the end of "The German Refugee" reveals the superficiality of Malamud's humanism placed in an historical context. This last switch to omniscience in "The German

Refugee," and a far more literal rendering of the Holocaust, signals Malamud's reverting to the assured narrative voice of "The Lady of the Lake" and his earlier misuse of Holocaust imagery. Five years later, Malamud's symbolic Jews are still unable to testify to the destruction of the Holocaust.

UNIVERSAL JEWS?

In her essay "A Liberal's Auschwitz," Cynthia Ozick maintains, "'Mankind,' 'humanity,' and 'universal'—these are among the most dangerous words in the language" (151). Ozick discusses the literary precedents for universalizing Jews (Shakespeare's Shylock) before moving to a discussion of more recent examples. Several years before he published *Sophie's Choice*, William Styron wrote an op-ed piece in *The New York Times*, arguing for an interpretation of Auschwitz as being *antihuman* as opposed to a narrower definition of *anti-Semitic*. Ozick forcefully argues that while being a gesture of good will and compassion, such humanistic and universalizing tendencies may end with "confusing the victim with the victimizer" (151).

Ozick concludes her remarks on the particularity of history saying: "Jews are no metaphors—not for poets, not for novelists, not for theologians, not for murderers, and never for anti-Semites" (153). Ozick's declaration is easily applied to Malamud's Holocaust fiction. In Malamud's symbolic system, the vengeful rabbi metonymically represents traditional Judaism and Orthodoxy. The rabbi isn't blamed for only the death of Frau Gassner in conquered Poland, but by extension he is also responsible for the gassing of Oskar Gassner in America. In attempting to universalize the suffering of his protagonists, Malamud does indeed end up confusing the victims of the third Reich with their victimizers.

In the first week of September 1939, Gassner finally completes his lecture on Walt Whitman, giving Goldberg a moment of suspended relief. He says: "The Nazis had invaded Poland, and though we were greatly troubled, there was some sense of release; maybe the brave Poles would beat them" (366). Maybe indeed. Goldberg's wishful and naive comments eerily parallel Malamud's own thoughts as a young man in the summer of 1939, recounted in a memoir shortly before his death. Malamud writes: "Possibly diplomacy was in progress. Perhaps there would be no renewed conflict. Many Americans seemed to think the threat of war might expire. Many of us hoped so, though hoping was hard work; nor did it make too much sense, given the aberrations of Adolph Hitler. We worried about the inevitable world war but tried not to think of it" (Cheuse and Delbanco, *Talking Horse* 27).

SONG OF WHOSE SELF?

Malamud is clearly modeling the narrator Martin Goldberg on himself as a young man. In so doing, he hopes for his readers to understand how he has matured as a writer and as a humanist. Lasher suggests that "The story can be read as an exploration of the relationship between history and narrative as Malamud invites the reader to be witness at the birth of the artist, as personal experience embedded in the web of history becomes moral understanding which is communicated, finally, through aesthetic form" (74).

We can now understand the aesthetic difficulty confronting Malamud in either guise—as a young, brash, and naive first-person Goldberg, or as omniscient and mature artist Goldberg—Malamud's raw materials for aesthetic form remain unchanged: symbolic Jews who cannot properly bear witness to the Holocaust. We can see the shortcomings of Malamud's mature aesthetic form in the concluding section of "The German Refugee." Gassner's speech on Whitman contains these famous lines from section five of "Song of Myself":

> And I know the spirit of God is the brother of my own,
> And that all men ever born are also my brothers,
> and the women my sisters and lovers,
> And that the kelson of creation is love. (367)

In attempting to universalize the Holocaust, Malamud has succumbed to the pre-Holocaustal optimism of which Whitman so eloquently sang. In so doing, the mature artist Malamud, much like the young Martin Goldberg, has refused to see the singularity of the Holocaust, attempting instead to ironically realize Whitman's promise of universal brotherhood in a communal grave rather than in life.

Malamud's attempt at representing the Holocaust through indirection, through addressing his difficult position as creative artist conjuring a lost world, is a noble pursuit, but as Baudrillard warns us, it is a dangerous one as well, one which may inadvertently demean and denature the images used to represent the Holocaust itself. Malamud's two Holocaust stories emphasize the fraught landscape facing any writer who attempts to create art out of the yawning gulf of the Holocaust. Toward the end of "The German Refugee" after hearing Gassner's lecture, Goldberg suggests that during that bleak summer of 1939 Whitman's "verses were somehow protective" (367). While it is true that Whitman's poetry and perhaps Malamud's stories may help salve the wound, this modicum of comfort is not gained without a commensurate cost to language's power of representation and a loss of Holocaustal imagistic power.[10]

In "The German Refugee" Malamud has not written "a parable of desertion and sacrifice" as Walter Goodman contends; rather, he has created a parable of the Jewish American author attempting to represent the horror of the Holocaust. "The German Refugee" and "The Lady of the Lake" do bear witness, but toward a type of testimony Malamud never imagined. These stories eloquently voice the perils of creating art out of the ashes of the Holocaust, and the dilemma of imbuing symbolic and assimilated characters with the weight of actual covenantal, or dialectical, history. Holocaust art might help a reader grapple with the enormity of the destruction, but Malamud, five years after "The Lady of the Lake" was published, in his short story "The German Refugee," perhaps inadvertently, reminds his readers—as well as himself—of the perils of attempting to draw any easy moral and humanistic lessons from the cataclysmic event of the twentieth century. As Ozick reminds us: "Blurring eases. Specificity pains" ("A Liberal's Auschwitz" 153). Malamud's attempt at creating a universal symbol of the Jew ultimately blurs the reality of what it means to be a Jew. Within his two Holocaust stories Malamud's continued attempt toward universalism ultimately obscures the reality faced by Jews in the Holocaust. Frau Gassner wasn't murdered because of a "vengeful rabbi," or because of her universal humanity, nor for any symbolic system, but simply for being a Jew.

CONCLUSION

Being a Jew isn't about universality, for once a Jew becomes a symbol she ceases to have a distinct history; Malamud's symbolic Jews once divorced from their culture cease to bear witness to their histories. Malamud would have us believe his characters are Jews because they have Jewish names or speak with Yiddish inflections. As Ozick insists:

"Biology levels. Ideas differentiate. Ideas differentiate because every idea, and every civilization which expresses it, is situated to history, and history—unlike organs, dimensions, senses, etc.—is singular" (150).

In recalling Berger's conception of the Jewish American writer's role as theologian, we should read Malamud's two Holocaust stories as cautionary tales: novelists should be careful of constructing symbolic abstractions, particularly when attempting to place on their characters' frail metaphorical shoulders the weight of history—specifically a Jewish history and identity as it relates to the Holocaust. If contemporary fiction writers observe Malamud's aesthetic warning, they will continue to confront the awesome legacy of the Holocaust without exhausting language's capacity for representation and without diluting and denaturing the profound, and singular, historical reality of the Holocaust.

Despite his compassionate empathy and generous view of his characters, Malamud's symbolic and universal Judaism blurs the witnessing within his Holocaust stories. Ironically Malamud's two attempts at representing the Holocaust do not testify to the historical event itself, but to the perils of creating art from its tragedy and loss.

CHAPTER 3

Bellow's Short Fiction: Something Jewish To Remember Him By

I didn't invent that; you know I got stuck with it. Suppose you had an uncle in the wooden handle business and the wooden handle business went out of date and was broke. And you got stuck with a big inventory of wooden handles. Well, you would want to go around and attach wooden handles to as many things as possible. I'm just an unfortunate creature who gets a lot of these handles attached to him. This whole Jewish writer business is sheer invention—by the media, by critics and by "scholars." It never even passes through my mind. I'm well aware of being Jewish and also of being an American and of being a writer. But I'm also a hockey fan, a fact which nobody ever mentions.

—Cronin and Siegel, *Conversations with Saul Bellow* 103

AMERICANIZATION/MENTCHIFICATION

Irving Howe maintained that by the 1960s Jewish American fiction had passed its high point. The great theme of Jewish American novels had been immigration: Jews becoming Americans for better or (usually) for worse. Howe's remark presupposes the idea that the great Jewish novelists of the fifties and sixties had immigration and Americanization as their one (and only) great theme. This supposition is shared by Bellow's official biographer James Atlas, who claims Bellow "was a novelist who was to make the process of becoming an American one of his major themes" (19). Putting aside for a moment whether or not Bellow ever actually thematically deals with the process of Americanization in his fiction, what is always of utmost importance to the Bellovian hero is not the process of Americanization itself, but the even more difficult personal journey of *mentchification*. Lee Siegel suggests, "Bellow's characters, Jewish or not, are Americans who are in the process of becoming persons" (79). Atlas and Siegel are both half correct. Bellow's fiction intertwines the process of Americanization with the process of *mentchification* or of becoming more fully human. In this chapter I will analyze this duality of Americanization/*Mentchification*; this dual theme can be most clearly seen in Bellow's short fiction: "The Old System," "A Silver Dish," and *The Bellarosa Connection*. "The Old System" is found in *Mosby's Memoirs and Other Stories*; "A Silver Dish" is found in *Him with His Foot in His Mouth and Other Stories*, and *The Bellarosa Connection*.

FROM PARIAH TO PRINCE:
A BIOGRAPHICAL DIGRESSION

Pariahs, thought Braun, with the dignity of princes among themselves.

—"The Old System" 48–49

"For this is an era of hardboiled-dom" (9): So begins Joseph's ruminations in Bellow's first book *Dangling Man*. Joseph leaps onto the American literary stage *kvetching* about Hemingway. Joseph (much like Bellow himself)[1] was born into a generation raised on a healthy diet of tough-guy machismo; America in the nineteen forties did not possess the delicate constitution required of soul searching and navel watching. In the midst of World War II, when Bellow enters the literary landscape, an American public in need of action, of energy, simply could not swallow notions of selfish inwardness. For example, in his 1997 novel *American Pastoral*, while summing up the postwar American sensibility, Philip Roth implores his readers (presumably those far removed from such notions) to "remember the energy. . . . The depression had disappeared. Everything was in motion. The lid was off. Americans were to start over again, en masse, everyone in it together" (40). With Roth's reminiscence in mind, it is not surprising that in the midst of such altruistic patriotism Joseph is worried about the selfish and unseemly act of keeping a diary.

With all of Bellow's postwar success as a novelist and short-story writer, it is hard to remember that Bellow leapt onto the literary scene not with Augie March's barbaric yawp, "I am an American, Chicago born" (3), but with the self-conscious ruminations of Jewish protagonists worried about not being American enough. Early in his career, Bellow seems obsessed by the idea of the writer as feminine, weak, and self-absorbed. Bellow has his hero Joseph explain this hardboiled Hemingwayesque pose as having been inherited from the figure of the English gentleman—cool and detached in the face of terror—and which Bellow suggests dates back to Alexander the Great, a monarch from the avowed enemies of the Jews, the destroyers of the Holy Temple in Jerusalem.

Similarly, in the opening pages of *Augie March*, Bellow contrasts the British Playboy mentality with the style of old world Jewish immigrants, associated in Bellow's memory with poor people desperately conniving to get ahead in American society. In the opening scene of *Augie March*, this "immigrant style" is used in procuring free eyeglasses for Augie's mother. Augie relates the story: "Coached by Grandma Lausch, I went to do the lying. Now I know it wasn't so necessary to lie, but then everyone thought so, and Grandma Lausch especially who was one of those Machiavellis of small street and neighborhood that my young years were full of" (4). Augie at the young age of nine already understood that it is the Jews versus *them*—everyone else. Augie's brother Simon, however, having gotten "English schoolboy notions of honor" was somewhat removed from the immigrant mindset.

In Bellow's early work, American hardboiledness, inherited from the English gentleman and having been bequeathed from classical notions of honor and civicmindedness, was an ideal far removed from the striving, conniving, Jewish immigrant milieu. Notions of postwar civility were better left to the moneyed and leisured classes of American (or British) high society. As Augie memorably sums up: "*Tom Brown's Schooldays* for many years had an influence we were not in a position to afford" (4). Or similarly, nearly forty years after the publication of *Augie March*, in a 1991 interview Bellow talks about the enslavement of American literature to English models (pre-*Augie*): "Leading the 'correct' grammatical forces was *The New Yorker*. I used to say about Shawn and *The New Yorker* that he had traded the Talmud for Fowler's *Modern English Usage*" (Cronin and Siegel, *Conversations with Saul Bellow* 282). Although by 1991 Bellow could look back and poke fun at the WASPish Jews who had separated themselves from their Jewish textual inheritance, his own literary record leaves an impression not dissimilar to *The New Yorker* mindset he lampooned in 1991.

The more literary success Bellow achieved, the further removed he became from the conniving, striving, immigrant generation of his youth. Once Bellow could afford English Gentlemanly behaviors, the more obscene and despicable the immigrant ways—the old world and its systems—seemed to the Nobel Laureate. Twenty-five years after *Augie March*, in "The Old System," an obscure short story which is just recently beginning to be recognized as a small masterpiece,[2] Bellow still carps at this same trope "us versus them," immigrant Jew in all his huddled ugliness, yearning to afford the gentlemanly manner of hardboiledness.

With twenty-five years passing between *Augie March* and "The Old System," we can begin to question whether Bellow revises his thinking on his major fictional theme and ask: has his representation and perception of Judaism matured as his career blossomed? Being the man of masks that he is, the answer will of course not be easily gleaned from the fictional portrait Bellow has left his readers and critics. However, in "The Old System," first published in *Playboy*[3] in 1967, we can begin to see Bellow's changing conception of Judaism, particularly as it relates to Orthodox praxis and ritual.

MR. BELLOW'S JUDAISM

> They had a hideous synagogue of such red brick as seemed to grow in upstate New York by the will of the demon spirit charged with the ugliness of America in that epoch, which saw to it that a particular comic ugliness should influence the soul of man.
>
> —"The Old System" 48

Except for Eugene Henderson, Saul Bellow's literary heroes (some might call them antiheroes) have been almost exclusively Jewish. Despite this fact, in his early work Bellow's characters are hardly recognizably, let alone obviously, Jewish. I was recently reminded of this peculiar fact while teaching Bellow's *Dangling Man* to an extremely bright group of New York University English majors who needed to be informed of Joseph's religion. Although never coming out and stating that Joseph is a Jew, Bellow implies Joseph's ancestry through several Old Testament references in *Dangling Man*. For example, in a moment of frustration Joseph's brother Amos refers to Joseph as being "stiff-necked" (60). Although in explaining Amos's remark Bellow quotes the prophet Isaiah who refers to the "stretched forth necks" of the "haughty daughters of Zion," Amos's remark more clearly parallels the end of the book of Exodus, the scene of the covenant when God describes his chosen people. After Moses comes down from Mount Sinai and sees his people worshiping the golden calf, in a fit of anger he breaks the Ten Commandments. Soon thereafter, while deciding the fate of his chosen, but sinful, people, God tells Moses to say to the Israelites: "You are a stiff-necked people (*am kishai oref*)" (Exodus 33:5). After speaking to the Israelites, Moses reminds God that he shall "visit the iniquity of parents upon children and children's children, upon the third and fourth generations" (Exodus 34:7), before begging God to forgive his chosen people: "Even though this is a stiff-necked people. Pardon our iniquity and our sin, and take us for Your own" (Exodus 34:9).

Despite a few semiveiled covenantal references, there are no outwardly Jewish moments either in *Dangling Man* or in *Seize the Day*. If one were not reading Bellow's early work with an eye toward Jewishness and Jewish-related themes, Joseph's (if not Wilky's) lineage might easily pass by even the most perspicacious reader.

However, in his best work, beginning with *Augie March* in 1953, Bellow is no longer afraid of outwardly Jewish characters; despite Augie's remonstrance that he is "An American, Chicago born," there is never a doubt from the opening page of just what Augie is: distinctively Jewish American, and not some WASPlike wannabe. If we are to take at face value James Atlas's assertion that "It was through Bellow's efforts that Jewish literature was to become American" (129), we are still left with the question of just what kind of Jewish characters has Bellow been portraying since Augie burst on the literary scene over half a century ago?

BELLOW'S HEROES:
FROM ASSIMILATION TO ORTHODOXY

Often, the Bellovian hero is a completely assimilated Jew, a person cut off from his history and identity much like Moses Herzog, a man who in pursuit of High Culture has traded in his Jewish religion for a pseudo-religion of the intellect. It isn't until his later work, beginning with "The Old System" in 1967 that Bellow begins to portray genuinely Jewish characters, characters immersed in Jewish culture, steeped in the tradition, and bound by the legal and ethical precepts of the Torah. In other words, it takes Bellow a quarter of a century before he gets around to creating the types of characters who are in Alan

Berger's phrase "covenantal" Jews. In this chapter I investigate just how Bellow has reworked his earlier conception and representation of Judaism, and how he has linked Orthodoxy and tradition, what he refers to as "the old system," with a broader critique of American culture, the postwar dissolution of the family, and most of all, the American embrace of the-future-at-all-costs with a concomitant amnesic attitude toward the past and any resemblance to cultural continuity.

Here I will demonstrate how Bellow uses traditional Judaism as a contrasting device through which he may politically, culturally, and philosophically critique the unfettered postwar American pursuit of capitalism. It is this "new system" of American capitalism, a callous economic system that must be pursued at all costs, which in Bellow's estimation has leveled all tradition and enfeebled the American family. Furthermore, we will see how Bellow's scathing critique of American values, which is often labeled archconservative,[4] is in fact more liberal than his critics from the left, stung by the publication of *Mr. Sammler's Planet*,[5] have been apt to characterize his project. For example, John Clayton, who felt betrayed by Bellow's turn against liberalism, read *Mr. Sammler's Planet* as a diatribe against the antiestablishment left of the 1960s. "The Old System," which was completed just a few years prior to Bellow's publishing *Mr. Sammler's Planet*, might be viewed as a dress rehearsal for the strident political statements Bellow made in his longer, and more well-known, work of fiction.

In previous chapters we analyzed how Henry Roth, early in his writing career, created stereotypically Jewish characters, and particularly how Roth's characterization of Rabbi Pankower in *Call It Sleep* borrowed from classical notions of anti-Semitism. Early in his career Roth viewed Judaism as an albatross around an immigrant's neck; the sooner it was tossed from the ship's deck in New York Harbor the better. In chapter 2, we examined how a generation later, Bernard Malamud, in order to make a broad humanistic statement appealing to ultimate redemption through suffering, created archetypically Christian characters masked as Jews.

In contrast, Saul Bellow has never created only symbolically Jewish characters. Although Bellow occasionally falls into the Malamudian trap in attempting to universalize the suffering and lives of his Jewish characters, as in the following example: "A vision of mankind Braun was having as he sat over his coffee Saturday afternoon. Beginning with those Jews of 1920" ("The Old System" 47), in general Bellow does not use his Jewish characters to make a larger humanistic argument. Although his early Jewish characters tend to be completely assimilated Jews, characters with only a vague remembrance of Jewishness and the old world, Bellow never uses his Jews to develop a Universalist theme. Additionally, unlike Malamud, we see Bellow's portrayal of Jewish characters, as well as his conception of Judaism, under constant revision throughout his career. In Malamud's work we saw how Judaism is used as a symbolic system of suffering by which Malamud universalizes his ghetto Jews into Christian archetypes of suffering and redemption, a concept alien to Judaism. Whereas Malamud's conception of Judaism was static, Bellow's Judaism is fluid and more complex; Bellow's "system" is under constant revision.

Judaism has meant different things to Bellow in different novels and short stories. For Joseph in *Dangling Man* Judaism meant one thing, for Augie March another. Still to Elya Gruner and Artur Sammler, Judaism becomes something else entirely. Within Bellow's ever-shifting Judaism, might a method or pattern emerge? Through examining several short-story "snapshots" of Bellow's evolving conception of Judaism, we might begin to understand what he means by "the old system" of doing things.

DR. BELLOW'S MEMORY: THE NOVELIST AS PHYSICIAN

Unlike Harry Fonstein, the founder of the Mnemosyne Institute and narrator of *The Bellarosa Connection* who finally "would like to forget about remembering" (1–2), Saul Bellow's capacious memory churns on. Being one of the twentieth century's great prose stylists, Bellow has been blessed (or cursed, depending on one's perspective) with the inability to forget. Consequently, what is worth remembering from the twentieth century may be glimpsed in Bellow's superb, if often overlooked, short fiction,[6] works that often feature the dual theme of memory and forgetting. As Gloria Cronin points out in her introduction to *Small Planets*, a collection of essays on Bellow's short fiction: "Bellow has been far more seriously involved in mastering the short fiction form than most of his literary critics have previously realized" (xi). Beginning with his first work *Dangling Man*,[7] all the way through *Seize the Day*, *A Theft*, *The Bellarosa Connection*, and *The Actual*, Bellow has periodically published novellas. Bellow has also been a prolific short-story writer; in addition to the recently published *Collected Stories*

(2001), which largely reprints previously published material, throughout his career Bellow has periodically returned to short fiction, publishing *Mosby's Memoirs* (1968) and *Him with His Foot in His Mouth* (1984). With the publication of his *Collected Stories* (2001), we can begin to clearly see the long trajectory of Saul Bellow's mature work in the short-story form. What becomes apparent is that after turning fifty, Bellow becomes increasingly obsessed (some might say haunted) by the issue of memory.

It is my contention that it is in the shorter fictional form—a place where Bellow has felt free to, in the words of John Clayton, "richly rework" his previous fictional material—that Bellow more honestly approaches the truth "of how things really are." This is particularly true in regards to the thorny issue (for Bellow) of Judaism. In his essay "Bellow at 85, Roth at 67," Norman Podhoretz, the editor of *Commentary*, goes so far as to suggest that Bellow's books are "almost always of surpassing brilliance and great fascination—forced into novelistic form" (41). Podhoretz suggests that the great prestige our society[8] holds for the novel "deflected" Bellow into becoming a novelist. Instead, Podhoretz laments, Bellow might have focused his immense talents on becoming a great essayist, or memoirist. The point of departure for Podhoretz's ruminations is the publication of Bellow's novel *Ravelstein*, a thinly veiled fictionalized portrait of Bellow's late friend, the archconservative critic Allan Bloom.

While I would agree with Podhoretz that often Bellow's novels become "monologues" and that Bellow suffers from "the compulsion to dress up as novels the fruits of his endlessly fascinating mind and magnificent literary gift" (42), I disagree with his contention that Bellow should have devoted himself to the craft of memoirist and nonfiction writer. Podhoretz points to the brilliance of Bellow's memoiristic essays in *To Jerusalem and Back* as exhibit A, while the roman a clef without the roman, *Ravelstein*, stands as exhibit B. While not disagreeing with most of Podhoretz's claims, I believe that what Podhoretz's formulation neglects is Bellow's superb mastery of short fiction, a form that contains some of his greatest, even most ambitious, writing. It is often only in the short fiction that we are fully drawn into the lives of characters who appear to us to truly live and breath, characters who are not merely mouthpieces for Bellow himself, or extended reflections on ideas long cherished by their creator/author.

Although Bellow's novels reflect his humanistic concern with what Alan Berger has termed "the covenantal relationship," I would suggest that, in addition to a covenant between God and Man, in Bellow's case there exists a special covenant between author and reader as well. L. H. Goldman has said that Bellow's late novels are "outspoken expressions of covenant Judaism" (qtd. in Berger, "The Logic of the Heart" 94). Although Goldman refers to the novels, this covenantal contract might best be glimpsed in Bellow's short works of fiction. In the stories both readers and characters begin to understand not just what is worth remembering, but more importantly Bellow's characters begin to answer the question of how one is to live one's life.

Consequently, in an effort to glimpse Bellow reworking his earlier conception of Jewish identity, in this chapter I will look at three of Bellow's short works of fiction: "The Old System," "A Silver Dish," and the novella *The Bellarosa Connection*. In so doing we may gauge Bellow's remarkable turn toward Orthodoxy and traditional Judaism as he hones his great twentieth-century memory. Just as Bellow himself gains sustenance from the act of writing, so too does the act of reading sustain Bellow's audience. In these stories and novella Bellow seems to be willing back to life that lost world of the "old system," all but destroyed in the Holocaust, all but forgotten by an increasingly assimilated American Jewish public.

MODERN ORTHODOXY IN AMERICA

> The rigid madness of the Orthodox. Their, haughty, spinning, crazy spirit.
> —"The Old System" 52

Through world-renowned geneticist Dr. Samuel Braun, Bellow has occasion to tell Isaac Braun's paradigmatic tale of Modern Orthodoxy in late twentieth-century America. If not for Braun's winter ruminations, Isaac's story would be in danger of being lost to the oblivion of time. While reminiscing on the older generation of his family, Dr. Braun unsuccessfully attempts to distill the essence of the "Jewish character." While reflecting on the similarities and ultimate differences between Isaac and Aaron, his two older immigrant cousins, Dr. Braun, "despite twenty-five years of specialization in the chemistry of heredity" (55), is unable to draw any conclusions concerning their personalities. Yet despite Samuel's ultimate failure, the concept of a genetic basis for the Jewish character type, an idea not without peril for a twentieth-century Jewish American writer, is incautiously broached in "The

Old System" when Braun ponders the influence of genetics upon character formation and the materialistic qualities of postwar American capitalism. "The Old System" raises the question of just how nature and nurture combine to form a new-world American success story.

Isaac is named after the paradigmatic Jewish conniver, the street-smart patriarch who knew how to "play the game" and deceive his father and inherit his brother Esau's birthright; and his straight-laced brother Aaron named after the biblical brother of Moses who was known as a *rodeph shalom*, a man who chased after peace. Braun the scientist says: "Aaron and Uncle Braun were drawn from the same genetic pool. Chemically, he (Aaron) was the younger brother of his father. The differences within were due possibly to heredity. Or perhaps to the influence of business America" (57). Bellow's story implicitly asks who has been truly influenced by "new system" business practices in America: the CPA Aaron, who with his "intercomed" (57) office and tailored suits possesses all the trappings of the American business success in the style of the English gentleman; or Isaac, with his beard and "kingly pariah derby," (57) the antithesis of the modern American businessman in appearance, but who truly represents the striving, conniving energy which Bellow sees as characterizing postindustrial America?

PLOT SYNOPSIS

A limited omniscient narrator whose attention is focused on the perspective of Dr. Isaac Braun, a middle-aged and unmarried world-renowned geneticist, chronicles "The Old System." Dr. Braun is a man who, in Sarah Blacher Cohen's words, is yet "another of Bellow's cerebral protagonists suffering from an overdeveloped brain and an underdeveloped heart" (109). On a dreary December morning, Dr. Braun awakes and contemplates his own wasted life and opportunities; soon his ruminations fall upon his long-deceased family, the Brauns of upstate New York: his uncles, aunts, and cousins whom he had spent much time with in his youth. Dr. Braun recounts the family history from the 1920s Coolidge era, casting back his memory to tell the story of how three generations of Brauns either made their fortunes or met their ruin in the New World they found in the Mohawk Valley. Braun recalls the family story of how playing by the New World rules, to the resentment of his siblings who failed to embrace the "new system" of WASPish American capitalism, cousin Isaac became an immensely wealthy American businessman while the rest of the family missed their opportunity at seizing greatness in the new world. Through the long history of the Braun family in upstate New York, Bellow constructs a postrabbinic *midrash*, or parable, on the dissolution of Jewish Orthodoxy and traditional values "in the void of America" (59).

ISAAC'S FAUSTIAN BARGAIN

The story turns upon a risky business deal that Isaac is forced to undertake alone. This deal, which founds Isaac's increasing fortune, over the course of many years leads to the increasing resentment of his siblings, especially Isaac's unruly sister Tina. Although Tina resents Isaac's immense wealth and blames him for not bringing them all into the real estate business, Tina's versions of events is not entirely accurate. In fact, Isaac had attempted to bring the entire family into what became the Robbstown shopping center, the basis for all Isaac's future wealth in postwar America. In truth, at a risky moment in the deal the entire family abandoned Isaac, forcing him to consummate the deal on his own. Old Ilkington who had led the Robbstown Country Club demanded a $100,000 bribe (in cash) under the table to allow Isaac and his siblings to develop the prime real estate in the center of an expanding Albany into a new, sprawling shopping center. In keeping with his increasing Orthodoxy, Isaac had found out about the real estate development deal from an old caddy master at the club when Isaac, doing a *mitzvah* (lit: a commandment, a good deed), "gave the man a lift, one morning of fog" (56) and was informed that the club was moving further into the countryside.

The four siblings agree to contribute $25,000 each for the bribe to Ilkington, but at the last possible moment they all back out leaving Isaac to fend for himself. Bellow's description of the shady business deal brilliantly showcases his firm grasp not only of immigrant Jewish family politics but the backroom business dealings of a sped-up industrialized postwar America. I'll quote it at length:

> The old goy, now seventy, retiring to the British West Indies, had said to Isaac, "Off the record. One hundred thousand. And I don't want to have to bother about Internal Revenue." He was a long, austere man with a marbled face. Cornell 1910 or so. Cold but plain. And in Isaac's opinion fair. Developed as a shopping center, properly planned, the Robbstown golf course was worth half a million apiece

to the Brauns. The city in the postwar boom was spreading fast. Isaac had a friend on the zoning board who would clear everything for five grand. As for the contracting, he offered to do it all on his own. Tina insisted that a separate corporation be formed by the Brauns to make sure the building profits were shared equally. To this Isaac agreed. As head of the family, he took the burden upon himself. He would have to organize it all. Only Aaron the C.P.A. could help him, setting up the books. The meeting, in Aaron's office, lasted from noon to three P.M. All the difficult problems were examined. Four players, specialists in the harsh music of money, studying a score. In the end they agreed to perform. (56)

At the last minute, however, Aaron, Tina, and Mutt decide that they cannot trust a non-Jew, a *goy*, leaving Isaac to raise the entire $100,000 on his own. Aaron tells Isaac: "You'll turn over a hundred thousand to a man you don't know? Without a receipt? Blind? Don't do it" (58). But Isaac does borrow the money, and two days later Ilkington comes through on his promise. In contrast, Aaron rejects Ilkington, and thus America's postwar promise largely passes him by. It is only by concurrently embracing his old-world system and new-world American business "ethics" and value system of under-the-table dealings that Isaac *makes it* in America.

The trope of the immigrant generations successfully mixing the old-world value system with the new-world order is seen time and again in Bellow's short fiction. Bellow underscores Isaac's successful navigation of the deal with juxtaposed images of Jewish and *goyish* values. First Bellow describes the way that Isaac worked his way up in the old European way "penny by penny, old style, starting with rags and bottles as a boy; then fire-salvaged goods; then used cars; then learning the building trades. Earth moving, foundations, concrete, sewage, wiring, roofing, heating systems. He got his money the hard way" (58–59). Next Bellow juxtaposes Isaac's hardscrabble childhood with Ilkington the "playboy capitalist" WASP. In Bellow's description of Ilkington's office, even the furnishings become piglike, unkosher: "Furnished in old goy taste and disseminating an old goy odor of tiresome, silly, respectable things. Of which Ilkington was clearly so proud. The applewood, the cherry, the wing tables and cabinets, the upholstery with a flavor of dry paste, the pork-pale colors of gentility" (59).

Ilkington remains so unemotional and detached that counting the $100,000 Isaac has given him is never a consideration; in fact, Ilkington doesn't even acknowledge the presence of the briefcase Isaac has filled with the payoff. Instead he coolly offers Isaac, at noon, a martini "Like something distilled in outer space. Having no color. He sat there sturdily, but felt lost—lost to his people, his family, lost to God, lost in the void of America" (59).

It is not by chance that Bellow has Isaac find out about the investment opportunity of building a shopping mall through his doing a *mitzvah*: "Isaac had learned this from the old caddie master when he gave him a lift, one morning of fog" (56). The word *caddie* is also punning on Tina's sly but cruel use of the word Caddy on the previous page to refer to Isaac's keeping in his Cadillac a Tehillim (a book of Psalms) to recite from while stuck in traffic. Tina scornfully, and quite wittily, opines: "He reads the Tehillim aloud in his air-conditioned Caddy when there's a long freight train at the crossing. That crook! He'd pick God's pocket!" (55).

The picture of Isaac reciting the Tehillim in his Cadillac while waiting for the "long freight train at the crossing" is as brilliant as any image in Bellow's mature work. The juxtaposition of old-world piety symbolized by the *sefer* (book) of Tehillim, is beautifully contrasted with the new-world symbol of prosperity, an air-conditioned Cadillac automobile. Furthermore the instrument that makes this scene possible is the long freight train at the crossing personifying the industrial success of America in the Mohawk Valley of the early twentieth century.

This image is given even more resonance when one recalls the previous scene in "The Old System" when Dr. Braun recounts Isaac's difficult courting process. Aunt Rose, Isaac's impossible mother, rejected all potential spouses for her son, characterizing each one with a memorably hyperbolic⁹ Yiddish phrase: "'A false dog.' 'Candied Poison.' 'An open ditch. A sewer. A born whore!'" (52). Isaac eventually marries the daughter of a Jewish farmer. When Rose protests that the woman's father is "ignorant, and common," Isaac assures her: "He's honest, a hard worker on the land. . . . He recites the Psalms even when he's driving. He keeps them under his wagon seat" (52).

In "The Old System," Bellow brilliantly tropes on the Tehillim, a classical Jewish text. In Bellow's story it is not only used as an example of Jewish continuity (a symbol of Isaac's increasing Orthodoxy), but it is also used to gauge the development of the Eastern European immigrant generation in America. In Bellow's symbolic system this immigrant generation is best understood through the many Jewish businessmen who traded in their horse-drawn wagons for air-conditioned Cadillacs. Yet despite this generation of immigrants' material rise in

America, their well-worn copies of the Tehillim made the arduous journey from under their farmer's rustic wagon seats in the *shtetl* to inside
their leather-lined glove compartments in American automobiles.[10]

Although Isaac was able to do business with the new-world
upstate *goyim*, he was still Cainlike marked by the old world with "a
long scar on his cheek" as a result of his mother having "given him milk
from a tubercular cow in the old country" (46). Through all of Isaac's
new-world dealings he remains physically marked, but more importantly Isaac is separated from the new world ethically, by his adherence
to the old-world values of Jewish Orthodoxy. As Isaac accumulates
wealth in the new world, he undergoes a concomitant return to his
immigrant roots through the medium of Orthodox Judaism. The more
wealth Isaac accumulates, the more of a *baal teshuvah* (literally translated as: "a master of repentance," a term used to denote someone who
has returned to an Orthodox lifestyle) he becomes. Yet in true biblical
fashion, despite Isaac's increased commitment to Orthodoxy, Bellow's
story dramatizes the reality that there is no such thing as an unadul-
terated good. The ugliness of improvement, of modernity, the callous
bald-faced horror of Isaac's shopping center, a monstrosity built upon
what used to be "Green acres reserved, it was true, for mild idleness, for
hitting a little ball with a stick, were now paralyzed by parking for five
hundred cars" (60) points to the pollution and debasement of the
America soil upon which Isaac and his immigrant generation were to
build their *New Jerusalem* in the Mohawk Valley. Isaac's monstrous
housing developments also underscore Bellow's critique of the unfettered materialism that he believes has weakened not only the American character, but the American environment as well.

TINA'S *MISHEGAS*

After Dr. Braun retells the story of Isaac's deal with Ilkington, "The
Old System" turns truly macabre. Years after the business deal with Ilkington is completed, Isaac's two brothers make up with him; however
his morose and bitter sister Tina refuses to make peace with her
brother.

There is a *halachah* (Jewish law) that before Yom Kippur (Day of
Atonement) before praying for God's forgiveness every Jew must first
ask *mechilah* (forgiveness) from other people—all those he may have
wronged during the previous year. Consequently, following the Ortho-

dox custom, each year before Yom Kippur Isaac drove over to Tina's house to beg her forgiveness. Each year when Tina would open the door and recognize her brother's scarred face, in full operatic range, she would curse Isaac, slam the door, and for one more year feed upon her anger and bitterness.

Interestingly, each year after this scene Tina would call her brother Aaron (who ironically despite his biblical namesake was unable, or unwilling, to affect a reconciliation between his siblings), and bitterly complain to him about Isaac. "She said she hated his Orthodox cringe. She could take him straight. In a deal. Or a swindle. But she couldn't bear his sentiment" (67). Tina's characterization of Orthodoxy as "sentimental" and weak is in keeping with Bellow's own long-standing antipathy toward Orthodoxy glimpsed in his early work when he equates Judaism with sentimentalism and feminine, emotion-laden soul searching.

Isaac, fleeing the awful scene with Tina, goes to the local synagogue on Yom Kippur eve, but even the prayer house cannot console his grief. The new modern rabbi is uncomfortable with the old-world emotionality of the immigrant generation:

> The new way was the way of understatement. Anglo-Saxon restraint. The rabbi, with his Madison Avenue public-relations airs, did not go for these European Judaic, operatic fist-clenchings. Tears. He made the cantor tone it down. But Isaac Braun, covered by his father's prayer shawl with its black stripes and shedding fringes, ground his teeth and wept near the ark. (67–68)

But finally after years of the continued battle, Tina becomes ill with liver cancer. Although Tina knows she is dying and all hope for a recovery is lost, she refuses to allow her brother Isaac to visit her in the hospital. When her brother Mutt urges her to allow Isaac to visit, Tina responds: "Why should I? A Jewish deathbed scene, that's what he wants. No" (68). But Isaac perseveres and daily calls the hospital; still Tina refuses to see him. Eventually Tina sends a message to Isaac: she will see him only if he pays her $20,000 cash, saying: "If he's got to come, that's the price of admission" (70).

Bellow contrasts Tina's operatic and Jewish emotionality with the silent WASP restraint of Ilkington Junior, whom Isaac (who was a member of the governor's pollution commission) meets on a boat tour of the polluted Hudson River. The young Ilkington behaves "with courtesy," informing Isaac that his father had lost all his "legitimate" money in bad investments, but that he was thankful Ilkington Senior "had a little something to fall back on" (72).

Isaac was moved that Ilkington Jr. did not begrudge him his fortune and he would liked to have shown his appreciation of Ilkington's graciousness, but Isaac realizes "what you showed, among these people, you showed with silence" (72). Reflecting on the operatic parody his sister was making of her death, Isaac began to "appreciate the wisdom" of WASP restraint.

When the Hudson River tour is concluded, Isaac, who is afraid of flying, takes a train to Williamsburg Brooklyn to ask his New York rebbe (modeled upon the Lubavitcher rebbe) whether he is allowed to make the payment to Tina. Isaac comes to Brooklyn seeking both *halachic* as well as ethical advice from the rebbe.

THE HOLOCAUST IN "THE OLD SYSTEM"

Bellow begins to cautiously approach Holocaust representation in "The Old System." While referring to Isaac and his wife's marriage, Bellow says: "It was an ample plain old-fashioned respectable domestic life on an Eastern European model completely destroyed in 1939 by Hitler and Stalin. Those two saw to the eradication of the old conditions, made sure that certain modern concepts became social realities" (64–65). We can see in this quotation Bellow's almost offhanded dealing with the Holocaust in his fiction previous to *The Bellarosa Connection*. Not only are Hitler and Stalin equated, but also Hitler's crimes seem to be reduced to the destruction of respectable "domestic life" and not the annihilation of a people. A few lines later, almost tongue-in-cheek Bellow says, "In America, the abuses of the Old World were righted. It was appointed to be the land of historical redress" (65).

This Holocaust theme is further developed when Isaac goes to visit his Williamsburg rebbe. We are told the rebbe is a Holocaust survivor, as are many of his Chasidim (followers). When Isaac tells the rebbe the story of the business deal with Ilkington and how his siblings deserted him at the last moment, the rebbe interrupts to say, "But that was also your good luck. They turned their faces from you, and this made you rich. You didn't have to share" (75). The phrase "turned their faces from you" seems an odd choice of words for the rebbe. Yet read with an understanding of traditional Jewish texts, and the historic Jewish response to tragedy, it is apparent that Bellow is choosing his ciphered words very deliberately.

HESTER PANIM I

The problem of the persistence of evil in the world has perplexed philosophers and biblical commentators for millennia. In the aftermath of the destruction of the Holy Temple in Jerusalem and the dispersal of the Jewish people, the redactors of the Babylonian Talmud attempted to account for the nature of evil in a world created by a benevolent God. The redactors of the Talmud discuss the concept of *Hester Panim*, literally translated as: a turning away of the face. The redactors conclude that, as a result of the sins of the Jewish people, God turns his face away from his chosen people, allowing evil to enter the world.

The Orthodox Chasidic world that had flourished in Eastern European *shtetlach* before World War II was decimated in the Holocaust. In the aftermath of the destruction of European Jewry, numerous Chasidic rabbis chose to interpret the Holocaust as one more historical instance of *Hester Panim*, of God's momentarily turning his face away from his people.

Once Bellow's story is read in the context of the long arc of Jewish literary responses to tragedy, its hidden meaning is revealed. The rebbe's remarks contain the key to understanding the true nature of Judaism, the meaning that eludes Dr. Samuel Braun. After hearing about Tina's illness, the rebbe turns philosophical for a moment. He tells Isaac: "Yes, a wasting disease. But the living can only will to live. I am speaking of Jews. They wanted to annihilate us. To give our consent would have been to turn from God" (75–76).

In the rebbe's remarks, again the phrase of "turning," this time man turning from God, appears. What the rebbe understands is that it is precisely the embracing of life in all of its embarrassing, even sometimes parodic, emotions which is the true vocation of a Jew. Not the restrained communication represented by both Jr. and Sr. Ilkington. Consequently, the rebbe urges Isaac to pay Tina's admission fee. He tells Isaac: "Our Jews love deathbed jokes. I know many. Well. America has not changed everything, has it? People assume that God has a sense of humor. Such jokes made by the dying in anguish show a strong and brave soul, but skeptical" (76–77).

Isaac follows the rebbe's advice, and when he arrives at the hospital, Tina reveals she never really wanted her brother's money after all. Not only does she refuse the payment, but also she gives Isaac their mother's ring for Isaac to give to his wife. What Tina desired was the emotions of the scene, the rest were mere props aiding in her life-embracing and emotionally unrestrained death scene.

The unemotional and distant Dr. Samuel Braun, and not Tina, is the tragic figure of "The Old System." Braun is unable to fully participate in the Jewish emotionality of his long-deceased relatives. Dr. Braun, as a world-renowned geneticist, is a full participant in the process of Americanization, but his lack of emotionality leaves him wanting in the process of *mentchification*; by rejecting and leaving behind the old-world system of Orthodox Judaism, unlike his cousins Isaac and Tina, Dr. Samuel Braun literally shuts himself out from a full participation in life.

BELLOW'S DEMOCRATIC LAUGHTER

> Sarah said, "God has brought me laughter; everyone who hears will laugh with me."
> —Genesis 21:6

During a scathing attack on James Atlas's biography of Bellow, Lee Siegel meditates on the conclusion to *Herzog*, noting Bellow's marvelous creation "of an existential harmony" in the concluding passage to one of Bellow's great works of fiction. Siegel remarks upon the accumulation of contrasting natural and artificial images which Bellow juxtaposes and that, at least momentarily, Herzog finally feels himself in harmony with. Siegel says: "Rearranging life's givens in such a way is a refusal to accept the tyranny of life's givens, and that is the essence of laughter and the function of art. It is also the promise of democracy" (76).

"The Old System" might be read as a parable of an America bereft of the old world yet not quite settled in any new system for doing things. Applying Siegel's definition of humor to "The Old System" reveals Bellow's terrifying vision of a world without order, a portrait of a people cut loose from the old world and not really having replaced it with a new system. The humor in "The Old System" is exposed during the narrator's (Bellow's) laughter at Braun's having succeeded in America, this world of nothingness; for despite all his success in the new world, perhaps as a result of his success, it is Dr. Braun and not Isaac or Tina who is the true tragic figure in Bellow's story. Unlike Isaac who lives his life based upon the precepts of the Torah, who is an old-system believer, and unlike Tina who despite her unhappy tongue and impious ways lives a life redolent of the old world[11] and its system, Dr.

Braun stands apart, adrift in the midst of his success. Cut off from any meaningful embrace of Orthodoxy and Judaism, he is bereft of any family whatsoever, all he has are the flickering memories of a distant and dead past, memories which fail to warm the frigid December day of his reminiscences.

BELLOW'S TWO JEWISH "TYPES"

In a recent interview[12] Bellow's interlocutor badgers him about the issue of Jewishness in his novels and stories. D. Venkateswarlu comments: "Your fictional people seem to be thinking about their past all the time. They keep talking about their parents, cousins and uncles—the family structure, in other words, figures very prominently in your work" (13).

Bellow's characteristic response has more than passing resonance to our discussion of "The Old System," particularly the character of Dr. Braun. Bellow responds:

> There are two kinds of Jews in the Western world. There are Jews who soon forget their history. The Jews who want to forget their history are the assimilationists, who want to rid themselves of their Jewish identity. But I think that would be a terrible mistake for Jews to turn away from their history. They mustn't. They have to be loyal to it even if they are not believing Jews; loyal to it, to the history of your people. (14)

Although in this interview Bellow never got around to defining the "other" kind of Jew in the Western world, one can easily imagine that unnamed second "type"—the kind of Jew who lives his history, who is true to his Jewish tradition, the kind of Jew personified by Isaac Braun. So here we have the two "types" Bellow spoke of in this interview: Traditionalist Isaac, Assimilationist Samuel. Although Bellow might have wanted to simplify things for the benefit of his interviewer, Judaism is never quite that neat and simple in Bellow's fiction, particularly in "The Old System."

TRIBAL GENETICS

Upon awakening, one of Dr. Braun's first recollections is tinged by his cousin Isaac's imperative of the importance of memory and Jewish tradition:

> Silent, with silent eyes crossing and recrossing the red water tank bound by twisted cables, from which ragged ice hung down and white vapor rose, Dr. Braun extracted a moment four decades gone in which Cousin Isaac had said, with one of those archaic looks he had, that the Brauns were descended from the tribe of Naphtali.
>
> "How do we know?"
>
> "People—families—*know*."
>
> Braun was reluctant, even at the age of ten, to believe such things. But Isaac, with the authority of a senior, almost an uncle, said, "You'd better not forget it." (49)

In this scene we can begin to glimpse why I refer to Bellow as a deeply *theological* writer. For without an understanding of the rich cultural heritage of the Torah, which Bellow time and again draws from and refers to in his fiction, many of the brilliant details and more subtle components of his social satire will elude the reader. On a basic level, this short scene between Isaac and Dr. Braun recalls the biblical admonition of God to his chosen people of the perils and punishments for forgetfulness. Throughout the Bible the Jews are repeatedly warned that forgetfulness will lead to complete annihilation and utter ruin:

> Beware lest you forget the Lord your God so that you do not keep his commandments and judgments and ordinances . . . lest you lift up your heart and forget the Lord your God who brought you out of the land of Egypt, out of the house of bondage. . . . And it shall come to pass that if indeed you forget the Lord your God . . . I bear witness against you this day that you shall utterly perish. (Deut. 8:11, 14, 19)

Although to my knowledge there are no critics who, even in passing, refer to this obvious biblical parallel, even far more interesting than the biblical allusion is the symbolism of the passage, unmentioned by the many critics who have written on this story. The Torah refers simultaneously to the five books of Moses, and to the *halachah*, the law or the path of the just that the upright Jews who follow the Torah's precepts always walk upon. In *midrash* Torah is symbolically called *mayim* (lit: water) since all life flows through the Torah. Since water is the sustenance for physical life on earth, so to is the Torah the sustainer of spiritual life. In the passage above, Dr. Braun is staring at the red water tank while he "extracts" this particular memory from oblivion. The water tank might be interpreted as a symbolic Torah scroll in this passage.[13] The "scroll" is "red," that is, bloodied through neglect by Dr.

Braun, but also as a result of the "twisted cables" which bind it, an obvious Holocaust image referring to the barbed wires that surrounded the concentration camps. The white vapor might also refer to the white ash that would continually flake over Auschwitz while the crematoria burned all day, every day. Out of this nightmare vision Dr. Braun "extracts" (49) a memory, an odd word choice, unless Bellow is purposefully recalling the extractions of teeth for gold, a well-known component of *Lager* life.

All this remembrance comes right after Braun has just begun to ruminate on his cousins in upstate New York. On the previous page, thinking back on all the disputes and rivalries of the Albany Jewish community, Braun thinks to himself: "Pariahs, thought Braun, with the dignity of princes among themselves" (48–49). In his thoughts Dr. Braun, the geneticist, has completely removed himself from consideration along with these "pariahs," a group of undesirables who have the audacity to think of themselves as "princes" in the new world. Dr. Braun doesn't say *ourselves*, instead using *themselves*[14] assuming the disinterested pose of the scientist. To dramatize the extent of Dr. Braun's assimilation into mainstream American culture, Bellow shows his narrator, even in his thoughts, falling back on his training as a geneticist, not as a fellow Jew, even while discussing not just his own "people" but other members of his own family, the Albany branch of the Brauns. Despite the familial similarities that the reader views in the opening page in which Braun clearly bears the "genetic" markings (his term) of his fellow Jews, in his mind Dr. Braun views himself as a disinterested outsider looking in at the terrific foibles of these decidedly unWASP-like, operatically overwrought Jews.

And so it is from the absolute depths of oblivion that Dr. Braun recalls Isaac's admonition that "[he'd] better not forget" that he is descended from *shevet* Naphtali, the tribe of Naphtali (49). Coming right after Dr. Braun has thought of the Jews of the Mohawk Valley as "pariahs," Bellow is aware of the Holocaustal images of the barbwired water tank, even if the assimilated Dr. Braun remains completely oblivious to the history he has been charged to safekeep. Ironically, like many Bellovian heroes, Dr. Braun, a material success in the new world, has mastered the first half of the Bellovian dyad: Americanization; he remains, however, in desperate need of the second part: *Mentchification*, of returning to the humanistic Judaism of his youth.

The real tragedy of "The Old System" is not the overwrought scene between Tina and Isaac, it is the loss of Jewish memory, the loss of "The Old System," which is not just symbolized by Isaac, but personified in his religious devotion and his piety and adherence to the Torah, the *oldest* system known to Jews. This loss represents a striking shift in perspective from a quarter century earlier when Bellow published *Augie March* when Americanization and "making it" seemed the all-important quest. In "The Old System" we see Bellow turning his penetrating gaze inward toward Jewishness and Orthodoxy. We can begin to trace the prominence of the theme of memory, both biblical and personal, in "The Old System" a theme that will be replicated in much of Bellow's subsequent work.

WOULD THAT BE *SHEVET* NAPHTALI, DR. BRAUN?

The Braun family is descended from the *shevet* (lit: tribe) of Naphtali, one of the original twelve tribes of Israel (49). Naphtali is translated from the Hebrew as *wrestling*. Jacob blessed Naphtali as follows: "Naphtali is a hind let loose, that bears comely fawns" (Gen. 49:21). Later, toward the end of the Hebrew Bible, Moses blesses the tribe of Naphtali as being "satisfied with favour, and full of the blessing of the Lord" (Duet. 33:23).

"The Old System" uses a complex narratorial strategy through which Bellow manages to interject his own peculiar *mishigas* or "crazy spirit." Bellow, as the narrator of this story is in effect the "hind let loose"; he becomes a figure to be contrasted with Dr. Braun, a man who has had all the "hind" socialized and assimilated out of his character. Dr. Braun bears no comely fauns; he is described as unmarried, without children or family. We can discern the distinct Bellovian consciousness when the narrative becomes interrupted by an editorializing voice anathema to Dr. Braun's cold, hard, scientific perspective. It is usually to make a rather rigid or caustic, sometimes even racist, remark.

Although Dr. Braun, through whose consciousness Bellow tells the story, is seen as an assimilated Jew, cool and detached in demeanor, Braun has not always been so WASPlike. In his narratorial asides Bellow makes clear that, as a youth, Braun was a classic *vilde chaya* (Yiddish expression for Wild Animal or unruly child), anything but WASPlike. From the age of seven he is involved in sexual dalliances with his much older cousin Tina, and although Tina is clearly taking advantage of the far too young boy, Braun, it would seem, immensely enjoyed these "agonies of incapacity and pleasure" (50). At another point in the story, young Braun, upset at being turned back toward the house by Isaac who wants to be left alone with his female companion, is seized by vengeful rage: "Little Braun then tried to kill his cousin. He wanted with all his heart to club Isaac with a piece of wood. He was still struck by the incomparable happiness, the luxury of that pure murderousness" (51).

Although Young Braun's emotions manifest themselves in cruelty and violence, at least as a youth he had, and was able to express, emotions. The tragedy of "The Old System" is not just the tragedy of the passing of the striving, energetic, conniving, immigrant generation of Jews who fled from pogroms, scratching and saving their way toward America. "The Old System" gains its power, its true emotional resonance from the conflicted son of that immigrant generation, Dr. Braun. Braun is a man who has been trained as an American intellectual, trained in the hard, cold facts of science. Almost all traces of Dr. Braun's past, through his rigorous education, have been systematically erased. Still, through the unrelenting process of assimilation, despite America's best efforts at transforming Sammy Braun from the rough-housing emotionally violent Jew into the hard man of science and world-renowned geneticist, vestiges of his Jewish immigrant past, flickerings of the "old system" remain. Thus Bellow's Dr. Braun, much like many assimilated American Jews, is a classic *luftmentch*, a man of the air, not comfortably tethered in either world: old or new.

While ruminating on his cousin Isaac and the story of his (Dr. Braun's) own birth, this state of indeterminacy, of *luftmentchlichkeit*, is revealed. Dr. Braun recalls that when Dr. Braun's mother went into labor, Aunt Rose sent Isaac to fetch "drunken Jones" a man who "practiced among Jewish immigrants before those immigrants had educated their own doctors" (47). We are told that during labor the rather unscientific (and drunk) Dr. Jones ties Braun's mother's "hands to the bedposts, a custom of the times."[15] These grim beginnings are contrasted with the present professional identity of Dr. Braun who is a product of the next generation. Braun has grown up to assume his post in an assimilated America and become a doctor in his own right, presumably to administer more scientifically to the needs of his, by now, mostly assimilated people who would be horrified by these old-world customs.

The following paragraph dramatizes the cultural and generational logic of American materialism. No sooner does Braun begin to remark upon the progress of the next generation, the product of the "new system" quantified by American science, than he falters. In a brief flash of lyricism Braun cannot help philosophizing; his old-world beginnings momentarily take control of his thoughts, sabotaging the promise of unbridled American assimilation:

> Having worked as a science student in laboratories and kennels, Dr. Braun had himself delivered cats and dogs. Man, he knew, entered life like these other creatures, in a transparent bag or caul. Lying in a bag filled with transparent fluid, a purplish water. A color to mystify the most rational philosopher. What is this creature that struggles for birth in its membrane and clear fluid? Any puppy in its sac, in the blind terror of its emergence, any mouse breaking into the external world from this shining, innocent-seeming blue-tinged transparency! (47–48)

Braun begins the paragraph as the next-generation improvement, the doctor who has replaced the "old world" Dr. Jones. No longer needing to rely upon small-town drunks, the Jewish community has created its own breed of doctors and lawyers, a professional class far removed from the old world of the immigrant experience. Dr. Braun begins as a rational scientist claiming man is no different from beasts, which in his medical training he has observed first hand. Yet once Braun makes that cold scientific deduction, he turns wistful. In a leap away from the scientific and intellectual heterodoxy of his training, Braun momentarily chooses the metaphysics of the philosopher, ending his memory on the unanswerable age-old conundrum "What is this creature?" This question, in an early section of "The Old System" referring to a puppy, will foreshadow the conclusion of "The Old System" when Dr. Braun becomes confounded by a half dozen unanswerable metaphysical questions concerning Jews and emotions, life and death. Although throughout his career Bellow has been labeled an "intellectual" writer, it is right here in Dr. Braun's ruminations concerning that puppy that Saul Bellow stakes his claim as not just an intellectual writer to be cerebrally appreciated, but rather as the supreme artist combining both intellect and emotions in his writing.

THEOLOGY OVER PHYSIOLOGY

In 1987 Bellow gave the keynote address at a Haifa University conference celebrating his work. In his talk, titled "Summations," Bellow, at seventy, on the cusp of old age, seems to be taking stock of his career.[16] Bellow tells a story of a recent conversation he had with a psychologist who was a researcher in the field of *hope*, who was "convinced that hope was a psycho-physiological phenomenon activated by a hope hormone" (190). This psychologist, who, in Bellow's words, "has lifted hope out of theology and taken possession of it in the name of physiology" (190), believes that this elusive hope hormone is regulated by optimistic or pessimistic projections. In his encounter with the psychologist, Bellow glimpses the roots of Western rational civilization, a civilization that is based upon the enlightenment ideal that "the only truths about human existence are scientific truths" (190).

As a bulwark against this belief stands Saul Bellow. As a fabricator of fictions he attempts to reanimate that old system by which people were able to feel and express emotion and power. In his later work Bellow contrasts Judaism as a type of system that allows interaction between feeling and rationality. Tina and Isaac are just such characters.

In his "Summations" Bellow makes clear the idea he tries time and again to dramatize in his stories and novels. Bellow believes that writers should pursue human emotions and experience, the kinds of things modern society shuns and closes access to: ". . . our modern enlightenment and its psychology, by the rational civilization that has brought us political and social gains and paid for them by sealing off our most significant impulses and powers" (196). It is into just such a cauldron of human powers and wants, emotions and feelings, that Bellow stirs his "old system" characters. The overbearing Tina once more pulls the staid and dignified Isaac back into this tumult of emotions. So too, through the memory of Isaac and Tina's story, does Dr. Braun becomes immersed in the world of the old system, characterized by "impulses and powers" all that which Bellow believes is parsed out of "rational civilization." As a writer, Bellow hopes to reconnect his readers back to those parts of humanity that he believes modern society has stripped from the world.

In "The Old System" even Isaac's Brooklyn Chasidic rabbi (who is modeled on Rabbi Menachem Mendel Schneerson, the Lubavitcher Rebbe)[17] is not immune to this trade off between Western rationality and the old operatic world of feelings and emotions. Although he is still comfortable in that old world and urges Isaac to embrace it as well, having studied at the Sorbonne, "the rebbe" is also a Western educated man of modernity. Despite his secular education, the rebbe does not close himself off from the old-world system.

In contrast to Isaac's rebbe (and Isaac himself), as an adult Braun has led a constricted life, closing himself off from his "Jewish" instincts: emotions and drama. Instead Dr. Braun has chosen the WASPlike "colorlessness" of Ilkington, the hard, unemotional life of the scientist. In renouncing his emotions in favor of his American capitalist success, Braun has also renounced his identity and his hold on the past, on his memory. Although he recalls his cousins' stories on this one particular afternoon, the reader is left with the feeling that Braun has little use for his past, or for his memory; other than this particular winter afternoon Braun rarely recalls anything about these people who happen to constitute his only family.

All that remains of Braun's youthful embracing of life, of feelings and emotions (even murderous ones) are small and sad little kinesthetic moments for the adult Dr. Braun: the smell of a newly punctured can of coffee in the morning, the shape of an icicle hanging from a barn, the ordering of dishes and saucers in a pantry. Much like Woody Selbst in "A Silver Dish," about whom we will read later in this chapter, Dr. Braun is a man of irresolvable contradictions. He is able to consciously understand the great tragedy of what has been lost in the transplantation of Jewish life from the *shtetl* to an assimilated America. Yet he is unable to attach any meaningful action upon that knowledge. In "The Old System" Braun's thoughts are similar to Joseph's diary keeping in *Dangling Man*, for in essence Braun is also a dangling man, literally a *luftmentch*: a man of the air. He has renounced his emotions and feelings, he has risen to the very top of his profession, he is a leading geneticist, yet he never really fits into the WASP mentality. He lives the life, but it is a life based upon a lie. Braun is always haunted by the specter of his immigrant relatives; he has rejected that life yet mourns for its loss even while being aware of its inaccessibility: he is barred access to that operatic immigrant world of feelings and emotions. He spends the story with his nose pressed up to the window of his youth, through which he can glimpse the unfolding Jewish opera. Yet even while he watches, before the performance has ended, Braun realizes that he will never enter onto the *Bimah*, the Jewish stage that was his birthright. This contradiction is vividly seen in the opening pages when Dr. Braun thinks about the problems with (post)modern American culture:

> But every civilized man today cultivated an unhealthy self-detachment. Had learned from art the art of amusing self-observation and objectivity. Which, since there had to be something amus-

ing to watch, required art in one's conduct. Existence for the sake
of such practices did not seem worthwhile. Mankind was in a confusing, uncomfortable, disagreeable stage in the evolution of its
consciousness. (44)

While in the midst of these bitter thoughts on the state of modern
man in a WASP culture, Braun ambles into his kitchen where he "was
well pleased by the blue-and-white Dutch dishes, cups hanging,
saucers standing in slots" (44). Braun is aware of his cultural dilemma,
but he remains unaware of the self-conscious realization of the irony of
his predicament. Braun lacks the raucous Jewish humor necessary to
make light of his present condition; indeed, if he were able to at least
laugh at his predicament, he might not be a *luftmentch* at all. He might
very well be a man with an identity with a past worth remembering,
and therefore in possession of a life worth living in the present.

Braun's detachment is underscored by the conclusion of the story
in which he attempts to comprehend, to intellectually analyze his emotions instead of allowing himself to just experience them. At the conclusion of *Seize the Day* Tommy is finally able to give in to his emotions, to weep for the sake of another man, for humanity. Not so Dr.
Braun, a man who has had all his Jewish emotionality bled out of him.
At the end of "The Old System" Dr. Braun is seen fighting back his
tears, trying to understand them, to intellectualize them without fully
experiencing them. Like Woody Selbst trying on Hinduism and Bud-
dhism for size, when Dr. Braun is overcome by emotion at the conclusion of Isaac's and Tina's operatic tale, he tries on a Yeatsian mask:
"And Dr. Braun, bitterly moved, tried to grasp what emotions were.
What good were they! What were they for! And no one wanted them
now. Perhaps the cold eye was better. On life, on death" (82).

Braun paraphrases Yeats's famous epitaph from "Under Ben Bul-
ben," which reads: "Cast a cold eye/On life, on death./Horseman, pass
by!" (344). However, none of these tough-guy postures seems to fit Dr.
Braun. Throughout the story Braun is seen trying on for size first one
then another modern, capitalist, American identity, like so many ill-fit-
ting suits. For example, early in the story we are told he has been "written up in *Time*, in all the papers, for his research," but we are also told
that Braun "did not much care for being first in his field" (45). Quite
tellingly, as Braun recalls this information and his antipathy toward
emotion of any kind, he launches into an attack on the Jewish immigrant type: "People were boastful in America. Matthew Arnold, a not
entirely appetizing figure himself, had correctly observed this in the

U.S. Dr. Braun thought this national American boastfulness had aggravated a certain weakness in Jewish immigrants" (45).

In attacking Jewish immigrant "types" Braun leans heavily upon that old standard bearer for anti-Semitism, Matthew Arnold; Braun's acknowledging that Arnold was less than a savory "type" himself doesn't excuse Braun's nasty thought that flirts with anti-Semitism as well. In fact, Braun tries on several other postures in this story, the sole criteria being that each "identity" be as far removed from old-system Judaism as possible.

But Braun is no more at home in Yeats's cold stoicism than Joseph was in Hemingway's tough-guy hardboiled-dom in *Dangling Man*. Immediately after attempting a disinterested Yeatsian posture, Braun begins to speculate on the scientific concept of "a cold eye," intellectualizing the entire prospect and thus rendering the identity meaningless. The geneticist reasons: "the cold of the eye would be proportional to the degree of heat within" (82). Braun's rumination on a cold eye brings us back full circle to the very beginning of Bellow's literary career, to Joseph's complaint of an age of hardboiled-dom, in essence, a Hemingwayesque, and therefore anti-Jewish, way of life, a life free of emotions, parsed of feeling and expression. Such a life would seem to be as colorless as the dry white martini that Ilkington mixes for Isaac in his "New World" office.

THE NEW SYSTEM: DEAL WITH THE DEVIL?

"The Old System" did not begin to garner critical attention until twenty-five years after it was published in 1967. No less a critic than Irving Howe, although including the story in his 1977 anthology *Jewish-American Stories*, dismissed "The Old System" as reading "like a compressed version of those leisurely family chronicles which European novelists wrote at the turn of the century; the characters in this story matter mostly as representative figures in the saga of a family" (9). Howe leaves the impression that he was compelled to include some work from the recent Nobel Prize winner; in retrospect it would seem that perhaps the anthology came to fruition as a result of Bellow's winning the Nobel Prize.

In contrast to Howe's dismissal of the story as slight, in one of the first articles written about Bellow's story, Alan Berger writing in 1993 summarizes "The Old System" as "a canny social history of Jewish assimilation: an insider's description of the 'old system' of *Ostjuden* (East European Jews) with its emphasis on feeling and emotion, and an emphatic portrayal of biblical and Hasidic components of Jewish identity" ("The Logic of the Heart" 94). Berger goes on to locate the central conflict of the story as juxtaposing "ancestral religion" against "a morally flaccid American culture, an infantilized and sterile notion of religion, and an American restraint which has use for neither feeling nor emotion" (95).

While I agree with Berger's observations, and Bellow's complex short story indeed does emblematize the eternal conflict between the old world and the new world, between assimilation and religious observance, in my reading Bellow's story goes well beyond another reworking of what Howe called the great theme of the earlier generation of Jewish American writers: immigration. In my view, Dr. Samuel Braun does not narrate "The Old System," as Berger suggests, but rather it is Bellow himself who narrates and who uses Samuel Braun as a narrative foil through which to tell his tale. I would say that far from one more story dramatizing the age-old conflict of old world/new world, Bellow's story hearkens back to the eighteenth-century notion of the sublime. "The Old System" is a terrifying and sublime comedy that leaves Bellow's twentieth-century (and beyond) readers not elevated on a higher plane, but rather as *luftmentchen* (people of the air), devoid of place of any kind.

"The Old System" does not simply dramatize America versus *Ostjuden*, or us (Jew) versus them (Gentile) as it had seemed at the outset of Bellow's career, for example in *Dangling Man*, or *Seize the Day*, *Herzog*, and so on. What "The Old System" brilliantly dramatizes is that the postwar American battle was no longer us versus them but had become an entirely civil matter. It was now America versus itself. The great assimilating beast of postwar America had become a simulacrum of itself. Examples within the story abound, but a few will suffice.

After Isaac makes his deal with Ilkington (who stands for the great American industrialist and colonialist—we are told Ilkington will be retiring to the British West Indies), he can finally begin to afford the expensive lessons of *Tom Brown's Schooldays* and assume the reserve and hardboiledness of a regular British Colonialist as well. Bellow distills this notion of the "nada-ness" of American postwar culture in the symbol of the martini, that uppercrust drink of British extraction, which Ilkington offers to Isaac after accepting the briefcase, stuffed with $100,000:

Ilkington did not touch Isaac's briefcase. He did not intend, evidently, to count the bills, nor even to look. He offered Isaac a martini. Isaac, not a drinker, drank the clear gin. At noon. Like something distilled in outer space. Having no color. He sat there sturdily, but felt lost—lost to his people, his family, lost to God, lost in the void of America. (59)

The America that Isaac inherits is no longer a typological land of milk and honey, a shining city upon a hill, the New Jerusalem that the Calvinist settlers envisioned. By the twentieth century what remains of America is a postindustrial colorless absence, pure nothingness. Isaac is no mere observer of these deadening trends in American culture; he pursues American capitalism with glee. On the golf course he puts a shopping center. In the name of progress and American ingenuity America itself has been impoverished. This irony is underscored throughout the story by Bellow's Jewish humor. Dr. Braun thinks Isaac's shopping center is particularly hideous. "Perhaps because he remembered the Robbstown Club. Restricted, of course. But Jews could look at it from the road" (59). Once Isaac is finished "developing" there isn't an elm tree in sight. There is nothing left but the sight of the brutal architecture of a shopping mall, and nothing left to hear except for the cascading sound of money pouring in.

To be sure Bellow is no sentimentalist, nostalgically mourning the loss of the racist Robbstown country club. He simply remarks on the constant flux of American business. The "Coolidge era sedans" which had filled the country club had holders in the rear window for artificial flowers, and the razing of the club led only to the destruction of machinery. Isaac's victory celebrates America having beaten itself. Instead of a baseball diamond and golf course, all that is left is "Supermarket, pizza joint, chop suey, laundromat, Robert Hall clothes, a dime store" (60).

Perhaps the best example in Bellow's fiction of the disturbing postwar trend toward a monocultural America, as decried in Pynchon's the *The Crying of Lot 49* or in DeLillo's *Underworld*, is Bellow's description in "The Old System" of the local synagogue. The old-world *shul* is long dead, and in its place has arisen a new-world temple: "Now there was a temple like a World's Fair Pavilion" (60). In the Mohawk Valley temple we see the completion of the simulacrum. A synagogue in the new world that is filled with characters *resembling* the old world, so much so that it comes close to looking like a synagogue built for the 1964 world's fair in Flushing Meadows Park, built to resemble something which merely looks like the old world. Bellow introduces this brilliant idea with these words: "The little synagogue was wiped out. It was as dead as the Dutch painters who would have appreciated its dimness and its shaggy old ped-dlers" (60). The old-world *shul* and its traditional Orthodox value system has gone from being a representation of the old system upon Rem-brandt's canvases, to becoming in Bellow's story a representation of a representation, a chimera which doesn't even rise to the heights of a world's fair pavilion, built as a representation of the old. The study house of religion, in America, has become morally bankrupt, a pure simulacra.

In John Updike's *Rabbit Run* a pivotal scene contrasts the new-world Episcopalian minister with an old-world Lutheran, a stand-in figure for the old traditions and all that has been lost in the rush toward modernity. In "The Old System," written less than a decade after *Rabbit Run*, Bellow describes the new rabbi as "The worldly rabbi, with his trained voice and tailored suits, like a Christian minister except for the play of Jewish cleverness in his face" (60). There is not much authen-ticity left in Bellow's nightmarish vision of postwar America. The global monoculture has reached its long hand even into the sanctum of the synagogue; it too has been "malled."

Even the great American dream of becoming a baseball star is no longer viable. For one thing the "bush league park where a scout had him (Mutt Braun) spotted before the war as material for the majors," has now been overtaken by a computer center. For another, the former major league prospect Mutt had taken a bullet in the head at Iwo Jima and came back "from a year in the hospital to sell Zenith, Motorola, and Westinghouse appliances" (61). "The Old System" dramatizes the giv-ing up of the open-field dream of America in favor of the simulation of the American dream: prosperity and progress viewed in the comfort of a well-appointed living room through a nineteen-inch Zenith.

Isaac, having come over from the old world, is not so far removed from "the old system" way of doing things to be completely lost in his one-handed embrace of America. After his new-system business deal consummated in Ilkington's office, Isaac increasingly retreats to the comforts of religion and family. Isaac becomes one more fairly Ameri-canized Jew to embrace Orthodoxy once more as a *baal teshuvah*. As Bellow tells us: "Isaac's Orthodoxy only increased with his wealth" (54).

BELLOW'S TWO-FACED JUDAISM

Bellow represents Judaism from opposing perspectives in "The Old Sys-tem." On the one hand, Judaism represents that licentious, free-flowing world of emotions, of graft, of a people without rules. For example, after young Sammy Braun is sent away from his cousin's Adirondack home for being such a *vilde chaya*, Bellow tells us that he later became an obedient young man and a good student. "Everyone was more civilized. Little Braun became a docile, bookish child. Did very well in school." While discussing the fate of young Sammy Braun, Bellow adds as a side remark on the Jewish people: "We were getting somewhere" (51). That *somewhere* was a place without Jewish customs brought over from the old world.

On the other hand, in "The Old System" Bellow laments the loss of Judaism. The destruction of the way of life symbolized by old-system Orthodoxy is a loss for humanity, certainly it is a terrible loss for someone like Dr. Sammy Braun who has had all of his "Jewishness" civilized out of him, and is left an empty container, a cerebral shell, lonely and isolated despite his professional glory in the new world.

BELLOW'S EVOLVING JUDAISM

What has Bellow learned in the twenty years between his creating Tommy "Wilky" Wilhelm and Dr. Samuel Braun? How has Bellow's attitude toward Judaism changed in his fictional representation of Jewish characters? The last lines of "The Old System" leave an, at best, ambiguous portrait. After the last light of the short winter day has finally faded, Braun rouses himself and goes to the window to look at the stars. Unlike the self-possessed Walt Whitman who, grown tired from hearing the learned astronomer intellectualize, wandered out from the lecture hall and in "the mystical moist night-air, and from time to time, / Look'd up in perfect silence at the stars" (226), Dr. Braun cannot just see the stars and appreciate their existence, feel them emotionally without, like Moses Herzog before him, *thinking* about them. The reader is told: ". . . he went to the dark kitchen window to have a look at stars. These things cast outward by a great begetting spasm billions of years ago" (83). Although these lines are purposefully ambiguous, the reader is unsure if these words are the narrator's (Bellow's) thoughts, or the narrator's reporting of Dr. Braun's reflections as he watches the stars. Despite the ambiguity, Bellow has left us some clues that may help decipher the coded last line of "The Old System." The concluding passage rejects the Jewish conception of the universe, the biblical creation story told in Genesis which relates that the world, approximately six thousand years old, was created by a purposeful God, and not by a mindless "begetting spasm" several billion years ago. This scientific reading, in essence a Big-Bang reading of the universe, would seem to coincide with Braun's thought patterns and not the narrator's (or Bellow's) Jewish conception of the universe as expressed throughout the story. Therefore the tragedy of "The Old System" is not in the story itself, the operatic story of Isaac and Tina and all the other dead relatives, but rather in Dr. Braun's inability, in essence the entire post-immigrant generation's inability, to make use of the old-world values bequeathed to them as their birthright. It is Braun's estrangement from Judaism and a conception of a Jewish world that is mourned by Bellow in "The Old System."

This reading is bolstered when one considers the Old Testament covenant between God and Abraham. When Abraham is concerned that he is without an heir, God appears to him in a vision and says: "'Look toward heaven and count the stars, if you are able to count them.' And He added, 'So shall your offspring be'" (Gen. 15:5–6).

In traditional Jewish texts stars always symbolize the Jewish people. This seminal event in Jewish history, where God told Abraham his descendents will be like the stars in the heavens, is immediately followed in the biblical text by the ultimate covenant in Jewish history: God's bequeathing the land of Canaan to Abraham as "the promised land." It is only after being "strangers in a strange land" that the Israelites were promised the land of Canaan. Bellow's "The Old System" ends with a sterile vision. Braun is childless; the old-world Jews like Isaac who practiced the old system are long dead. Dr. Braun's cold rational eye surveys the stars yet he no longer comprehends the symbolism of what he gazes upon, nor does he understand what the stars traditionally symbolize to the Jewish people. But despite Braun's separation from the old-system Judaism of his deceased relatives, he also lacks the cool detachment of Yeats, as well as the "perfect silence" of Whitman. All Braun is left with is a sterile vision of the future, a future based upon a mindless and "great begetting spasm billions of years ago" (83).

COMMUNAL ACTION

Despite Bellow's best efforts to memorialize the preglobalized "malling" of Jewish American life, the old system of Jewish life, "The Old System," through its *meshugah* laughter does postpone the inevitable. Yet the collective memory of the Jewish people may only be preserved through collective action, and not through Dr. Braun's late afternoon reminiscences. As Yerushalmi argues: "The collective memories of the Jewish people were a function of a shared faith, cohesiveness, and will of the group itself, transmitting and recreating its past through an entire complex of interlocking social and religious institutions that functioned organically to achieve this" (94).

It is through this lack of communal action that Bellow rebukes himself and the American Jewish community in *The Bellarosa Connection*. Before examining the nature of this mussar (rebuke), let's take a short peek at "A Silver Dish," which dramatizes the failures of memory and what is necessary on a personal level before tackling the communal responsibilities that *The Bellarosa Connection* conjures. When we turn from "The Old System" to "A Silver Dish" found in *Him with His Foot in His Mouth and Other Stories* we see Bellow once again looking at the *Tanach*, the Christian Bible, as well as the passing of the immigrant generation in America. Bellow once more dramatizes a search for roots in a rootless America, a place where one may reinvent oneself out of nothing, while perhaps becoming a simulacrum in the process.

Just like Isaac is Bellow's paradigmatic figure for Modern Orthodoxy in postwar America, so too is Dr. Samuel Braun Bellow's paradigmatic figure for the assimilated American Jew, a man who has lost his memory of what is important in life, a man who is no longer in touch with the old system for doing things. Dr. Braun's *luftmentchlichkeit*, his state of indeterminacy at the conclusion to "The Old System," might best be compared to another of Bellow's lost souls. Like Dr. Samuel Braun, Woody Selbst in Bellow's short story "A Silver Dish" is a man who is cut off from his past and separated from Judaism: Woody is a man in need of memory.

SLIPPING INTO FREEDOM:
EMANCIPATING THE SELF IN "A SILVER DISH"

Although it is the many South Chicago church bells which batter Woody Selbst's soul the first Sunday morning his father spends in the ground and which set his memory whirling back to his youth, the clear persistence of those church bells—"metal [clanging] on naked metal" (198)—holds no promise of salvation for Woody Selbst. Church bells bring with them reflection, quiet contemplation, and visions of cloistered monks meditating in tranquility. Woody is a *macher*, a businessman, a contemporary free thinker, a seemingly self-made man stuffed with real information, a man in step with the "steel-making, oil-refining, power-producing" South Chicago of his birth. Woody is a man of action; but he is also a man of contradiction. Deep within his soul, although he likes to call himself an agnostic, Woody is, above all else, a firm and true believer. As a young man in the seminary he was seized by the idea "that this world should be a love world, that it should eventually recover and be entirely a world of love" (199). And so Woody Selbst, man of contradictions, is in trouble.

After the death of his father, Woody feels rootless. Cut adrift from his usual chores Woody wakes this first Sunday morning after his father's funeral perplexed by an overwhelming feeling of stagnation, of inactivity. Woody has spent his adult years much as he had spent his childhood: in the perpetual service of those around him. He is a man who is constantly on the move—Woody has been taken by the hand and seized by his myriad responsibilities. Even after Morris's funeral, Woody slips into his usual routine. The narrator tells us that "Then for the rest of the week Woody was busy, had jobs to run, office responsibilities, family responsibilities" (194). Woody takes care of his wife from whom he is separated, doing the shopping for her on Fridays, before discharging his numerous chores undertaken for his mistress Helen. Traditionally, Saturdays were spent shopping for his mother—a convert to Christianity—before taking care of his mentally unstable sisters, whom he has ferried in and out of institutions for years.

It is on Sunday morning, the day he had always devoted to caring for his father, that the emptiness of his present state seizes Woody. As the sound of the church bells wash over Woody, he becomes aware that he is cut from his moorings. Numerous critics have maintained that the key action of "A Silver Dish" takes place during the tumultuous wrestling scene between father and son, which lies at the center of this story. However, the main conflict of this text, despite the horrific and violent action that swirls and eddies around the father and son conflict is actually an internal quarrel within the mind and soul of Woody Selbst as he attempts to mourn the loss of his father.

EDUCATION VERSUS BLOOD

At the outset of this story, Woody, although sixty years old and in perfect physical health, the owner of a successful tile business, is not a man who is in possession of his self. Woody acts reflexively and we are told that when an unpleasant feeling overtakes him, rather than dealing with the underlying issue he is in the habit of "taking something for it" (195). This "something" presumably refers to drugs or alcohol. Woody lives in what I would call a state of perpetual childhood—as someone who has been seized and taken by the hand. Although it appears as if all those family members rely upon his services, in reality it is Woody who is dependent on these people—dependent on them to give order to his life, to keep him so busy running around with responsibilities that he never has the chance to stop and reflect on just who is in possession of the life he has been given. All this changes once his father dies, when Woody has an epiphanic moment of reflection as the church bells ring; immediately his thoughts return to the first primal scene of the wrestling with his father.

This issue of overcoming a state of perpetual childhood in order to assume a sense of freedom animates Bellow's story and forms the core inner action which drives Woody on his quest of remembrance and mourning for his father. If Woody can mourn for his father, then just maybe he will be able to seize control of his identity and truly emancipate himself. In order to accomplish this, however, Woody is forced to once again choose, just as he was forced to choose as a young man, between his Jewish blood and his Christian schooling which had left him rootless—he cannot possibly mourn his father properly without making that choice. He must, in the words of that other great American writer obsessed with fathers and sons, William Faulkner, give in to "the old, fierce pull of blood" (*Collected Stories* 3) and return to his roots in order to gain possession of his life for the first time.

It is the freedom of choosing Judaism, of electing to live the life of a Jew and in so doing choosing to honor his history, however meager that history might appear in the context of American materialism (his father in this context is a failure in the New World), that Woody, finally, might be made a man, a person with a distinct identity. In Bellow's fiction, possessing a sense of self and an awareness of one's history might be the highest good a person can hope for. As Emmanuel Levinas suggests in his book *Difficult Freedom*, Judaism is the promise of precisely such an individualist's difficult freedom confined within the religious proscriptions of communal action and consciousness:

> One cannot, in fact, be a Jew instinctively; one cannot be a Jew without knowing it. One must desire good with all one's heart and, at the same time, not simply desire it on the basis of a naïve impulse of the heart. Both to maintain and to break this impulse is perhaps what

constitutes the Jewish ritual. Passion mistrusts its pathos, and becomes and rebecomes *consci*ousness! Belonging to Judaism presupposes a ritual and a science. Justice is impossible to the ignorant man. Judaism is an extreme consciousness. (Levinas, *Difficult Freedom* 6)

Following Levinas's conception of Judaism, in "A Silver Dish," it is precisely Woody's omnipresent consciousness which defines his embracing both Judaism as well as his grief over the loss of his father.

PLOT SUMMARY

"A Silver Dish" begins soon after Woody Selbst, a successful Chicago businessman, has buried his long-suffering Jewish father Morris. Waking up the first Sunday morning after the funeral, the day he usually devoted to Morris, Woody contemplates the meaning of mourning and laments his inability to properly mourn for his father. While listening to the many church bells surrounding his warehouse, Woody recalls a scene from his youth in the 1930s when his father Morris, a gambling, thieving, drinking ne'er-do-well who had abandoned his family years earlier, convinces Woody to take him to visit his benefactress, a wealthy Christian woman whose life's aim was to convert the Jews and who was at the time supporting Woody's mother and sisters, as well as paying Woody's seminary tuition in hopes of his eventual conversion to Christianity and his becoming a minister. When Mrs. Skoglund goes into her office to pray to Jesus to ask whether she should grant Morris's request of a fifty-dollar loan, Morris pries open a glass case and steals an expensive silver dish. Woody seeing his future in doubt pleads for his father to return the dish. When he refuses, Woody attacks his father and they begin wrestling on the floor for the silver dish. Woody, however, is unable to pry the dish loose. Finally, exhausted, the two hear Mrs. Skoglund returning and Morris tells Woody to distract her in the other room while he puts back the dish. Of course Woody is played for a fool when Morris doesn't put the dish back. Consequently a few days later Woody is accused of thievery and thrown out of the seminary. He is forced to fend for himself in the midst of the Great Depression.

FREEING WOODY?

Throughout "A Silver Dish" Woody searches for a means of mourning for his father. After recalling this scene from his youth, Woody is finally able to properly mourn his father. The story ends with Woody's remembering the more recent wrestling match, which takes place in Morris's hospital bed.

"A Silver Dish" is Bellow's adult version of a *bildungsroman*. Woody must revisit the violence of his youth to be able to comprehend just what he has lost when his father dies. He will only begin to feel, to mourn his loss, and thereby to truly live when he silences the many voices competing in his head and finally listens to what Morris has been telling him all along: "From those people," Morris had continually told Woody, referring to the Mrs. Skoglunds of the world whose sole aim in life is to convert the Jews, "you'll never find out what life is" (221).

In his essay "Mainmise" Jean-Francois Lyotard sums up the concept of Humanism with the expression "man is something that must be freed" (Lyotard and Gruber 3). In the process of defining freedom Lyotard analyzes feudal legal terms, which, surprisingly, may be relevant in our analysis of "A Silver Dish." Lyotard says: "The name *manceps* designates someone who takes something in hand so as to possess or appropriate it. . . . And *mancipium* refers to this act of taking in hand by the manceps" (1). The *mancipium* also designates the person or object that is literally and figuratively "in the hands of another." In a fascinating play on words Lyotard refers to childhood as a state of being where a child is defined as "one who is held by the hand." In the case of Woody Selbst we might take this reasoning a step further: his childhood, and the defining act of that childhood "never ceases to exercise its *mancipium*" (1), or ownership, over him. Thus despite being sixty years old and believing himself to be a free man, Woody, after the death of his father, is in desperate need of emancipation. The root of the word *mancipate*, according to the OED, comes from the Latin and is a Roman legal term, which means: "to take or seize by hand." In order to emancipate himself, or "to release himself or [be] set free from the *patria potestas*," Woody must literally take in hand his roots—those parts of himself which he had shied away from so many years before. Judaism has a similar concept concerning ownership: in *Halachah*, Jewish law, a "laying on of hands" connotes a *kinyan*, a legal action symbolizing ownership. It is an act which Woody was unable to fulfill nearly half a century earlier in Mrs. Skoglund's parlor, but one which he must complete if he is to emancipate himself from his state of advanced childhood to become fully free and human.

Bellow's story with its double-billed wrestling brings to my Yeshiva-trained mind an image of another famous wrestling match.

Before there was Woody versus Morris, there was Jacob versus God's messenger—the feature event in an all-night match. Unlike Woody, Jacob, that first Jewish wrestling champion was not afraid to get down and dirty and grab that angel by the loins. The Bible says of Jacob's encounter with the angel:

> And a man wrestled with him there till daybreak. When the man saw that he could not get the better of Jacob, he struck him in the hollow of his thigh, so that Jacob's hip was dislocated as they wrestled. The man said, "Let me go for day is breaking," but Jacob replied, "I will not let you go unless you bless me." The man asked, "What is your name?" "Jacob," he answered. The man said, "Your name shall no longer be Jacob but Israel, because you have striven with God and with mortals, and have prevailed. . . . Jacob called the place Peniel, "because," he said, "I have seen God face to face yet my life is spared." The sun rose as Jacob passed through Penuel, limping because of his hip. That is why to this day the Israelites do not eat the sinew that is on the hollow of the thigh, because the man had struck Jacob on that sinew. (Gen. 32:24–32)

As a result of Jacob winning this wrestling match with the angel of God he is given the name of Israel; as a result Jacob is called upon to assume the role of patriarch for a great nation.

In contrast, Woody is the king over a vast empire of emptiness and human misery. This is how the narrator describes the extended Selbst clan: "Everybody had diabetes and pleurisy and arthritis and cataracts and cardiac pacemakers." As if these punishments of biblical proportion were not enough, Bellow adds with a flourish: "And everybody had lived by the body, but the body was giving out" (193). Bellow's story is peopled by a group of *mancipiums*—characters that are not living fully human, and therefore not fully free, lives. At the head of this odd conglomerate stands Woody, who like everybody else leads an isolated, lonely existence. Bellow's narrator tells us: "He lived alone; as did his wife; as did his mistress; everybody in a separate establishment" (194). This is hardly a description of emotionally satisfying human relationships.

Let us return for a moment to the primal scene in Mrs. Skoglund's parlor. After Morris picks the lock of the étagère and steals the silver dish, Woody implores his father:

> "We're going to put it back now. Give it here."
> "Woody, it's under my fly, inside my underpants. Don't make such a noise about nothing."

> Before he knew it, Woody had jumped his father and had begun
> to wrestle with him. (212)

Yet for all his gumption Woody is rendered powerless. Instead of the victorious Jacob, Woody assumes the role of the vanquished angel forced to clutch his father close and hold on for dear life. The narrator says: "Woody recognized that to have wrestled him to the floor counted for nothing. It was impossible to thrust his hand under Pop's belt to recover the dish" (213).

Woody is overcome by the feelings of delicacy engendered in him by his fellow seminarians and the Episcopalian Mrs. Skoglund with her supposed high breeding. Mrs. Skoglund's socializing has only been reinforced by his convert mother's English airs and her numerous efforts at civilizing Woody. He cannot force himself to lay his hands on that which is his, and Woody is thus relegated to a life as a *manceps*, a life of serving others.

The first wrestling match with Morris was a failure for the young boy. To force his father to return the silver dish Woody needs to reach down to his father's "sinewy thigh" as had Jacob with his angel. In Woody and Morris's wrestling, Woody stops short of reaching down into his father's pants—that would be too improper for the young seminarian. And so he relents and his father wins the battle—it is only years later that Woody truly lays on his hands fully grasping his father's body in an attempt to keep him from "slipping into death" (221). Bellow's story forces us all, and not just Woody and Morris, to contemplate not just the price of freedom, but the lifelong cost of not pursuing freedom, of not being fully human. Bellow reminds his readers that Woody's failure during his first wrestling match with his father in Mrs. Skoglund's parlor has repercussions not only for his own development but also for his entire extended family.

SLIPPING AWAY?

Our ongoing discussion in this chapter of the first two of three Bellow short fictions should sufficiently explain why in my introduction I refer to Bellow as a deeply theological writer. In these two stories and one novella, Bellow is clearly building upon postrabbinic Jewish literature. In these works we see Bellow writing a modern *midrash*, a commentary on the Torah. In his foreward to *Zakhor*, Harold Bloom suggests that ultimately all writing that may be called Jewish aims to interpret the

Bible: "What Jewish writing has to interpret, finally, and however indirectly, is the Hebrew Bible, since that always has been the function of Jewish writing, or rather its burden: how to open the Bible to one's own suffering" (xxiii). Bloom goes on to comment on this open-endedness of postrabbinic literature saying:

> The Hebrew Bible, in contrast to the New Testament or the Koran, never has been closed, it does not end with Second Chronicles, or with the *Kuzari* of Judah Halevi, or with *The Great Wall of China* of Kafka, or with the *Three Essays on the Theory of Sexuality* by Freud. The desire to be Scripture is hardly in itself Jewish; Dante and Milton each believed himself to be uttering prophecy. But to trust that you join yourself to the Hebrew Bible by opening it further to your own pathos does seem to me a peculiarly Jewish ambition for a writer. (xxiv)

In my introductory chapter to *American Talmud* I said that: "twentieth- and twenty-first-century Jewish American fiction writers have been codifying a new Talmud, an American Talmud," and I argued that we should view "the literary production of Jews in America . . . as one more stage of rabbinic commentary on the scriptural inheritance of the Jewish people. The defining hallmark of rabbinic literature is its attempt to interpret the history the rabbis were given." I quoted Yosef Hayim Yerushalmi who noted that the rabbis "did not set out to write a history of the biblical period; they already possessed that. Instead they were engrossed in an ongoing exploration of the meaning of the history bequeathed to them, striving to interpret it in living terms for their own and future generations" (*Zakhor* 20). Is this not exactly what Bellow is doing in these three fictions? If further proof were needed for this assertion, we should look to Rashi,[18] the medieval commentator on the Pentateuch, who has a fascinating comment on the derivation of the Hebrew word *gid hanasheh*, "the sinew that is on the hollow of the thigh" (Gen. 32:33), which is particularly relevant to our discussion of "A Silver Dish." Rashi's commentary on this section of Genesis reveals the deep theological discussion operating on a subtextual level within Bellow's fiction. In these short fictions he is seen creating a modern *midrash* on the textual inheritance of the Jewish people.

In his commentary on Genesis 32:33 Rashi asks:

> Why was it called *gid hanasheh*? Because it slipped (*nasheh*) from its place and went up. It (*nasheh*) denotes "leaping" (out of its place); and similarly (Jer. 51.30): "Their might has slipped" (*nishteh*) (failed); and

> similarly (Gen. 41.51): "For God hath made me to slip away (*nashani*) all my toil." (*The Pentateuch and Rashi's Commentary: A Linear Translation into English*, Ben Isaiah, Gen. 32:33)

It is not coincidental that Bellow uses the English translation of this biblical term *nasheh* (slipped), in two climactic moments of "A Silver Dish." The first reference to *nasheh* comes early in the story when Bellow fleshes out Pop's youth and difficult formative years. Bellow says:

> Morris had been a street boy in Liverpool. . . . Morris's Polish family, on their way to America, abandoned him in Liverpool because he had an eye infection and they all would have been sent back from Ellis Island. They stopped awhile in England, but his eyes kept running and they ditched him. They *slipped away* [italics mine], and he had to make out alone in Liverpool at the age of twelve. (198)

This exposition sets up the climactic ending of Pop's last struggle and the ending of the story.

Once again in the concluding scene when Woody climbs into bed and wrestles with his dying father one last time, Bellow repeats the phrase *nasheh* (slipped) once more: "Pop, whom Woody thought he had stilled, only had found a better way to get around him. Loss of heat was the way he did it. His heat was leaving him. . . . Then, as Woody did his best to *restrain* [italics mine] him, and thought he was succeeding, Pop divided himself. And when he was separated from his warmth, he *slipped* [italics mine] into death" (221).

TWO NATIONS IN ONE WOMB

If one is not entirely convinced by my argument that through these references to *nasheh* (slipped) Bellow is alluding to and *drashing* on Genesis, one should also note that Bellow is not only alluding to the *gid hanasheh* aspects of the Jacob story, but perhaps more importantly, he is slyly leading his readers toward a means of interpreting, and being fully conscious of, Woody's mournful Jewish victory after the death of his father.

To fully understand the meaning of "A Silver Dish," we must look further into the biblical story of Jacob's name change. Again, Rashi explains the etymology of Jacob's name by referencing the biblical story of the birth of the twin brothers, Jacob and Esau. The following is Rashi's comment on the name change in Genesis 32:29 the biblical phrase of "*Lo Yaakov* (Not Jacob)": "It will no longer be said that the blessing came to you through insinuation (similarity of *akev* and *yaakov*) and deceit, but through prevailing (similarity of *saar* and *yisrael*) and openly" (331). In his interpretations and commentaries on the Hebrew Bible, Rashi would often allude to the numerous *midrashim* told of different biblical stories. Rashi confidently assumed that his students and readers were well aware of these midrashim and so could just obliquely allude to them with an economy of words.[19] The story of Jacob's birth is told earlier in Genesis, and might be thought of as beginning when Sarah is told by God that "Two nations are in thy womb . . . and the one people shall be stronger than the other people; and the elder shall serve the younger" (Gen. 25:23). As Genesis says, Yaakov (Jacob) received his name because Jacob's "hand had hold of Esau's (baakev) heel" (25:26.) Rashi explains this story further: "And Jacob came to restrain (yaakov) him (Esau) so that he would be the first to be born . . . and would take the birthright legally" (243).

There are two interesting connections between Jacob's birth story in Genesis and Bellow's character Woody in "A Silver Dish." First, Bellow uses the biblical word *restrain* to speak of Woody's desperately holding onto his father in the final deathbed wrestling scene—this is hardly an accidental use of the word *yaakov* (restrained). Perhaps more importantly, ordinarily we think of Jacob's restraining his brother's heal as being a duplicitous act of trying to switch places with his brother. Therefore, in his interpretation, Rashi takes the time to explain that Jacob's act was the exact opposite of deception; it was, in fact, an act of honesty. Jacob restrained his brother from within the womb out of desperation at not wanting to have to resort to dishonesty and theft later on in his life. In his commentary Rashi is, of course, referring to the later episodes recounted in Genesis of Jacob's trickery in first getting Esau to sell him his birthright (Gen. 25:29–33) and then the even more questionable act of Jacob's and Rebekah's conspiracy to trick an aged Isaac into believing he was giving his blessing to Esau when in reality he was blessing Jacob disguised as Esau (Gen. 27:19–29).

In Rashi's commentary, Jacob is seen as a man who hates duplicity of any kind. Similarly, in "A Silver Dish," Bellow describes Woody's character as he listens to the church bells ringing:

> Woody was moved when things were *honest*. Bearing beams were honest, undisguised concrete pillars inside high-rise apartments were honest. It was bad to cover up anything. He hated faking. Stone was honest. Metal was honest. These Sunday bells were very straight.

They broke loose, they wagged and rocked, and the vibrations and the banging did something for him—cleansed his insides, purified his blood. (195)

Since he lost the first wrestling match with his father in Mrs. Skoglund's parlor Woody has been living with the contradictions of containing "two nations" within his one body. This split in his character is manifested in a constant search for authenticity, for what is true and pure in life.

WRESTLING FOR MANCIPATION

Unlike his first wrestling match with his father, which Woody lost as a result of his misguided ideas of propriety, in his second wrestling match with Pop, Woody overcomes this reticence, and like his progenitor Jacob, he can become the literal child of Israel. This second wrestling match signals the beginning of Woody's regeneration as a subjective Jew, a man who while not ironing out the contradictions in his nature may in fact, as Levinas suggests, revel in the consciousness of those ambiguities. He has exited his prolonged apprenticeship or childhood, and is finally able to mancipate himself, become a man who is fully aware of where he has come from; a man in full possession of himself, a person who is able to fully embrace life. In his jumping into his father's deathbed, Woody has finally leapt into life from what had been a sort of prolonged slumber, a life filled with nearly mindless activity and responsibility.

Philosopher and novelist Rebecca Goldstein, remarked in a recent interview (see appendix) that to her "Judaism is about love of life." Quoting I. B. Singer she said: "Jews suffer because they love life too much." Woody Selbst is only able to suffer and mourn once he understands and is fully conscious of how much he loved his father, how much he will miss Morris's peculiar brand of tough-minded selfishness.

SLIPPING INTO FREEDOM

At the end of the story, only after Woody has relived the experience of the first wrestling, can he recall the more recent death struggle with Morris. This time, although having failed to postpone the inevitable onslaught of death, Woody is victorious in his ability to mourn his loss in full consciousness. Seeing his feeble father writhing in his hospital bed with the sides raised up like a crib, Woody takes off his shoes and climbs into the hospital bed beside his dying father "and held him in his arms to soothe and still him" (221). This time Woody is not overcome by Episcopal convention or Mrs. Skoglund's "high breeding." When the disapproving nurses come in and look askance at the two grown men hugging each other in the bed, tubes splayed out all around them, Woody, unable to spare a hand, motions with his head for them to leave—he knows they are treading on holy ground.

Having dabbled in paganism on his trip to Africa at the beginning of "A Silver Dish," barely escaped conversion to Christianity as a youngster, flirted with Buddhist meditation in the middle of the story, at the conclusion, having "striven with God and with mortals, and hav[ing] prevailed" (Gen. 32:28), Woody finally returns to his roots. He emancipates himself from his prolonged apprenticeship and is finally restored to the God of his father and forefathers. Now Woody, like Jacob before him, is ready to assume leadership of his own life, a new life. Emmanuel Levinas, quoting traditional Jewish textual sources, in his essay "Judaism" says: "One follows the Most High God, above all by drawing near to one's fellow man, and showing concern for 'the widow, the orphan, the stranger and the beggar', an approach that must not be made 'with empty hands'" (*Difficult Freedom* 26).

A JEWISH WOODY

And so even in that last struggle Morris, in his own deathbed, has something up his sleeve for his son. Once again Woody loses the wrestling match with his father; however, this time he wins a far more important battle. Woody Selbst has found something quite rare and extraordinary. Having jumped into bed with his father and wrestled to the death, he has unwittingly slipped back into being a free man in full ownership of his self. Consequently, Woody finally has the satisfaction of being able to properly mourn his father. Seizing his Jewish roots with full hands Woody is comforted by a humanitarian vision of transcendence. He says "that the goal set for this earth was that it should be filled with good, saturated with it" (220). He has seized control of his own life. And so that first Sunday after his father's burial, as Woody sits beneath the ringing church bells and is finally able to mourn his father, Woody is emancipated into the difficult freedom which is his birthright. Levinas suggests that it is precisely this "difficult freedom" which Judaism entails. Although Woody loses his father, perhaps this is necessary for his becoming a Jewish man in possession of himself. In his essay "Loving the Torah More Than God," Levinas says: "The just man who suffers for a justice in which there is no victory is the living embodiment of Judaism" (83). Already, in the midst of our study of two Bellow short stories, we are beginning to recognize that this is also the difficult freedom and "suffering for justice" that Bellow's shorter fiction makes implicit.

THE BELLAROSA CONNECTION

In a review of Cynthia Ozick's *The Messiah of Stockholm*, Robert Alter criticizes Ozick for not directly dealing with the Holocaust in her novel. Shortly thereafter, Bellow sent a letter to Ozick, which, while dismissing Alter's complaints, also reveals his own misgivings about his treatment (or lack thereof) of the Holocaust in his work. James Atlas quotes the letter at length in his copious *Bellow: A Biography*. In this letter Bellow traces not just his own failing, as a Jewish American writer, to recognize what was occurring in Europe, but perhaps more importantly, connects his personal reflections with the Jewish American community at large. Due to its importance, particularly in regard to our discussion of memory in this chapter, I'll quote from the letter at length:

> It's perfectly true that "Jewish writers in America" (a repulsive category!) missed what should have been for them the central event of their time, the destruction of European Jewry. I can't say how our responsibility can be assessed. We (I speak of Jews now and not merely writers) should have reckoned more fully, more deeply with it. Nobody in America seriously took this on. (546–47)

Later in the same letter Bellow switches from a national perspective to a more personal account:

> I was too busy becoming a novelist to take note of what was happening in the forties. I was involved with "literature" and given over to preoccupations with art, with language, with my struggle on the American scene, with claims on the recognition of my talent or, like my pals of the *Partisan Review*, with modernism, Marxism, New Criticism, with Eliot, Yeats, Proust, etc.—with anything except the terrible events in Poland. (547)

This letter reveals Bellow's long-standing and well-documented antipathy to the term "Jewish American Writer"; at the same time it demonstrates Bellow's unerring identification with the Jewish people even while chastising himself (and other American Jews) for not properly responding to "the central event of their time." This is doubly true when we consider the recipient of this missive: Cynthia Ozick. Bellow and Ozick represent two-thirds of the late twentieth-century triumvirate (the third member being Philip Roth) of indispensable Jewish American writers.[20]

Although, as we have previously seen, Bellow began making thematic use of the Holocaust at least as early as 1967 in "The Old System," it is not until 1989 and the publication of his novella *The Bellarosa Connection* that he attempts an artistic mea culpa to the above self-leveled charge of his not having made enough of the Holocaust, the "central event" of his time.

In the underappreciated masterpiece *The Bellarosa Connection* we see Bellow's fascination with Jewish American identity, his conception of Jewish history, his unflinching interrogation of Orthodoxy and what remains of Jewish memory in a postwar America all coalesce in a tale of ephemeral beauty. In *The Bellarosa Connection* Bellow revises his own inability to deal with the Holocaust in his earlier fiction. In this novella Bellow suggests that secular America is a diaspora within a diaspora, and implicitly asks: can the Jews survive Americanization? Or as his character Sorella phrases the question: "The Jews could survive everything that Europe threw at them. I mean the lucky remnant. But now comes the next test—America. Can they hold their ground, or will the U.S.A. be too much for them?" (65).

PLOT SYNOPSIS

The Bellarosa Connection tells the story of Harry Fonstein's rescue from Nazi-occupied Europe by Broadway impresario Billy Rose's underground operation. When he finally arrives in America, all that Harry wishes to do is to personally greet and thank his savior Billy Rose. However the despicable producer has no interest in speaking to the Jewish immigrant he has saved, thus relegating Harry's assimilation into American culture incomplete. Meanwhile, Harry's overbearing wife Sorella comes into damaging information concerning Billy Rose and in an effort to persuade Rose to speak with

Harry, who for his entire life in America has been obsessed with thanking his savior, attempts to blackmail him with the damaging information.

MEMORY

"I the Lord am your God who brought you out of the land of Egypt, the house of bondage" (Exod. 20:2). Throughout the Bible the Israelites are charged time and again "Remember this . . ." Consequently the idée fixee for the unnamed narrator of Saul Bellow's *The Bellarosa Connection* is not so much a historical imperative or set of cultural concepts he must transmit. Rather he repeatedly asks of himself: What is worth remembering?

Yet the narrator is wary of remembering the Holocaust. As Sorella tells him the specifics of the murder, torture, and humiliation of the Jews in concentration camps, he begins to tune her out. He says: "I didn't want to hear this." Then a few lines later: "First those people murdered you, then they forced you to brood on their crimes. It suffocated me to do this" (29).[21] He continues:

> Hunting for causes was a horrible imposition added to the original "selection," gassing, cremation. I didn't want to think of the history and psychology of these abominations, death chambers and furnaces. Stars are nuclear furnaces too. Such things are utterly beyond me, a pointless exercise. (29)

As Yerushalmi says: "ancient Israel knows what God is from what he has done in history" (9). Thus for the Jews, from the very beginning, memory becomes all-important. Bellow's *The Bellarosa Connection* is about Jewish memory in America: will Jewish memory, without which Jewish culture would have ceased centuries ago, survive in the *Goldena Medina*?

But just how Jewish is Bellow's unnamed narrator of *The Bellarosa Connection*, the founder of the Mnemosyne Institute and hero of memory? As Yerushalmi observes, Israel is commanded by God to be a Holy nation, yet nowhere does God say, "become a nation of Historians" (10). What kind of memory does the founder deal in? Is it Jewish memory or something else entirely? First we need to define just what constitutes a Jewish memory. Jewish history is not about remembering glories of the past in the way Herodotus's histories recalled. Jewish history is about imbuing the past with meaning. Jewish history is the very idea of a dialectical relationship between God and his chosen people.

We know and thereby get close to God, *davek*, or cling to God, by understanding and remembering his past actions. Thus the past is imbued with meaning beyond itself, it represents a dialectical relationship: a promise of future fealty from the chosen people in exchange for God's protection.

The founder of the Mnemosyne Institute has amassed a professional reputation based upon developing tricks for remembering, but his own memory misses all that is important: his memorization tricks cannot imbue what is being recalled with *meaning*—the prime element of a Jewish conception of memory. Ironically, Billy Rose, a producer of Broadway musicals, does not understand this concept either. The only people who remotely understand this basic tenet of Jewish belief are the survivor Harry Fonstein and his overbearing wife Sorella.

Jewish history separates from the Greek notion of gods battling one another to a dialectical conception of God's desire and Man's free will to either obey or rebel. Thus Jewish history is the record of this dialectic of God's intervention in the affairs of men. In *The Bellarosa Connection* Billy Rose assumes this Godlike role in the lives of those he rescues from the Holocaust. Consequently, Harry Fonstein needs to record the dialectical experience between himself and Billy Rose; he cannot relive it. What Harry wishes is to move his experience of survival from the pagan memory of myth to the Jewish conception of historical time. Pagan and primitive societies reject the importance of a historical moment; the only real time is the time of performing ritual or a reenactment of a primal scene of beginning or birth. Through ritual one can experience the moment of birth and therefore live again during that ritual. Jewish history is the concept of this dialectic, the give and take that will consecrate the past and make it truly historical; it will thus be finished and not reenacted over and over again. Throughout the novella, Billy Rose's refusal to even acknowledge Harry's existence relegates the survivor's experience back to the level of myth. Billy Rose's denial bars Fonstein from participating in the dialectic tradition of Jewish historiography. Until acknowledged by Billy Rose, his story of survival will remain myth and not historiography.

HESTER PANIM II

Bellow's enigmatic novella dramatizes the classical Chasidic response to tragedy: *hester panim* when God turns his face away from this chosen people. Yet Bellow sardonically subverts this by representing Billy Rose, the prime mover of his story as an awful, gluttonous, whoring, foul-mouthed, thieving hanger-on—hardly an image of Jehovah worth preserving. Bellow has Billy Rise repeatedly turn his face away from Harry Fonstein, the man he rescued during the Holocaust.

SURVIVING AMERICA

In the end the narrator has made it in America, but is left alone, he is made fun of and belittled by the new generation of intellectuals for whom everything is just a game, an exercise in futility, nihilism. That is what America has bequeathed to the next generation of Jews. The novella ends with the narrator attempting to contact the Fonsteins. When he is finally able to contact the Fonstein residence he not only discovers that both Harry and Sorella have died, but an intelligent and wisecracking housesitter also berates him. This housesitter is a young man of the next generation, a generation far removed from the narrator's generation, who possesses an overabundance of intelligence, but his brain functions as an intelligence without memory; he is stripped of the weight of Jewish history and the dialectic of God and his chosen people. The young housesitter's memory is in opposition to the type of memory personified by the Fonsteins. Thus in Bellow's system, although the "the lucky remnant" of Jews can survive Hitler, *The Bellarosa Connection* suggests that they cannot seemingly survive America with their cultural inheritance intact.

Why does Harry Fonstein really need Billy Rose in order to complete his story of flight and miraculous survival? Harry knows all the facts and events as they transpired, shouldn't that be enough?

BROADWAY MUSICAL VERSUS BIBLICAL HISTORY

If we look to biblical history telling, it isn't so much the events themselves conveyed in all their detail; instead the *what* that occurred is generally secondary in the stories to the *how* an event occurred. Harry possesses the *what* of his survival, what only Billy Rose can fill in is the *how*, and that, for over half a century Rose has steadfastly refused to do. And so Sorella makes a Herculean effort on behalf of her husband to fill in the blanks of his story. In reaching out to Billy Rose, Sorella recreates the dialectic of Jewish memory and the particularity of Harry's Holocaust history.

CONCLUSION

In these short fictions Bellow has named the malady which not only afflicts Jewish Americans, but which has become a universal American epidemic: an amnesic memory. It is through rejecting the false promises of a completely sterile intellectual life, or a stultifying and deadening capitalist existence, in favor of an embracing of the past, of an identity rooted in something beyond oneself, that human dignity may be salvaged in a post-Holocaust world. Only through memory and through an understanding and appreciation of their immense cultural history will Jewish Americans ever hope to create a distinctive Jewish American culture in the diaspora. Although American Jews have assumed a prominent position in contemporary culture and they have fully integrated themselves into the highest reaches of society, Bellow's short fiction stridently and repeatedly proclaims that it is only through an engagement with Jewish memory, through a reenactment of Jewish culture, that diasporic Jews may become more *mentchlich*, more fully human in conjunction with their becoming more fully Americanized. As Yerushalmi plaintively notes: "The decline of Jewish collective memory in modern times is only a symptom of the unraveling of that common network of belief and praxis through whose mechanisms . . . the past was made present" (94). Yerushalmi, as a historian, sees himself as relatively powerless, more "pathologist, than physician," able to point out what ails the Jewish community in America but unable to halt the spread of the amnesic disease.

If the historian may be thought of as a cultural pathologist, then perhaps the fictionist can serve not only as theologian, as I've argued earlier in this study, but as physician as well. As a writer Bellow can at least temporarily heal this cultural disease through his life-affirming humor. From the *mishegunah* Billy Rose and Sorella, crazy Pop and Woody wrestling in the Skoglund's parlor, to Isaac and Tina's operatic deathbed scene, Bellow has all these *meshugah* Jews going about their *meshuguh* lives. But in the humorous process Bellow obliterates the sadness of the realization that life will never live up to the expectations of his sensitive, and thereby noble, characters. Despite this awful realization of the tragedy of life, Bellow's characters are able to laugh, and in so doing remember a thing or two and in that process create a reconstituted self after the obliteration of their biblical laughter.

The cultural work that great fiction performs—and Bellow's is in my estimation the most powerful—is organically life affirming. While it cannot heal the wounds which history has inflicted, Bellow's fiction can, for a moment, re-imagine life restored. In Bellow's three separate deathbed scenes we see Jewish memory working its magic, helping to reconstitute both individuals and communities. For a moment, at least as long as Bellow tells his tale, all is made whole once more and Jewish culture in post-Holocaust America is revived.

CHAPTER 4

Rebecca Goldstein:
The Ethics of Second-Generation Witnessing

> The Holocaust has already engendered more historical research than any single event in Jewish history, but I have no doubt whatever that its image is being shaped, not at the historian's anvil, but in the novelist's crucible.
> —Yosef Hayim Yerushalmi, *Zakhor* 98

> In *Mazel* my character Sasha sees a young I. B. Singer walking down the street and overhears him saying something, something which he actually had said in a story—a woman asks him: "Why are we Jews so doomed?" And he answers: "Because we love life too much." And that to me somehow says so much about our history. You know not to see us only in terms of that tragedy, and not to feel the victim because that is not about us, that is about them. That is what they did to us, but that's not what we're about. We're not about being martyred, and we're not about suffering, and we're not about victim-hood: we're about celebration.
> —Rebecca Goldstein, October 2000 Interview[1]

INTRODUCTION

Renee Feuer, the first-person narrator of Rebecca Goldstein's novel *The Mind-Body Problem*, wanders into a small restaurant in Vienna faint from hunger. Renee has been following her husband Noam Himmel, a world-renowned mathematician, across the European continent on an academic journey that doubles as their honeymoon. When Renee notices that the waitress's arm bears the blue tattoo of a concentration camp survivor, amazed to find a survivor living in Austria, she asks the waitress: "And you still live here?" (109). The waitress replies: "I lived in America for a few years after the war, in New York's

Washington Heights. . . . But I am Viennese. . . . In spite of it all. In spite of the fact that I can look out into this square and remember when it flowed with blood. I am Viennese" (109).

What was it that drew Renee Feuer to that cafe of all the many she and Noam had passed that afternoon? When it comes to imagining and representing the Holocaust, as well as the rich texture of Jewish history, Rebecca Goldstein cannot help but dream Jewish dreams.

Being an ethical, humanistic writer in the aftermath of the Holocaust, Goldstein repeatedly asks: How can we not attempt to represent this monumental loss to world history? As it did for Renee, for many of Goldstein's characters, the Holocaust, either through familial history or by historical import, becomes a centering force. During a recent interview Goldstein was asked to discuss the centrality of the Holocaust in her work. She replies:

> I know that it looms large in my psyche. In some sense it was something I actually wanted to get past, for example, in writing *Mazel*. I think that we have been scarred, all of us collectively, the world, not just Jews, although particularly Jews, scarred by the trauma, that we forget what their lives were like before. We see them in terms of their end and the tragedy and we forget about the fullness and the richness of that culture—and the joyfulness, the sort of life-embracing, vivid, intense celebration of life. (Interview)

Until her teens Rebecca Goldstein believed that her father was a concentration camp survivor. She held this belief despite the fact that her father had immigrated to America in the early 1930s. In the same interview she says:

> Now my father was Polish and for some reason throughout our childhoods my younger sister and I somehow connected, we thought somehow that he had gone through the camps. There was something about him that made us really think that he had . . . so if I am not a child of survivors, I think I have very much the sensibility, to a certain extent, of a child of survivors. There was such a sense of the hurt, of the betrayal, of the broken lives in our family. (Interview)

Goldstein's childhood beliefs reinforce Arthur Cohen's observation in *The Tremendum* that American Jews are the Holocaust witnesses who "bear the scar without the wound" (2). Goldstein is a writer on the front lines of a generation of writers who in Cohen's words feel "the obligation, self-imposed and self-accepted (however ineluctably), to describe a meaning and wrest instruction from the historical" (2). The nexus of ideas that animates Goldstein's lyrical prose swirls around the issue of memory both private and historical. Thus the Holocaust, both as moral educator and as personal history, is often at the center of her short stories and novels.

Goldstein is a writer and philosopher concerned with the many ways in which people balance the competing claims of mind and body, reason and desire. It is therefore not surprising that Goldstein, as a Jewish American writer and as someone profoundly interested in her characters' personal philosophy, is drawn to the darkest aspects of humanity and the history of her own family in the Holocaust. Concurrently, Goldstein, through her philosophical and fictional universe, wrestles with the dilemma of bearing witness to the Holocaust from a generational distance. Indeed, as dramatized in much of her fiction, but perhaps most poignantly in her short story "The Legacy of Raizel Kaidish," her haunting and unparalleled evocation of the psychological consequences of Holocaust survival and the bequeathed emotional legacy with which the second generation must somehow reckon, Goldstein lays bare the costs of both emotional detachment in the face of trauma and terror, as well as the perils of emotional involvement, all the time forcing the reader to contemplate the awesome demands which are a consequence of each position. In the end the reader is left pondering whether these two philosophical positions are as mutually exclusive as Goldstein's thwarted and frustrated characters would have us believe.

Concerned with the long and proud history of her people, Goldstein is not satisfied with a fictional universe that limits itself to portraying only the twelve years of the Third Reich. In her novel *Mazel*, which won both the National Jewish Book Award and the Edward Lewis Wallant Award, Goldstein gives voice to the pre-Holocaust culture of the Jews—focusing on the vibrancy and culture that was largely destroyed by the Nazis. Unlike many second-generation writers dealing with the Holocaust, rather than focus entirely on the destruction of European Jewry, Goldstein attempts to reanimate that lost world by moving back into prewar Poland to show the rich and varied cultural life that flourished in Warsaw before the war. In the tradition of Aharon Appelfeld, who in *Badenheim 1939* shows the calm before the storm in a resort community in Austria on the eve of the Holocaust, Goldstein's *Mazel* chapters set in prewar Poland create almost unbearable tension within her readers who are aware of what in a few short years will befall European Jewry and engulf Goldstein's characters.

Goldstein was born in 1950 into a traditionally Orthodox home in White Plains, New York. Her father was, in Goldstein's words, "a *shtickele chazzan*" (a minor cantor), who immigrated to America in the 1930s. He was to have a profound and lasting influence over Goldstein's life and work. Goldstein attended an Orthodox *Beis Yaakov Yeshiva* for girls. The Yeshiva's antifeminist teachings have also left their mark on Goldstein in her dual roles as a mother and writer. After graduating from *Beis Yaakov*, Goldstein, against her mother's wishes (it was unacceptable for a traditional Jewish girl to go to college), enrolled at Barnard College where she earned her B.A., before going on to Princeton where she earned a Ph.D. in philosophy. After completing her Ph.D., Goldstein returned to Barnard where she taught in the philosophy department for ten years. Goldstein has won two Whiting Awards, a grant from the American Council of Learned Societies, a "Genius Grant" from the MacArthur Foundation, and most recently a second National Jewish Book Award.

In speaking of her family's Holocaust history, Goldstein says: "My father was born in a *shtetl* in Poland (Lemberg). He left before the war. He was one of the youngest in a large family, so they came over. His older sister is the only one who married and settled over there so she and her four children, four of my first cousins, of course, died. That was on the Polish side. On my mother's side, the Hungarian side, my Grandmother had come over by herself from Hungary. She had a huge family, very artistic, very prominent, very wealthy; they almost all died. There were a few who managed to survive from this very large family." Those few who did survive would often come to stay with Goldstein's family in White Plains. Memories of these immigrant survivors, the few remnants, were formative for the young Goldstein. She says:

> There was one in particular, Zanvil, who really impressed me because he was so arrogant. He would order my mother and us girls around, do this and do that. He was a shriveled up broken little man. And my mother did not like to be ordered around [but] she did it. She picked up after him. She did everything. And I said, "He's so obnoxious, why are you doing this?" And she would say, "You don't want to know. You don't want to know." And I was always hearing this: "You don't want to know." She'd say: "He was in the camps." I'd ask: "What does that mean?" She'd say: "You don't want to know." So I got the sense of these people that something incredibly horrible and

mysterious had happened to them. I remember my mother saying of this guy: "He used to ride around on his white horse, he was a prince surveying his land, and now look at him." (Interview)

Goldstein's father had been studying for his doctorate in German literature at City College before the war. Years after the Holocaust he refused to help his daughter with her German homework while she studied philosophy; he refused to speak the language, calling it "*Farfluchtah* Deutsche," accursed German:

> It was sort of an ultimate denial—he wouldn't even speak the language. I came to understand that he had such a deep sense of betrayal. One of the things about Jews, I think European Jews, and I inherited this very strongly, is a love of German culture. I mean, we love German culture, my father loved it, and we *loved* it. And it didn't love us back quite clearly. So there's a sense of betrayal on top of everything else that this culture had so let us down. (Interview)

THE PHILOSOPHY OF ETHICAL FICTION

Goldstein's voice is unique in contemporary fiction; she is seemingly able to write elegantly on any scientific or intellectual topic: quantum physics, mathematics, as well as Orthodox Judaism and philosophy. Goldstein is a writer perpetually enchanted by the ethical; she is obsessed with the issue of morality in a post-Holocaust universe. Her fiction is marked by a ceaseless interrogation of traditional Judaism and history, a history that has the Holocaust as one, but only one, among many of its defining moments.

Goldstein, unlike her thwarted intellectual characters, urges her readers to embrace the ambiguities of life, to somehow forge a reconciliation between their bodies and their minds. In her numerous forays into the Gothic, for example her short story "From Dreams of the Dangerous Duke" in *Strange Attractors* and her most recent novel *Properties of Light*, Goldstein reminds her readers that her roots, although transplanted from Europe, have found fertile soil on American shores. Goldstein is a worthy heir to Nathaniel Hawthorne. Numerous intellectuals, characters who, much like Arthur Dimmesdale, are caught between reason and passion, body and mind, populate her novels. Yet rather than draw from Hawthorne's Puritan past, Goldstein takes her inspiration from an even older tradition: Orthodox Judaism.

Despite her seemingly endless fictional topics and philosophical themes, Goldstein time and again returns in her fiction, often obliquely, to the subject matter of the Holocaust. Goldstein evokes the Holocaust through indirection, always approaching the carnage aslant. For example, in her first novel the specter of the Holocaust rises before her characters Renee and Noam while touring Europe on an academic conference. While in her second novel Goldstein depicts the horrors of the war through the reactions of a second-generation perpetrator: her protagonist is the daughter of a famous Nazi musicologist who has moved to New York to escape her family's evil legacy.

Goldstein's fictional universe hovers in the questioning and ephemeral space between the old world of received traditional Judaism marked by blind faith and adherence to a patriarchal world-view, and a doubting skeptical, scientific new-world order of super-string chaos theory and relativity. Goldstein's lyrical fictional universe gently hovers between these opposing viewpoints, questioning, searching, and always self-consciously aware of these two traditions: one inherited by birth, the other gained through rigorous and sustained rational analysis.

In *The Mind-Body Problem*, Renee Feuer inhabits this twin tradition. She is named after Renee Descartes, the father of modern philosophy and rationality, and her maternal great-grandmother Reine, a name that connotes spiritual purity. As Goldstein tells her readers, Reine was "married at twelve and lived to have sixteen children and sixty grandchildren before she was carted off, at ninety-four, to Auschwitz" (179).

In an age of increasing relativism, when Deconstruction and post-structuralism hold sway and metaphysics seems quaint, Goldstein's work stridently proclaims the human will. In Goldstein's fictional universe truth becomes a moral imperative leading her characters and readers to ask the right questions, the big questions, those concerning faith and doubt, history and responsibility.

Her first novel deals obliquely with the Holocaust. The war seems grafted onto what is essentially an academic (Barnard, Columbia, and Princeton) satire. The honeymoon in Europe seems more an opportunity for Goldstein to tentatively enter the actual European site of the Holocaust than an occasion to reflect on the consequences of the Holocaust both historically and emotionally. A reader in search of the emotional residue, still actively evolving for the second generation of not just survivors but the victimizers' children as well, would have to wait until 1988 and the publication of Goldstein's second novel *The Late Summer Passion of a Woman of Mind*. In this novel Goldstein attempts to stretch her readers' compassion and empathy to the narratological breaking point. She demands that her readers empathize with Eva Mueller, the daughter of a Nazi theorist and musicologist, who becomes a rationalist philosophy professor and flees to New York to escape the burden of her familial history. It is only after Eva corresponds with a *Yad Vashem* Holocaust scholar in Israel and reads her father's Nazi-ideology-laced treatise on Wagner, that Eva can begin to fully enter the world of the living for the first time. Goldstein's novel poignantly warns of the importance of memory and an accounting of history for the second generation.

In *The Dark Sister* Goldstein forages into the shadowy recesses of her characters' minds, in the process reinventing both William and Henry James as literary characters and giving new meaning to the term "Jamesian" novel. Through the eccentric writer Hedda, Goldstein once again dramatizes the struggle between remaining aloof and uninvolved in the emotional life of others and therefore of oneself, or of venturing into the world of passion and feeling and therefore compassion for others. For Hedda's sister Stella, in the conclusion of *The Dark Sister*, this empathic choice may open the way toward memory and a more balanced life of the mind and spirit.

In *Strange Attractors* Goldstein plays with voice, tone, and point-of-view; in these multilayered and often interlocking stories she shows her remarkable range as a writer. In the first two stories of this collection "The Editor's Story" and "From Dreams of the Dangerous Duke," Goldstein is primarily interested in tone and style and in representing how women's genius has been quashed in different ages. But this collection shines in Goldstein's stories that dramatize the theological questions, both moral and philosophical, which swirl and eddy around the Holocaust. Goldstein has said that she is wary of any direct aesthetic representation of the Holocaust. This is a stance she rigorously adheres to and her Holocaust stories are all the more powerful for her position that the ground of the martyrs is holy and not to be trod upon lightly, in fact for someone who considers herself akin to a second-generation survivor, perhaps not to be trod on at all. Instead, Goldstein forces her readers to ponder the philosophical and moral questions left to the next generation. Chief among these are questions of transmission, of the *mesorah* of Jewish history: what must be told to the next generation, and what must remain silent.

Silence in Goldstein's work, the phrase "over there," the only Holocaust marker, often points to the "unspeakability" of the crimes against not just the Jews but against all of humanity. Goldstein's short story "Mindel Gittel," collected in *Strange Attractors*, wrestles with what historian Peter Haidu has termed "The Dialectics of Unspeakability," the challenge of aesthetically representing the Holocaust. Haidu remarks that "Silence can be the marker of courage and heroism or the cover of cowardice and self-interest; sometimes it is the road-sign of an impossible turning" (278). In Goldstein's complex moral fictional universe silences are often suffused with the meaning of all that cannot, or will not, be said.

Goldstein forces her readers to account for the silence of Mindel Gittel's parents. Is it self-preservation within a hostile postwar *goyish* Connecticut? Is it merely expedience or personal preference that closes off intergenerational communication? Or is their silence an act of mercy, of not wanting to taint this golden child of the new world with all the unspeakable horror of the world left behind in their transatlantic flight? Perhaps their silence symbolizes the world's silence that greeted many survivor tales with both hostility and disbelief. Survivor stories were often not openly talked about until a second generation had come of age, a generation somewhat removed from the horrific events of the Holocaust.

In pondering these questions Goldstein's fiction begins a low murmuring dialogue within each of her readers, an intertextual conversation which obliterates that silence—at least that part of silence that is destructive, which is filled with fear and self-hate, pity and embarrassment. Through her morally complex stories, Goldstein urges her readers to never succumb to easy answers be they stridently called forth or silently ignored.

In her dual role of philosopher and fiction writer Goldstein recognizes that how the Holocaust will be remembered by future generations, those without a direct link to the first-hand witnesses, is the awesome responsibility of her generation. Goldstein's fiction travels the tortuous route between representing the Holocaust and its legacy, and doing so without prurient description of the unspeakable horror and without needlessly diluting Holocaust images. Aesthetically and narratively it is a difficult road to travel, particularly in an age that demands increasingly macabre elements to satisfy its passion for blood and guts, yet Goldstein never allows her fiction to ask easy questions, and she would hope no less for her readers as well.

SLANT REPRESENTATION

> Iris Murdoch said somewhere that "False consolation is bad art."
> And that rang so true to me. Art is supposed to open you up to
> the world. It's not supposed to close you off with false, easy
> answers: that's morally and aesthetically wrong. I've spent most
> of my life thinking about things that are irreconcilable, and if
> they're good questions, there are no easy answers and you want
> to do justice to that.
>
> —Rebecca Goldstein, Interview

In contrast to Bernard Malamud's unsuccessful attempts at representing the Holocaust directly, Goldstein, as a second-generation writer,
uses allusion and slant representation of the Holocaust not only as an
aesthetic decision but as a moral one as well. She asks:

> How can the Holocaust not dominate one's consciousness as a
> Jew, or with anybody as a citizen of a civilized world? How do we
> deal with that in fiction? The ethical problem seems to be it seems
> too large, too significant, and too important to be subverted in any
> way for aesthetic effect. And yet you want to. Part of what it means
> to be a Jew today is that the Holocaust lies in our path. (Interview)

For a fiction writer, in addition to the ethical problem stands an
equally troubling aesthetic dilemma. Goldstein asks: "How do you do
justice to this? I have always been very impressed with the way that
Aharon Appelfeld deals with it: he will never, ever be in the Holocaust;
it will always be before or after. And that is what I did in *Mazel*" (Interview). Goldstein would never dare tread upon the ground of the Holocaust. She believes that indirection is the only way to do justice to the
enormity of the Holocaust. She calls the space of Holocaust victims,
both physical and aesthetic, "holy ground." "I wouldn't dare. They're
martyrs. I wouldn't bring my, in comparison, trivial goals as a novelist
onto that ground. But to somehow indicate how large, by skirting
around it—I think it's very effective" (Interview).

This is precisely the aesthetic choice Goldstein uses in her evocation of the difficulties faced by the second generation and the nearly
impossible choices that the survivors were forced to make as they
Americanized their children. One of the more striking instances of this
aesthetic and moral choice is glimpsed in Goldstein's powerful story
"Mindel Gittel." In referring to the horrors of the Holocaust, Goldstein's narrator Sol can't even bring himself to mention the continent

which was the site of the Holocaust; instead he ominously repeats the vague phrase "over there."

Goldstein has said about Sol and his euphemistic use of "over there" that she was thinking about the silence that shut down any Holocaust discussion in her home:

> Just the enormity, the reticence. The reticence that I grew up with in my own family. It was: "You don't want to know. We can't say. We can't do justice. . . ." This is where language breaks down. It's where everything breaks down; it's the black hole of all values. There is no language adequate to it. It's either "over there," or there's silence—which is what I had experienced. (Interview)

Perhaps the most obvious instance of Goldstein's combining her philosophical and fictional writing modes is her short story "The Legacy of Raizel Kaidish," which dramatizes the emotional toll bequeathed from the survivors to their children before being passed on to the third generation. The story is told from the perspective of the daughter of a survivor of Buchenwald, a woman named after a martyr, Raizel Kaidish, who died in an act of courage. As Raizel narrates: "My mother's moral framework was formed in Buchenwald. Forged in the fires, it was strong and inflexible. One of her central concerns was that I should come to know, without myself suffering, all that she had learned there" (*Strange Attractors* 229). The story turns upon the unbearable moral decisions survivors were forced to make in the camps. Goldstein's story forces the reader to suspend judgment on the mother who at the story's conclusion reveals that far from being the hero of the episode, she actually was the informer who betrayed Raizel Kaidish.

"Raizel Kaidish" brilliantly dramatizes the weakness inherent in any ethical system not tuned to the humanistic, to the case-by-case situation. Goldstein's short story reveals the difficulties of drawing easy moral conclusions from our vantage point of three generations removed from the Holocaust. Goldstein says she wrote this story, her first piece of fiction, as a pedagogical tool for a class on ethics at Barnard College:

> I was teaching a course on ethics, and I was making the claim to my students that rules often don't do justice to the ethical situation, that you often need to have the narrative, you have to have the story. A rule-oriented ethics is not fine-tuned enough. I was trying to think

of a situation that I could use to explain this to my students, and that's how that story came to me. I was trying to solve this pedagogical problem in a class of ethics. Of course the Holocaust preoccupation came out in that story. (Interview)

Being a philosopher as well as a fiction writer, Goldstein is in a position to not only write evocative and emotionally challenging works of fiction, but to codify an aesthetics of Holocaust representation as well. Consequently Goldstein, through her forays into representing the Holocaust in such stories as "Mindel Gittel," and "The Legacy of Raizel Kaidish," manages to involve her readers fully in the lives of an other. This is especially true of her second novel *The Late Summer Passion of a Woman of Mind*, where Goldstein attempts the nearly impossible: that her readers will have utmost compassion and empathy for the progeny of a Nazi theorist. Goldstein's work is vitally important in order to understand the difficult second-generation response to the Holocaust as well as its evolving moral and aesthetic difficulties.

Described by Cynthia Ozick as "brainy and versatile," there is no doubt that Goldstein is one of only a handful of contemporary American fiction writers engaged in a project of dramatizing ideas. In her essay "Visits to Germany in Recent Jewish-American Writing," Susanne Klingenstein surmised: "Goldstein's novels are more interested in the philosophical positions they expose than in psychological realism" (554). While this position may have some relevance to Goldstein's early work, her more recent fiction has managed to convey a deep appreciation for philosophical ideas without sacrificing any psychological realism or emotional power.

Writing about *Mazel* Andrew Furman says that Goldstein's work affirms the notion that "Jewish identity is one that is worth both preserving through ritual and transmitting through art" (*Contemporary Jewish American Writers and the Multicultural Dilemma* 99). Goldstein is a writer more in the European tradition of philosophical fiction. Because she defies easy categorization, many American reviewers and critics do not know quite what to make of her. Still, much of the reception of her work has been extremely positive. Goldstein is one of only a handful of writers engaged in asking what Harold Bloom has called "the large questions." Goldstein's philosophical fiction forces her readers, living just a few generations removed from the European carnage, to embrace the ambiguities of a post-Holocaust world. She is a writer descended from a direct line of questioning Jewish skeptics and writers of overt paradoxes. Goldstein, with her feminist challenge toward Orthodoxy and her ethical aesthetic principle concerning Holocaust representation, is firmly within the avant-garde of the Jewish American cultural tradition. Her work is one freshly forged link in the great chain of Jewish tradition stretching back thousands of years.

CHAPTER 5

Four Questions for Allegra Goodman

INTRODUCTION

As a crossover best-selling success Allegra Goodman is a leading voice on nearly every major issue confronting modern Judaism in the diaspora. For almost twenty years Goodman has been writing fiction that covers the full spectrum of diasporic Jewish life in America, from Orthodoxy and feminism to Holocaust representation and liberal ideology. Goodman is as comfortable writing an uproarious academic satire as she is precise in skewering Chasidic communities and expatriate Orthodox Honolulu Jews. Earlier in *American Talmud* we discussed first- and second-generational witnessing to the Holocaust; this chapter explores Goodman's important third-generational representation of the Holocaust, before turning to her groundbreaking fictional representation of Orthodoxy.

Writing about the biblical matriarch Rachel, Allegra Goodman observes: "It does not matter how much commentary has been written; questioning and speculation are a part of reading this text. The questions cannot end, because gaps are integral to the story; the text will never be exhausted, because it can never be filled" ("The Story of Rachel" 174).

Although Goodman is referring to the troubling episode of Rachel's theft of her father's idols, she might just as easily be speculating on her own representation of the Holocaust within her fiction. Goodman is a writer who is concerned with asking the right questions if only to remind her readers of the tremendous gap that the Nazi era has left not only within Judaism, but also within contemporary culture.

Goodman is a discriminating observer of social mores and a chronicler of domesticity in the tradition of George Eliot. A satirical writer who relies on her readers to cut through layers of social nuance to glimpse the kernel of wisdom embedded within each of her stories and novels, Goodman is also, despite her Victorian roots, a writer with a decidedly postmodern and feminist sensibility. Her fictional universe is peopled with seekers; her characters are inevitably engaged in a cultural conflict in their attempt to transcend the quotidian of contemporary American society and connect to some deeper theological meaning. This quest often ends ambiguously because Goodman is more interested in setting up a problem than in seeking a solution. Thus, much of Goodman's work focuses on the religious conflicts, alienation, and displacement of the second and third generations of assimilated Jewish Americans, many of whom are descended from Holocaust survivors. This displacement, either as a result of the Holocaust for Andras and his children in *Kaaterskill Falls*, or the crippling effects of American assimilation for Ed and Sarah in *The Family Markowitz*, sends Goodman's characters in a search for higher spirituality. Though Goodman has never dealt with the Holocaust head-on in her fiction, she alludes to it in a troubling way, allowing her readers to view how her characters, whether they are assimilated or Orthodox, are disturbed by their personal and historical legacies.

Goodman was born in Brooklyn, New York, in 1967, but grew up in a small Jewish community in Hawaii where her parents taught at the University of Hawaii. Goodman remembers having worn a traditional floral muumuu at her *bat mitzvah*. She began publishing and also gained recognition for her writing at a remarkably young age—her first story appeared in *Commentary* when she was a freshman at Harvard University, while her first book of short stories was published before her graduation at the age of twenty-one. Goodman would go on to earn a Ph.D. in English Literature from Stanford University.

Much of Goodman's writing is semiautobiographical and draws upon the exoticism of her upbringing. At the end of her first story collection *Total Immersion*, for example, Goodman appends a glossary of words, not only for the Yiddish and Hebrew phrases, but also for the Hawaiian words and phrases that trickle into her prose.

SATIRICAL REPRESENTATION

Goodman's first book *Total Immersion* is a collection of stories that satirize Jewish American mores and assimilation. Goodman's sharp, witty writing showcases her remarkable penchant at cutting through layers of socialization to expose the unvarnished truth of her characters' lives. The Holocaust pervades this collection perhaps more for its absence than by its presence. One of the few references to the war in *Total*

Immersion occurs when a Jewish American who served during World War II remembers the letters he wrote home while in the Navy. Although he weeps as he remembers that "We all had no idea whether we'd make it through the war," Goodman quickly undercuts his tears, informing her readers that Max "had a small problem with his eyesight" and that he looked "as unconcerned as a man chopping onions" (137–38). The Holocaust is never mentioned during this American Jew's World War II remembrance. Later in the story even the rabbi emeritus of the community, while reflecting on his time as military chaplain in Hawaii during World War II, remembers their own "hardships and shortages" without mentioning the Holocaust or what befell their European brothers and sisters: the Holocaust doesn't even enter into the equation. This type of caustic, biting satire distinguishes Goodman's early stories.

Goodman's second book, *The Family Markowitz*, is a series of interlocking stories in which the Holocaust serves as subtext for many of her characters' lives. In "Fannie Mae," the first story of the collection, Rose becomes infuriated when the daughter of her deathly ill second husband comes from Israel to sleep on her sofa. Rose wants to send Dorothy back to Israel where she can no longer pester Maury about his past. She complains bitterly to her Washington Heights neighbor Esther: "I was seven years old when I came to England, and I was all alone with no one in the world to look after me. . . . And she can never know what I saw and went through." For added emphasis she explains: "My own parents sent me away. . . . In the name of safety they abandoned me" (12).

As in all her writing Goodman treats the Holocaust with a deft touch; through small details she reveals her characters' histories while concurrently showing the influence the Holocaust has had on the second and third generations. Goodman's fiction bears more than a passing resemblance to the work of Chaim Grade, whose work Goodman says "is always the elegiac record of times past. Even Grade's prewar work bears the shadow of the Holocaust" ("Writing Jewish Fiction" 269). Appropriating Grade's technique of foreshadowing the Holocaust, Goodman weaves Holocaustal images into works set in prewar Europe: the previous passage, readers find out in a later story, deals with Rose's family history during World War I; Rose's displacement is in fact not a consequence of the Holocaust.

Many of Goodman's stories dramatize the ways in which modern Americanized Jews have turned Holocaust commemoration into a cliché. If, as Francine Prose observed some time ago, the Holocaust is "the pin with which to stick yourself," that pin has begun to blunt. In Goodman's fictional universe, the Holocaust and the issue of Holocaust memory, indeed of any meaningful Jewish past history, is tied up in a larger search, often a futile search, for spirituality within the morass of assimilated America.

The following exchange is emblematic of Goodman's concerns. Henry, an aesthete who has moved to England, visits his brother Ed, an academic and terrorism expert in Washington, and they go to a *shabbos* service at the local synagogue.

> "What did you think of Congregation S.T.?" Ed asks.
> "Not bad. Not bad at all. Except for the ghastly Holocaust sculpture. The air conditioning was splendid."
> "I meant—you know—spiritually," Ed says.
> Henry looks at him questioning. (154)

In "The Persians," collected in *The Family Markowitz*, Ed and his wife Sarah search for a suitable bat mitzvah gift for their friend's daughter. Their simple trip to the local bookstore becomes transformed into a test of wills that dramatizes the political fallout from renewed Holocaust interest among assimilated Jewish America and its literature. Sarah rejects Philip Roth's *Goodbye Columbus* as being "too 50'ish," I. B. Singer's *Collected Stories* as "too kinky," and Saul Bellow's *The Adventures of Augie March* as "too hard for a twelve-year-old." When Sarah proposes *The Diary of Anne Frank*, all Ed can think to say is "Oh, very original." When Ed accuses Sarah of "honing in" on Holocaust books, Sarah offended, responds: "I am not! I'm just looking for the Jewish ones" (170).

In "The Four Questions," also from *The Family Markowitz*, Ed, a Middle East expert, is so conscious of political correctness he ensures that the only word of the Haggadah that he doesn't translate into English is *Mizrayim*. Instead of saying *Egypt*, Ed sticks to the ancient Hebrew so as not to taint the current political scene. Once the traditional four questions are read, Goodman really turns up the heat. When Ben reads, "But for the assimilated child . . . it is up to us to open the discussion," rather than engage in an actual conversation about the significance of the Haggadah, Ed says, going against the *halachic* prohibition of adding to the commandments of the Torah, "We can meditate for a minute . . . on a fifth child who died in the Holocaust" (196).

Instead of this moment of silence linking the Markowitz clan to family history, or it being an occasion of genuine Holocaust commemoration, Ed's addition to the ancient Haggadah is simply self-serving. Goodman's narrator tells us: "They sit silently and look at their plates." A moment later Miriam, the *baalat teshuvah* (lit: mistress of repentance; a recent returnee to Orthodoxy), the affiliated but angry Orthodox daughter says: "So much for discussion at the seder" (196). It is this difficult assimilated American response to the Holocaust that Goodman invokes in her early fiction. Her treatment of the Holocaust, however, takes a decided turn in her more recent work.

In the opening pages of Goodman's first novel *Kaaterskill Falls*, Andras, a child-survivor of the Holocaust, and his wife Nina argue over his responsibility to bear witness to his personal trauma. Frustrated over his inaction, befuddled by his lifelong reticence on the topic of his childhood displacement during the war, she implores him: "Survivors are witnesses, and when they are gone there will be nothing left." World-weary Andras can't even summon the energy to respond to his wife's chastisement. The omniscient narrator reports: "But how can he describe a vacancy, an absence?" (46).

Goodman, writing from a third-generational remove from the Holocaust, has her character Andras, although a child-survivor, epitomize the third-generational bind. Deeply affected by their grandparents' suffering, third-generation witnesses are removed from testifying to the atrocities of the Holocaust, yet are often compelled to represent those events which even sixty years later are at the center of their familial history and legacy. In *Kaaterskill Falls* Goodman attempts to represent the moral complexities of living an Orthodox life within the demands of modernity while being aware of the responsibilities to Jewish History, particularly the Holocaust. Goodman has said, "it was a matter of creating this moment that would make the reader think, and feel troubled" (Kreilkamp 80).

In her novel *Paradise Park*, published in 2001, Goodman once again represents not the Holocaust itself, but the ways in which assimilated American Jews respond to its legacy, both in preserving its history, and in marring the historical record for personal use. *Paradise Park* follows the self-absorbed, unreliable first-person narrator Sharon Spiegelman on a twenty-year journey through spiritual reversal, disappointment, and ultimate rebirth. Goodman uses the occasion of Sharon's receiving a letter from her old boyfriend Gary (who has become a *baal teshuvah* and moved to Jerusalem where he is studying at the Torah Or Institute) to satirize much of American Jewry's simple knee-jerk response to the Holocaust. Goodman explains that after Gary was "persecuted," that is, "dumped" by his German girlfriend, he wanders around Holland and finds himself in the Anne Frank house where he receives a spiritual epiphany: "That he was a Jew like Anne. He was Jew enough to be killed for it. As soon as he realized he was Jewish, Gary took off for Jerusalem" (144).

Goodman uses the seemingly innocuous occasion of Sharon's taking a religion seminar midterm to satirize her trivializing of the Holocaust. When the proctors collect the booklets before she has finished the exam, Sharon exclaims: "It was like I was in some labor camp trying to scribble out my last words, and the guards snatched away my scrap of paper" (166). Goodman often has her characters abuse genuine Holocaust memory to satirize the ways in which both her Orthodox and her assimilated characters, through their debilitating self-absorption, misuse Holocaust images and history. Similarly, after Sharon has moved to Jerusalem to be with her supposed *bashert* (destined mate) Gary, and is unhappy studying *halachah* (Jewish law) with her teacher Morah Zipporah, she bitterly complains to Gary: "She's a Nazi" (181).

Perhaps the most disturbing scene in the novel, from the perspective of a reader concerned with Holocaust memory and history, is the late afternoon walk Gary and Sharon take in Jerusalem's old city. Gary explains to Sharon his epiphanic moment in the Frank house. In a satirical reworking of Thane Rosenbaum's "Cattle Car Complex," in which an American child of survivors experiences a psychotic flashback to the Holocaust in a midtown Manhattan elevator car, Gary is dragged out of the Anne Frank House. Gary says:

> It was a moment of sheer terror. . . . I was standing in the Anne Frank house, and I felt deep in the pit of my stomach that my identity was her identity. Her fate was my fate. We shared one blood. . . . I was a Jew! I was gasping for air, and I was crying out. And the security guards came for me but I couldn't stop screaming. . . . They began to drag me away. (182)

In this section Goodman mocks the easy pieties of her assimilated American Jewish character, a narcissistic man who equates his own neurosis and rootless identity with the unimaginable (and unrepresentable) suffering of Anne Frank. Through her satiric rendering of Gary's tainted Holocaust memory, a trivializing distortion of history, Goodman stridently and ironically defends true Holocaust witnessing.

Sharon's response to Gary's overwrought tale is reminiscent of Bernard Malamud's seminal grocery store debate on Jewish identity between Morris Bober and Frank Alpine in *The Assistant*. Even the unstable and self-absorbed Sharon questions Gary's simple formulations: "How could you not have realized before you were a Jew?" Gary's answer to Sharon's question is important for it begins to reveal Goodman's methodology behind her representation of the Holocaust. He replies: "No, Sharon! Don't you see? Before I had no history. I had no knowledge. I had no learning. And at that moment. In one split second in the Netherlands. My history came home to me. That was what happened" (183). Goodman's short, incomplete, and staccato sentences reveal the imperfection of Gary's logic. The six years of the Holocaust cannot become a substitute for millennia of Jewish history and culture. In keeping with Goodman's caustic satire, both Gary and Sharon are blissfully unaware of the shortcomings of their distorted view of Jewish identity and culture. Goodman's characters remain ignorant of the horrific parody Gary has made of the Frank family's seizure by the Gestapo.

REPRESENTING ABSENCE

Rather than probe the limits of representation in attempting a Holocaust literature, Goodman concerns herself with the ways in which American Jews have made use of the Holocaust: ethically, historically, and most of all, personally. Goodman's omniscient narrator in *Kaaterskill Falls* eerily evokes Cynthia Ozick's conception of a post-Holocaust Germany. Ozick says, "What stands in witness for Germany is not the Germans, but an emptiness, an absence—the ones who are not there" (qtd. in Klingenstein, "Visits to Germany in Recent Jewish-American Writing" 546). Any writer who thematically represents the Holocaust is in the words of Norma Rosen "a witness through the imagination." Goodman, as a third-generational witness, is an outsider thrice removed from the Holocaust. Yet she is a writer who has never shied away from the innate difficulties of being a third-generation witness.

Goodman's major contribution to Holocaust representation has been and continues to be her wry and often disturbing evocation of the uses—historical, personal, often selfish, and always conflicted and complicated—which her Americanized Jewish characters make of Holocaust memory. In the short story "Sarah," Goodman says of the

Markowitz clan's matriarch: "Rose did not suffer in the wars directly, but she imagines she did, and in her mind's eye sees them sweeping away the world she loved" (*The Family Markowitz* 217).

Numerous philosophers, including Berel Lang, have debated whether the Holocaust is beyond the limits of aesthetic representation. Goodman never probes the limits of representation which Lang discusses; her work never engages this debate. Instead Goodman turns her attention to the ways in which assimilated and affiliated American Jews, as well as non-Jews, incorporate Holocaust awareness into their bifurcated, modern identities. For example, in her story "Mosquito," a German Christian theologian attending a conference on interfaith relations asks for forgiveness from the Jews assembled in a circle around her. She says:

> I do not take it for granted—I am a Christian, and a German one—what it is to sit down with you who are Jews. This is a privilege for me . . . it is a lesson to us who have residing on us the guilt of our history. So I must deeply thank you. (*The Family Markowitz* 128).

Never actually describing the camps or their conditions, Goodman writes obliquely of the Holocaust. She is concerned with representing the legacy of the Holocaust not just for the survivors themselves but also for the second and third generations as well.

Although Goodman has yet to write what a previous generation of Jewish American authors would call a "Holocaust Literature," almost all of her work is informed by the awesome legacy that the Holocaust has bestowed on Jews living in both Israel and the Diaspora. Goodman is one of the most forceful and eloquent voices speaking for the third generation of survivors who try to warily circle the legacy of suffering bestowed on them fifty years removed from the events of the Holocaust.

As Sanford Pinsker says, Goodman's "social realism and moral seriousness" leads her to a unique perspective on American Jewry. In her best stories Goodman manages to combine an awareness of the lingering effects of the Holocaust along with a nuanced Israeli sensibility. In "One Down," the concluding story to *The Family Markowitz*, two sets of parents all from the second generation discuss the impending marriage of their children. The usual small talk about their children's future takes a dark turn when Zaev reflects on his own difficult upbringing raising chickens in Palestine and wonders about his third-generation son: "If anything ever happens in this country, is he going to survive?"

Zaev's despairing thought leads to a recounting of his mother Ilse's Holocaust history. He continues: "People laugh when I say this, but my mother . . . she came from a very wealthy family, and they lost everything." A moment later Ilse continues her sister's story of displacement and loss as a result of the Holocaust: ". . . one to England, one to New York, I to Palestine escaping, and one perishing in Dachau" (249–50).

Goodman's social realism assumes its full dimension in the figure of Rose, the Markowitz matriarch. While listening to Zaev and Ilse's story Rose can't help but feel jealous. She feels that her family's displacement during World War I should take precedence in the recounting. "In her mind's eye, with her background as a reader of historical romances, she can't help believing that if there is a greater trend or larger story to be told, then it would have to be her story writ large" (250). In "One Down" Goodman's retelling of the Holocaust history of one particular family becomes a modern *Midrash* on the nature of family stories, particularly Holocaust family stories, and the ways in which they become altered by the vagaries of time and memory.

REPRESENTING ORTHODOXY

While we have seen how in her fiction Goodman tackles the difficult issues associated with Holocaust representation we have yet to explain her singular achievement, her attempting an honest representation of Orthodoxy in America. In the pages that follow I will assess Goodman's complex fictional representation of that mythical figure in Jewish American fiction: the Orthodox Jewish American character.

There may be no better way to begin this investigation than by analyzing Goodman's handling of what Yosef Hayim Yerushalmi calls the "quintessential exercise in Jewish group memory" (44), the *Pesach* (Passover) seder. Once we have thoroughly examined Goodman's use of the seder ritual, we may then be in a better position to tackle the thorny issue of Goodman's representation of Orthodox characters in her fiction.

The Passover seder is the ritualized ceremony of collective memory for the Jewish people. In the seder communal liturgy and ritual are combined with a familial and culinary experience orchestrated to pass on the collective memory of Jewish history. It is therefore not surprising to find that numerous Jewish American writers,[1] often in strikingly different contexts, have turned to the seder within their fiction. In the pages that follow, before delving into Goodman's more recent representations of

Orthodoxy in her novels *Kaaterskill Falls* and *Paradise Park*, I will look at two contemporary fictional seders: one in Goodman's short story "The Four Questions," and the other, Thane Rosenbaum's title story to his Edward Lewis Wallant award-wining short-story collection *Elijah Visible*. Through this comparison of the seder ritual we will begin to understand how contemporary Jewish American writers are critiquing and satirizing contemporary Jewish American culture, not from the exotic position of "outsider" peering in from afar, but as insiders writing as participants sitting around the Passover table. But first, along with a short historical overview, I will explain the seder ritual's centrality in the Jewish calendar.

THE PASSOVER SEDER

For even the most assimilated Jewish American family there are two liturgical rituals which are still scrupulously enacted: reciting the Kaddish prayer for the death of a family member and the Passover seder, the ritualized reenactment of Jewish history performed each year around the dining tables of millions of Jewish homes across America. These two rituals are nearly polar opposites: one commemorates the dead, the other is a ritualized celebration of community and continuity—the telling of the story of freedom from oppression and the rebirth of a vibrant Jewish nation.

Both the Kaddish ritual and the Passover seder have become major tropes in American literary culture as well as mainstream popular culture; examples of Kaddish recital abound in popular culture: from Archie Bunker reciting the ancient Aramaic over his friend Stretch Cunningham, to Rocky Balboa bidding a tearful (and transliterated) goodbye to his beloved manager Mick. In her essay "Liturgy in Contemporary Jewish American Literature," Hana Wirth-Nesher suggests that the Kaddish has become "a religious text turned marker of ethnic origin" (123).

Easter is the only Christian holiday that is not set on a specific day. According to church doctrine Easter falls on the Sunday after the first full moon of the vernal equinox. As Wirth-Nesher argues, the reason for this singular dating method in the Gregorian calendar was attributed to "the church father's [wanting] to separate it [Easter] irrevocably from Passover, always celebrated at the full moon" (119). Wirth-Nesher cites the First Council in Nicaea in 325 C.E., which decreed, "celebrating Easter with Passover constituted an act of heresy" (119).

From at least as early as the time of Mary Antin and Henry Roth, Passover has been a major trope for Jewish American fiction writers. Perhaps, as Wirth-Nesher points out, its centrality to Jewish American ethos as well as its prominence in fiction is a result of its having become "entangled with [both] the Christian world and the American Puritan rhetoric" (118). As a result of Passover's "entanglement" with Puritan typology in which America became the *New Jerusalem*, precisely on a holiday which celebrates the Jewish people's freedom from slavery in Egypt and their return to the Promised Land of Israel, Wirth-Nesher points out, Jews in America have been required to renounce their claims for Israel being the promised land, in deference to America becoming the *New Jerusalem*, a "city upon a hill."

This commingling of Jewish and Christian holidays and Puritan typology has formed a major theological trope in Jewish American fiction since its infancy. The pull of history and tradition remains strong, and seder scenes are prevalent in contemporary Jewish American fiction as well as in contemporary films. For example, even Woody Allen,[2] who in previous work had been prone to the very worst stereotyping of Jewish American characters and mores, uses the seder in a pivotal flashback scene in his Academy Award–winning 1989 movie *Crimes and Misdemeanors*. In the title story to his collection *Elijah Visible*, Thane Rosenbaum takes these cultural trends a step further when he combines the Kaddish and the seder rituals. In so doing, Rosenbaum brilliantly intermingles Jewish continuity with Holocaust memory.

"ELIJAH VISIBLE": THANE ROSENBAUM'S SEDER GUEST

In her short story "The Four Questions" we see how Goodman deftly constructs a tableau of Jewish Americanization around the Markowitz's Passover seder. In Thane Rosenbaum's equally powerful evocation of lost roots in his title story to the collection *Elijah Visible* we see the continued withering of a Jewish American family's already tenuous connection to Jewish tradition and ritual.

Goodman's story reverses the roles for the family; she allows her newly *baalat teshuvah* character Miriam to question the changing face of American Judaism, forcing her father, the oldest member of the family, to ask of himself a series of four questions. In comparison to Goodman's Markowitz clan with their asides on world oppression and blessings for third-world nations, Rosenbaum's Posner family seems downright traditional and Orthodox: "The four questions went unasked, as though the Posner family didn't want to know the answers, and were sapped of all curiosity" (91). To underscore this sorry state of affairs (as if any emphasis were needed) Rosenbaum writes: "A stack of matzo lay idly by amidst slices of yeast-infested pumpernickel" (91).

Whereas Jewish roles and feminism formed the main backdrop of Goodman's "The Four Questions," Rosenbaum's "Elijah Visible" becomes a parable of Jewish history and the ways in which carelessly cynical and assimilated American Jews ignore tradition and mangle ritual. In the Haggadah a prayer is recited to hasten the arrival of the prophet Elijah who, traditionally, is believed to visit each and every seder ceremony around the world. During Rosenbaum's fictional seder Elijah's presence takes on the spectral form of a survivor named Artur, a European cousin who inexplicably arrives, heralded by a letter, to "save" the Posner family from themselves, and in particular Adam Posner who in his study of death and Holocaust history has retreated from life. Although it would appear that much like Adam Posner the Markowitz's are in need of a savior, as we will soon discern, no spectral presence appears to enlighten the Markowitz's Long Island seder.

"THE FOUR QUESTIONS"

The 1954 Ranck house in West Hempstead represents all the kitsch "tradition" of Long Island. All the period details have been kept exactly as designed by Sam Levitt, a few miles down Sunrise Highway. Although the Markowitz's strictly adhere to the kitsch tradition, the Jewish tradition of the Haggadah has been discarded in favor of recitations of contemporary political correctness. The Markowitz's leftist ideology is a much shorter recitation of the traditional Haggadah, and is used as a ploy to shorten the seder ritual so that the family can move quickly through the Haggadah and start on the *shulchan orech*—the festive meal portion of the seder.

SETTING

Goodman's setting of "The Four Questions" becomes extremely important in contextualizing her characters. Although Ed once again sits at the head of the table directing the recitation of the Haggadah, and he appears to be in command of his family, in reality it is the women who control family relations. Goodman tells us that whenever middle-aged Ed and Sarah come to stay with Sol and Estelle they sleep in Sarah's childhood bedroom: "There is a creaky trundle bed to wheel out from under Sarah's bed, and Ed always sleeps there, a step below Sarah" (184). In her satirical stories Goodman never misses an opportunity to mine social conventions for thematic value. A dinner-table seating chart as well as her character's sleeping arrangements becomes emblematic of heightened feminism in Goodman's work. Setting becomes so important in Goodman's work because it sets the stage for her social satire. Each detail becomes one more piece of evidence for indicting her characters, showing their "gentle madness" through the accumulation of each detail.

FOOD AS ETHNIC MARKER

> I dragged my belongings over to Grandmother's, my books, my music stand, and my violin. The table had already been set for me. Grandmother sat in the corner. I ate. We didn't say a word. The door was locked. We were alone. There was cold gefilte fish for dinner with horseradish (a dish worth embracing Judaism for), a rich and delicious soup, roasted meat with onion, salad, compote, coffee, pie, and apples.
>
> —Isaac Babel 48

In Goodman's fictional world, food, particularly baked delicacies, take on monumental importance. In the dedication of Goodman's first novel, we understand where this thematic interest springs from: Goodman dedicates her first novel to the memory of her mother whom she calls "a baker extraordinaire."

Cooking, but especially baking, in a Goodman story, is a hallmark of a "Good Jewish Household." One could go so far as to rate the level of Jewish observance by the quality of the baked goods contained within a Jewish home. A perfect illustration of this "Baking=Jewish Observance Principle" is an early scene of "The Four Questions," when we see Ed munching on a second-rate éclair—one which is apparently filled with bad-tasting custard. It seems that the top-of-the-line kosher bakery has been bought out by a large consortium. In foreshadowing the pivotal seder scene, Goodman transforms a before-dinner snack into a *midrash* (parable) on the dissolution of Jewish culture in America.

Although Ed has already been warned by Estelle, his mother-in-law, that he must watch his weight, he decides to indulge in an éclair after all. The omniscient narrator follows Ed's consciousness closely:

> Estelle always has superb pastry in the house. Sol had started out as a baker, and still has a few friends in the business.
> "Are these from Leonard's?" Ed asks when Sol comes in.
> "Leonard's was bought out," Sol says, easing himself into a chair.
> "These are from Magic Oven. How is the teaching?" (187)

Although the Markowitz family seems incapable of accepting even the most obvious truths, whether they be concerning food or their sorry spiritual state, the old Jews at the nursing home, whom Ed's youngest daughter Yehudit visits in "The Four Questions," are the only ones who, perhaps because of a lack of tact and their not having been indoctrinated in the ways of political correctness, say the unvarnished truth in the story. An old man at the home Yehudit visits complains about "Oyfn Pripitchek," a *schmaltzy* song that an assimilated American culture believes to be truly representative (much like the Hollywood version of *Fiddler on the Roof* as opposed to the real Shalom Aleichem) of old-world Judaism.

Yehudit's gentle constitution raised on an "Oyfn Pripitchek" culture of American Judaism cannot accept this cold hard dose of reality when she goes to visit the old-age home. She recounts the entire episode during the *shulchan orech*, the "meal" portion of the seder. Having previously claimed to be too sick to sit at the table and participate in even the shortened version of the ritual Haggadah recitation, Yehudit makes a miraculous recovery and appears as soon as the meal begins. At the first sign of food, "Yehudit toddles in from the den with the afgan trailing behind her" (198). After asking for some "plain salad" she tells the story of how she got sick. Food once again plays a main role in this scene. The "plain salad" that Yehudit requests is counterbalanced by the following dialogue:

> "This fish is wonderful," Sol says.
> "Outstanding," Ed agrees.
> "More," says Ben with his mouth full.
> "Ben! Gross! Can't you eat like a human being?" Avi asks him.
> "It's Manishevitz Gold Label," Estelle says. (198)

One must have read Goodman's other stories (if one doesn't have the requisite Jewish grandmother who labors full afternoons to create a gefilte fish with the perfect ground-by-hand balance of pike, whitefish, and matzo meal) to fully appreciate the meaning with which Goodman imbues Estelle serving canned gefilte fish during the Pesach seder.

Since Estelle does not keep a kosher kitchen, she would be determined to blame Miriam, her only grandchild who keeps kosher, for having to serve canned gefilte fish instead of homemade (not an option in a nonkosher kitchen). But that would be an evasion. In a Goodman story, any Jewish matriarch worthy of the name would be embarrassed to serve canned gefilte fish. The debasement of Jewish cuisine in West Hempstead, Long Island, is symptomatic of the accommodations assimilated American Jews have made to the prevailing secular American culture. Goodman underscores this cultural bankruptcy in the next paragraph when Yehudit explains that she became ill when she went to sing at the Jewish Community Center for seniors. Estelle predictably remarks: "It's nice that you do that. . . . Very nice. They're always so appreciative" (198). It is here that Goodman separates herself from countless other writers telling tales of good deeds done by Jewish youths and appreciative seniors dumbly nodding along to the songs. As Yehudit explains:

> Yeah I guess so. There was this old guy there and he asked me, "Do you know 'Oyfn Pripitchik'?" I said, "Yes, we do," and he said, "Then please, can I ask you, don't sing 'Oyfn Pripitchik.' They always come here and sing it for us and it's so depressing."
>
> Then when we left, this little old lady beckoned to me and she said, "What's your name?" I told her, and she said, "You're very plain, dear, but you're very nice." (198)

It is precisely this complete reversal of expectations, both of the old people at the Senior Center and then of the Markowitz's denial of the truth of the old Jews' rude observations, which drives Goodman's best fiction. The prepackaged gefilte fish has found its corollary in the canned *schmaltz* of the Yiddish song "Oyfn Pripitchik," which in Americanized Jewish culture is meant to represent the old world of pre-Holocaust Europe with all the pain and loss associated with that destroyed world. In reality, as the old man (and Goodman) understands "Oyfn Pripitchek" is as realistic a portrayal of the destroyed European *shtetl* life as *Hava Nagilah* is of contemporary Israeli culture.

Instead of seeing the stark truths revealed by the un-politically correct old people, the Markowitz's quickly ignore the obvious truth and move back to a "safe," and boring, discussion of Miriam's wedding. The only person who seems in deeper reflection is Ed, who while not concerned with the larger truths of his assimilated Jewish American family, instead daydreams about his past omnipotence and frets over the usurpation of his familial power which has, in Goodman's feminist plot twist, shifted to his strictly Orthodox, and soon to be married, daughter Miriam.

FEMINISM

Sarah and Ed went to a local one-woman performance of "A Room of One's Own," and it occurred to Sarah as she left the theater that Virginia Woolf never had any children.
—*The Family Markowitz* 220

Instead of the traditional four questions asked at the seder by the youngest (and therefore supposedly weakest) person present at the seder, Goodman brilliantly reverses the "traditional" roles and power structure of men, women, and children. In Goodman's story it is not the youngest child who ends up asking the four questions. Instead Ed, the Markowitz patriarch, ends up asking four questions of his own. Tellingly, in Ed's rendition the questions become a silent meditation more reminiscent of the *Shemoneh Esrei* prayer than with the Haggadah recitation—its raison d'etre is to be read aloud to begin a discussion among the seder participants. Since the entire family cannot wait to get to the meal portion of the seder, Ed is seen quickly flipping through the Haggadah reading one or two portions outloud which he has hastily translated into English. Finally Miriam,[3] disgusted, comments: "This is ridiculous. The seder is getting shorter every year" (197). In response to his daughter, Ed silently asks three questions before finally asking his fourth question out loud. These four questions form a running commentary on the changing face of American Judaism.

In "The Four Questions" Sarah seems to be trying on her new-found power. In answer to her husband's question, she replies: "I have nothing more to say to you" (203). While on the phone with his difficult and demanding mother Rose, arguing over whether she may invite her friends to Miriam's wedding, Ed grows impatient and irritable. Finally Ed shouts at his mother:

"This is Miriam's wedding. For her. Not for you, not for Estelle. Not for anyone but the kids."
"You are wrong," Rose says simply. (205)

Goodman's fiction reveals that power has no need for flexing its muscles; in "The Four Questions" Ed, the father of the family, surrounded at the seder by increasingly powerful Jewish women, is silently immobilized at the dinner table.

Not only do Goodman's women truly control family relationships, but in *The Family Markowitz* they are already beginning to assume control of religious ritual, as well. While eating dinner at the seder, Ed can't help but begrudge not only his daughter Miriam's newfound Orthodoxy but also the power and leadership her religious knowledge entails. Goodman's narrator remarks: "Ed is looking at Miriam feeling that she is trying to undermine his whole seder" (199). Yet what has Miriam done to undermine Ed's authority and the traditional gender roles? She has simply sat at the dinner table reading the Haggadah (all the parts that Ed skipped in order to more quickly get to the dinner) silently to herself. It is Miriam's silent rebellion against an assimilated, politically correct Haggadah service that so rattles Ed. Much like Goodman's novel *Kaaterskill Falls*, "The Four Questions" shows women commanding a powerful presence just through their silence and patient manipulation of the power structure from within—from the inside of Judaic rituals and observance.

Goodman's feminism is fought on the front lines of the culture wars. She has no patience for the high-minded theories of feminists; what concerns her are, as they say in the Middle East, "facts on the ground." Goodman reserves her most caustic satire for women who call themselves feminists but who only preach about equality without undertaking any corresponding actions to achieve that equality. Goodman is particularly vicious at undercutting Ed's nonsense academic jargon. Goodman's *true* feminist characters are those women, who like Elizabeth in *Kaaterskill Falls*, slowly go about their lives making incremental changes in the role of women within Orthodox Judaism. In contrast, a character like Sharon Spiegelman from "Onionskin," rather than actively seeking redress, would, much like Ed Markowitz, be content to spout jargon and mantras obsessively using the word "patriarchal."

ZIONISM

Although the state of Israel is barely mentioned in the work of canonical Jewish American writers, this obvious fact has largely gone unnoticed by literary critics.[4] If Israel is acknowledged at all, it is usually in the form of a brief remark about the great divide between modern Israeli society and the diasporic Jewish community. For example, Saul Bellow in a short aside in "The Old System" (discussed at length in chapter 3), comments on Isaac's prayer recitation: "And in Hebrew with a Baltic accent at which modern Israelis scoffed" (66). This is about the extent of the fictional representation of previous generations of Jewish American writers' engagement with the state of Israel.

In contrast, a new generation of Jewish writers is more than tangentially engaged by the state of Israel. Goodman is an important contemporary voice on diasporic Jews' understanding and engagement with the state of Israel. For example, in her story "One Down," Goodman deftly dramatizes the competing allegiances and viewpoints between expatriate Israelis who have made *Yiridah* (lit: the act of going down, moving from Israel used in opposition to the term *Aliyah*, lit: raising up, moving to Israel) and Ed Markowitz an expert on terrorism and the Middle East. These opposing camps debate the prospects and hopes for a peaceful conclusion to the conflict that has plagued Israel since the moment of its inception in 1948.

SATIRE

If satirists are the self-appointed guardians of a culture and tradition, one must marvel at the *chutzpah* displayed by Allegra Goodman. At the ripe old age of twenty-one she began censuring, ridiculing, and generally bringing ironic scorn upon those would-be theologians, academics, and assorted grandiose characters who would, through their pride and hypocrisy, impugn and otherwise bring a *chilul hashem* upon Orthodoxy and a Torah-true lifestyle.

That Goodman was raised in the Orthodox tradition makes her sustained critique (two collections of stories and three novels) all the more remarkable. Resisting an Orthodox woman's role of acceptance and piety, Goodman has quickly become a writer of moral weight. Although she might cringe at the suggestion, through her sustained satire on topics as varied as academia, Orthodoxy, Zionism, the Holocaust, and locales as diverse as Hawaii, Oxford, Brooklyn, Jerusalem, Tel Aviv, and Manhattan, Goodman has fast become that rare breed of writer: a guardian of the culture and high standards, while also becoming a best-selling author.

THE NOVELS

Ironically, it is precisely that which makes Goodman's short stories so memorable and fun, which is an inherent weakness in her novels. Goodman's sharp, biting satire, so wonderfully paired to the short-story form, has an opposite effect in a novel where the reader is expected to take up residence with a character for a sustained length of time. A novel is fed by the inner life of a character. You cannot poke fun at a character for four hundred pages (as Goodman does to Sharon Spiegelman in *Paradise Park*) and expect the reader to empathize with that character's plight. Goodman often uses the ironic stance and satiric form as a means of exclusion, of detachment; she stands apart from her characters while revealing their shortcomings. This narratorial stance hardly engenders the type of empathy a novel requires of its readers.

Despite these shortcomings in Goodman's novels, there are short sections of the longer works of fiction in which Goodman summons the sharp satire that characterized her early work and *The Family Markowitz* stories. Her evocation of Chasidism in the Bellevue section of *Paradise Park* rises to the high standard Goodman has set in her penetrating and satiric short stories.

THE CHASIDIC SECTION OF *PARADISE PARK*

While driving in from the Sea-Tac Airport, Sharon first sees the Bellevue Bais Sarah Institute atop a large hill. The house is described as a marvelous old Victorian mansion, "all red brick and turrets . . . with a slate roof and bay windows" (236). Described from a distance as a grandeur-filled castle, the Yeshiva house is rotting away from the inside out, much like the termite-infested Hawaiian mansion in Goodman's *New Yorker* short story "The Closet." Once the rabbi lets Sharon into this Victorian castle, she is led into a "vast entrance hall with curving stairs, and everywhere was marble and carved wood, except the walls were peeling and stained yellow." Sharon observes, "The mansion was seriously run-down, but no one seemed too worried" (236).

The Bais Sarah serves as a metaphor for the state of organized religion in the digital age: hollowed out from the inside. In Goodman's fictional universe the architecture of organized religion is still extant, standing as formidable as ever; it is the internal, the spirit, which, having been left to rot, is missing.

BIALYSTOKER/LUBAVITCHER

As we have previously seen in chapter 3 during our discussion of "The Old System," the Lubavitcher Rebbe has proven to be a popular fictional rabbinic model. Like Bellow's Brooklyn rabbi, Goodman's Bialystoker rabbi is also an exact replica of Rabbi Menachem Mendel Schneerson, "The Rebbe," the spiritual leader of the Lubavitcher Chasidim. The Lubavitchers are an important and influential Chasidic group whose headquarters are in Crown Heights Brooklyn, but who have outposts all over the world—even in the most remote locales. Although Goodman calls her "fictional" Chasidim "Bialystokers," they are obviously Lubavitchers.[5] In fact Goodman takes the name of her "fictional" Chasidim from the Eastern European city where many of the Lubavitcher Chasidim originally hail from. This is similar to the way in which Goodman "fictionalized" the German Jewish Washington Heights community in *Kaaterskill Falls*, where the real-life Breuer clan becomes the Kirshners (more on this topic later in chapter 5).

The Lubavitch sect of Chasidim began with Rabbi Shneur Zalman of Liadi (1745–1812) who founded Chabad (an acronym for Chochmah [wisdom], Binah [understanding], and Da'at [knowledge]. "Chabad is distinguished by its unique philosophy of Judaism which combines the best of Torah scholarship with personal piety and selfless love for the Jewish people" (www.chabadelpaso.com).

Ironically, although the Chasidic movement originated with the Baal Shem Tov (lit: Master of the Good Name) as a revolutionary movement within Judaism designed to liberate Torah scholarship from a repressive elite class who regarded the vast majority of Jews as second-class citizens, in *Paradise Park* Goodman shows how the movement has become as repressive as many other revolutionary movements in history. Goodman compares the repression of Chasidism (at least for Chasidic women) to life under communist rule. As Sharon observes the portrait of the rebbe she says: "Above the fireplace there was the rebbe again, like Chairman Mao, watching from his picture frame" (237). Even more telling than the huge picture of the rebbe above the fireplace is the fact that the portrait niche in the wall "looked like it had been designed for an even bigger painting" (236) as if the rebbe cannot quite fill his allotted space and live up to the enormous expectations of his followers. In her shrewd description of the picture niche, Goodman is referring to the messianic strand of Lubavitcher Chasidism.

The last Lubavitcher rebbe, Rabbi Menachem Mendel Schneerson, assumed the role of spiritual leader of his people in 1951. Rabbi Schneerson, who was (and still is) simply referred to as "The Rebbe," died in 1994 at the age of ninety-two. As the Rebbe became old and frail his followers began likening him to a messianic figure. After his death many Lubavitcher Chasidim took this allusion a bit further and proudly proclaimed Rabbi Schneerson as *mashiach*, the one and true messiah.[6] Goodman's overly large picture frame recalls the impossibility of Rabbi Schneerson's living up to his followers' expectations of his extrahumanness.

Additionally, Goodman immediately taints Sharon's new adventure, her assuming a Chasidic lifestyle, with impropriety. A wealthy woman from the community, Alice Rosensweig, has donated the old Victorian mansion to the Chai Center. When Sharon hears this piece of information from the rabbi she innocently asks: "You mean, she didn't have any kids?" The rabbi answers: "'She did have kids . . . but she left the estate to CHAI of Bellevue.' And he put up his hand like nothing more should be said" (236).

While expounding on a section of the *Tashma*, Goodman's clever renaming of the *Tanya* (1797), a famous work of Chasidic thought and ethics written by Rabbi Shneur Zalman, the founder of Lubavitcher Chasidim, the rabbi concurrently discloses the two-tiered hierarchical structure of *Chasidus*. Inadvertently through his sophistic reasoning the rabbi dismisses feminism and women's liberation as aberrations of Madison Avenue advertising, suggesting that these social movements are predicated upon selling women more products (239–41). Goodman's satire of contemporary Lubavitcher Chasidim's perversion of Rabbi Shneur Zalman's ideas reveals her deep understanding of traditional Jewish texts. In the *Tanya* Rav Zalman taught that man

> serves God with mind, heart and hand. The mind understands, the heart feels, and the hand performs. The Chassid, he maintained, was to train himself for a life of faith and service to God by using all his faculties. Moreover, of the many people who flocked to him, the Rav demanded more than just the unquestioning adherence required by the other schools of Chassidic thought. Whereas their ideology centered on the tzaddik (righteous man) as a person of supernatural powers, he viewed the tzaddik as a spiritual guide, a teacher rather than a miracle worker. (*www.chabadelpaso.com*)

The title of the *Tanya* literally means *We Learn*, or *It Has Been Taught*, alluding to the dialectical aspect of Chasidism between a *rebbe* (teacher) and his *talmid* (student). In contrast to Rav Zalman's ideals contained in the *Tanya*, Goodman ironically changes the name to *Tashma*, which translates as the imperative *Listen!* Rav Zalman's philosophy of spiritual individuality is replaced in *Paradise Park* by blind adherence to a rigid communistlike doctrine.

Furthermore, in *Paradise Park's* Bellevue section (a name almost uniformly associated with insanity) Goodman shows her rabbi Simkovich to be quite skillful at manipulation. The rabbi sells his own "brand" of lifestyle choice; instead of a Madison Avenue lifestyle, Simkovich sells an Eastern Parkway, Crown Heights version of diasporic Chasidism. While lecturing his frighteningly malleable female students on the evils of materialism and modernity, he suggests modern culture is about "technology, and money, and materialism," which he claims can be reduced to advertising.

Yet Goodman's Chasidic leader Simkovich is as skilled a salesman as the most sophisticated Madison Avenue huckster. He effortlessly equates feminism and free choice with rootlessness, thereby immediately honing into his female audience's major weakness: lack of community. Using feminism as a scapegoat, Simkovitch places the responsibility for the misery of these women, many of whom are drug addicted or have previously been in abusive relationships, squarely on the women's liberation movement.

In the midst of an endlessly long speech, soon after he angrily dismisses both materialism and capitalism, Simkovich easily invokes banking metaphors while making his plea for the Chasidic lifestyle: "It's a very simple question. Where do you want to invest your life? In the cheap fly by night? Or in Hashem?" (240). In Simkovitch's zero-sum game he urges his girls (in the CHAI house all unmarried women, even those who are middle-aged, are called "girls") to choose the brand name "the God of Abraham, Isaac, and Jacob," the rabbi reasons, is the exclusive designer label.

In Sharon's odyssey, Goodman has Simkovich continue his investment metaphor: "In material things, or in the holy law, halacha? Do you want to take that time and spend it on quick pleasures? Or do you want to move that time from checking into savings? And invest it all in the Torah?" (240). Not yet done, the rabbi concludes his rousing revival-style preaching with a quote from Rav Hillel urging each of his girls to ask of themselves: "If not me, who? If not now, when?" (240). Of course Simkovich's quotation from the sayings of Rav Hillel leaves out all the ethical parts, such as Do unto your neighbor what you would have him do unto you.

What makes Goodman's satire and critique of Orthodoxy so trenchant is her taking her characters seriously. She never settles for the easy send-up. It would be far simpler to paint an uproariously funny caricature of CHAI house and its group of wandering Jewish women rejects much along the line of Henry Roth's *cheder* rabbi in *Call It Sleep*. Roth's rabbi is limited by his physical characteristics. He portrays Pankower as a simpleton who is unkempt both physically and mentally, and not as someone who rises to the level of satire but someone in need of ridicule and broad-brushed caricature. Instead Goodman's Simkovich is imbued with humanity even while Goodman shows him manipulating his impressionable "girls."

CONSTRUCTING ETHNICS: THE PECULIAR CASE OF STIFF-NECKED ORTHODOX CHARACTERS

Momentarily putting aside theological and political considerations, perhaps the overriding reason there have been so few fictional representations of Orthodoxy in Jewish American fiction is simply because it is so difficult for a writer to convincingly depict Orthodox characters without lapsing into caricature. While creating a modern Orthodox character, a number of aesthetic dilemmas must be grappled with. Perhaps of foremost concern is the question of how to depict a modern Orthodox Jew without that character seeming undifferentiated from an average white middle-class American. On the other hand to dress up Orthodox characters in the way Philip Roth did to Eli in "Eli the Fanatic," is to run the risk of oversimplifying what is essentially a very complex mediation between tradition and modernity. In short, it is no easy task, and most contemporary Jewish American writers, let alone earlier practitioners of the form, have shied away from even making the attempt at representing Orthodoxy in fiction. Thus Allegra Goodman's fiction is all the more remarkable not so much for her attempt, laudatory as it might be, but more for her relative success in representing a Modern Orthodox community in her first novel *Kaaterskill Falls*.

KAATERSKILL FALLS

After publishing *Kaaterskill Falls*, Goodman was praised "for allowing her readers a nuanced look at a cloistered community." Indeed, since the appearance of her first book of stories *Total Immersion*, Goodman has often been praised for representing Orthodoxy and its varied communities with a subtle imagination, a knowing wit, and a gentle satire. However, when one reads her entire oeuvre a less-balanced portrait emerges.

Although Allegra Goodman is one of only a handful of writers engaged in representing Orthodoxy and contemporary Jewish life from the inside, on occasion she is not above caricaturing the Orthodox community. To be fair, in Goodman's fiction there are not many characters who are not skewered at one point or another upon the sharp barb of her satiric pen. However, one senses extra vehemence when Goodman has an Orthodox character within her sights. Also, much like her Jewish American predecessors, Goodman occasionally falls prey to simplifying tendencies. These oversimplifications can be seen from the first pages of *Kaaterskill Falls* where she describes in clearly demarcated lines the division between the *goyish* Washington Heights world and the Kirshner clan's Jewish enclave huddled together within the Heights.

Even fine writers such as Rebecca Goldstein and Nathan Englander[7] occasionally resort to oversimplification and downright distortions when presenting Orthodox characters. In *Kaaterskill Falls* Goodman's opening chapters do not give a reader much hope for anything better than the Orthodox stereotypes (as already seen in previous chapters of this study, for example in the work of Henry Roth and Abraham Cahan) which have already appeared in Jewish American fiction for over a century. In the opening sections of her first novel Goodman describes the many long staircases that link the entire Washington Heights Jewish enclave: "Everyone takes these stairs to get up and down, as if the neighborhood were a single house" (4). Goodman provides architectural and structural relief to her demarcated division between *goy* and Jew: "No Kirshners climb up to Fort Tryon Park or go to the museum there, the Cloisters, with its icons and crucifixes, its medieval sculpture carved in cool gray stone. The Kirshners never think of the Cloisters. They are absorbed in their own religion" (4). Goodman rounds out this observation with a lyrical description of her principal characters, the Kirshner clan: "Although they have no paintings, or stained glass, or sculpture, they array themselves with gorgeous words" (4).

This description would probably not realistically portray an actual medieval Jewish community let alone a modern Orthodox or even an ultra-Orthodox or Chasidic community in 1976 (the time setting of *Kaaterskill Falls*). Goodman falls prey to a sentimentalizing description of her characters. Her characters, as we shall soon find out, do not "array themselves with gorgeous words" any more than an average American community does.[8] Goodman's 1998 oversimplification in *Kaaterskill Falls*, perhaps as a result of its extremely positive portrayal, is in reality just the flip side of the negative stereotyping we saw in Henry Roth's 1934 novel *Call It Sleep*. Both writers remain on the surface of their chosen communities: for Roth the Yeshiva world of the turn-of-the-century Lower East Side, for Goodman a late twentieth-century Jewish community summering in the Catskill Mountains. Neither writer realistically approaches their Orthodox communities.

Goodman feels the need to imbue her Orthodox characters with these hypertextual and literate qualities. As we have seen in previous chapters, earlier generations of Jewish American writers created Orthodox characters with stereotypically anti-Semitic features, a highly negative portrayal of both physical and personal characteristics. Goodman's ridiculously holy and pious descriptions of the Kirshner clan—"they array themselves with gorgeous words"—is a mirror image of Henry Roth's Reb Pankower, who might have been described as a man "who arrayed himself with vituperative Yiddish phrases." Goodman's hyperpositive spin accomplishes the same thing: distorting realistic portrayals of Orthodox Jewish characters.

Of course all novels, in attempting to draw a reader powerfully into the life of a character (someone or something outside a reader's frame of reference) oversimplify. A novel must conjure an entire world within only a few hundred pages, and the aesthetic need for compression requires a certain amount of generalizing. But this feature, common to all fiction writing, becomes more problematic in the case of *ethnic* fiction, a fiction that purports to represent a special enclave, religious, or racial group. Such fiction thrives upon difference; where none exists, the writer is compelled to create striking dissonances with the dominant society and culture. In *The Invention of Ethnicity*, Werner Sollors explores the cultural construct of all ethnicities: "By calling ethnicity—that is belonging and being perceived by others as belonging to an ethnic group—an 'invention,' one signals an interpretation in a modern and postmodern context" (xiii). According to Sollors, most studies dealing with ethnicity take this concept for granted without analyzing its obvious cultural (and thereby artificial) construction. Sollors's study uncovers ethnicity as "not so much an ancient deep-seated force surviving from the historical past, but rather [as] the modern and modernizing feature of a contrasting strategy that may be shared far beyond the boundaries within which it is claimed" (xiv).

In her Orthodox fictional world Goodman attempts to create "otherness" within her ethnic characters while at the same time she hopes to allow the wider culture to understand her ethnic cultural referents. Isaac, Goodman's *Kaaterskill Falls* character perfectly illustrates this duality. When we meet Isaac at the outset of the novel he is described as wearing "a black felt fedora, even in the summer . . . clean shaven, almost modern looking, with neither beard nor peyes" (4). It is that phrase "almost modern looking," seemingly dropped inadvertently into the midst of a physical description, which jolts the reader. Isaac, like all of Goodman's Orthodox characters, is indeed different, other, but not *too* much. But can a writer overly concerned with the "translatability" of her ethnic characters really ever hope to capture the essence, let alone the nuances, of a late twentieth-century Jewish American Orthodox community?

Goodman is a writer very attuned to the reality that successful fiction must not create too great a divide between character and reader. Goodman is aware that fiction is one of the most powerful vehicles for the creation of difference, and she uses the otherness of her characters to great advantage. Indeed, reviewers of *Kaaterskill Falls* wrote (incorrectly) that Goodman's first novel sheds light on a previously cloistered and secretive Chasidic community of Jews.[9] The secretive aspect connotes something illicit and is always good for sales. Indeed Goodman's novel was an international bestseller and was a finalist for the National Book Award.

GOODMAN'S DOUBLE BIND

The problems with Goodman's ethnic characters are built into the reader's expectations of a realist novel. In *Kaaterskill Falls* Goodman constructs such an exact realism that one could use her novel literally as a road map in order to get to Tannersville, New York. This only makes her complete lack of verisimilitude in regards to her Orthodox characters and community that much more glaring, and disappointing. One could say that it doesn't matter if she "gets it right" as long as she is consistent within her fictional universe. But here too Goodman's fictional Orthodox community is found wanting. There are several egregious mistakes in representing Orthodox rituals in *Kaaterskill Falls*. For example, a strictly kosher character is seen eating a Hebrew National hot dog, which would be considered *trayf* (unkosher) by even a lenient

Orthodox standard.[10] Goodman certainly knows this; however, she is also aware that most of her readers will be ignorant of this fact. She realizes that the words "Hebrew National," for the vast majority of her American readership (who can forget that heavenly voice in the prime-time commercial), practically spells *kosher*. These types of literary "accommodations," glimpsed throughout Goodman's oeuvre, weaken the artistry and literary merit of her fiction, while at the same time increasing her sales exponentially.

Goodman is not alone in this dilemma. Numerous ethnic fiction writers surely share this problem of balancing competing claims of the majority culture with fealty to their fictional ethnic enclave. This is not merely a Jewish American phenomenon. Although numerous contemporary Jewish American writers come immediately to mind, including Tova Mirvis, Eve Nomi, and Myla Goldberg, this issue crosses ethnic boundaries. The Dominican American writer Junot Diaz confronts this issue directly on the opening page of his award-winning novel-in-stories *Drown*. The book begins with the following quote from the poet Gustavo Perez Firmat:

> The fact that I
> am writing to you
> In English
> already falsifies what I
> wanted to tell you.
> My subject:
> how to explain to you that I
> don't belong to English
> though I belong nowhere else.

For Diaz this question of which language to write in (Spanish or English?) takes precedence. Language is often the only true homeland a writer ever has, so Diaz's dilemma also beddeviled an earlier generation of Jewish American immigrant writers (for example: Abrahan Cahan and Henry Roth) who often had to choose between writing in Yiddish or English. Jewish immigrant writers were often blessed with no homeland but filled with the sadness of the perpetually exiled. In his brilliant memoir, *Survival in Auschwitz*, the Italian Jewish chemist Primo Levi calls this emotion "the ancient grief of the people that has no land, the grief without hope of the exodus which is renewed every century" (16). Having been born and educated in America, Goodman need not concern herself with the question of which language to use for her writing. It is difficult to imagine Goodman spending much time questioning this issue when she began writing *Kaaterskill Falls*: Yiddish or Hebrew was hardly a major concern. However, all contemporary ethnic writers, Goodman included, face a similar problem of balancing the desire for authenticity to their ethnic enclave (and their compatriot ethnic readers) with the competing demands of the wider American literary marketplace.

PAROCHIALISM

As Gloria Cronin suggests, when attempting to contextualize Goodman's work, one might be tempted to place Goodman within the milieu of American religious writing. She would "most naturally [be] compared to Flannery O'Connor" ("Immersions in the Postmodern" 247). Yet this comparison does a disservice to both writers. Although both ostensibly deal with religion in their work, according to Cronin the comparison stops there. Cronin suggests O'Connor's characters are "religious seekers [who] operate within the Protestant Bible Belt and Roman Catholic Christian traditions of the Agrarian South" (247). In contrast, Goodman's characters operate "within the combined traditions of university-educated discourse communities, Yiddish comedy, and urbane *New Yorker* social satire" (248). From such characters, who not only have undergraduate degrees, but often doctorates as well, leads Goodman to a vastly different type of dialogue and satire than that found in O'Connor's stories.

Despite her highly educated characters, in numerous interviews, see for example *The Daily News* and *Publisher's Weekly*, Goodman repeatedly suggests that she has embraced "parochialism" as a philosophical credo of fictional creation. What Goodman means by this is the specificity of her cultural material, which she believes is a hallmark of all literature, not just multicultural or ethnic literature. In her conclusion to her powerful statement in defense of Jewish American fiction, "Writing Jewish Fiction In and Out of the Multicultural Context," Goodman surmises: "Ultimately, I believe all writing is ethnic writing, and all writers are ethnic writers grappling with great ambitions and a particular language and culture" (274). Goodman further develops this idea when she suggests: "Every writer works to develop and express ideas and emotions in the language of the particular and the mundane, to say something new and use what is old. Each strives to make a specific cultural experience an asset instead of a liability" (274). Goodman's expansion of the concept of ethnic writing would seem to bolster Sollors's argument concerning the "inventiveness" or cultural construction of all ethnicity.

In a letter to critic Sanford Pinsker, Goodman has phrased this concept or literary credo as "the universality of parochialism." Goodman suggests that without the universalizing component of all specific fictional communities we might not be able to understand where a character is coming from let alone be able to empathize with a moral or philosophical crisis as we are asked to do time and again in her complex fiction.

Goodman's fiction is universal, not despite its parochialism, but because of its embrace of the specificity of the textual Jewish tradition. Goodman's fiction parodies academic philosophies and theories that seek to disunite her readers. Unfortunately, much of the criticism written on Goodman's work misses this point entirely. A striking example of this trend would be the short story "Wish List," collected in Goodman's *Total Immersion*. Post 9/11, Goodman's short story should be required reading for anyone attempting to understand academia's failure at a rational analysis of terrorism and its root causes. Goodman parodies Ed Markowitz, who in "Wish List" is seen attempting to respect and understand the "terrorist's perspective" as well as the terrorist's "forms of communication" (i.e., suicide bombing). Despite Goodman's obvious antipathy toward academic jargon, in discussing "Wish List," numerous critics resort to the same type of empty phrases used by Ed Markowitz, for example using the terms "issues of otherness" and "intercultural understanding," while analyzing this story. This is precisely the kind of jargon-filled academic language that Goodman has so much fun attacking in her best satirical short stories.

The majority of critics tend to agree with Cynthia Ozick, who, while Goodman was still an undergraduate at Harvard, proclaimed: "This Goodman is a marvel." As a result of her attention to mores and her biting social satire, Goodman has often been compared to the great Victorian novelists. Generally eschewing postmodern narrative pyrotechnics, Goodman's work is indeed reminiscent of an earlier period. C. Beth Burch simply refers to Goodman as "a Jewish Jane Austen with an edge" (91). Similarly, critic Sanford Pinsker said that *Total Immersion* "is a satire so delicately balanced, so precise, that one harkens back to Austen or to Eliot for its models" (188). While Ivan

Kreilkamp, in an interview in *Publisher's Weekly*, writes: "In the tradition of authors from Balzac to Faulkner, Goodman creates the effect of a fully developed alternate world, in which her characters move from story to story like familiar acquaintances" (77). Andrew Furman may be the first critic to remark upon Goodman's trenchant engagement with the state of Israel, suggesting that "Although Israel emerges as a refuge for Jews in the aftermath of the Holocaust, Goodman also explores the tangled conflict between the Israelis and the Palestinians that currently divides the Jewish American community" (*Contemporary Jewish American Writers and the Multicultural Dilemma* 140).

Goodman won a Whiting Award for her first book *Total Immersion*, while her widely acclaimed second book *The Family Markowitz* was a *Los Angeles Times* bestseller and a *New York Times* notable book of the year. Continuing her remarkable ascendancy, Goodman's third book and first novel, *Kaaterskill Falls*, was a National Book Award finalist in 1998. Goodman's second novel was praised in *Commentary* where John Podhoretz called *Paradise Park* "a bravura performance." In *The Daily News* Sherryl Connelly says, "Goodman's aptitude for finely shaded comic writing grounded in acute observations on faith and faithlessness, makes *Paradise Park* a divine read."

CONCLUSION

Goodman has been praised for each new development in her career, and she is almost universally considered one of the most important fiction writers of her generation. She eloquently voices the perils of unfettered assimilation, the withering of roots and the loss of memory that is often attendant with pursuing the American dream. Her morally serious work warns of the political misuse American culture has often made of Holocaust commemoration. Despite her occasional missteps in representing Orthodoxy, Goodman creates a more complete and nuanced portrait of American Orthodoxy than previous Jewish American writers have ever before managed. Goodman's work points to the exciting future of Jewish American fiction in the twenty-first century. Goodman continues to dramatize the complex lives of her American and Israeli Jewish characters, while powerfully rendering the conflicts that inevitably arise between tradition and modernity, memory and history.

CHAPTER 6

Henry Roth's Second Novel: Mercy for a Rude Youth

INTRODUCTION

Attempting to understand Henry Roth's monumental literary shifts over the long arc of his career might confound even the most dedicated student of his craft. From Communism to Zionism, from lyrical high modernism to unadorned realism, from Shakespearean influenced Yiddish translations in *Call It Sleep* to the redolent, biblical inflections of *Mercy of a Rude Stream*, Roth's literary life and art present a seemingly insoluble conundrum.

When Roth published *Call It Sleep* in 1934 as a young man of twenty-eight, the immigrant world he so memorably conjured was still bloomingly alive both in the downtown tenements of the Lower East Side and upon the tough uptown streets of Jewish and Irish Harlem. Many of Roth's relatives, those who still awaited passage to the *Goldena Medina*, were living in the *shtetlach* of the Austro-Hungarian Empire or huddled (for the most part) in the pale of settlement across Europe and Russia. By the late 1970s, when Roth finally begins his second novel, those relatives are all gone. Roth's relatives not lucky enough to immigrate to America had already been murdered in the Holocaust decades before he began working on *Mercy*. Thus Roth's monumental paradigmatic shift between his two novels might be seen as not only an aesthetic decision but a moral one as well; Roth's inelegant style in *Mercy of a Rude Stream* might be attributable to a eulogistic pose for a lost world, an attempt to recreate that lost world of the *beis hamidrash* (study house) viewed only in sepia photographs and an old (exiled in New Mexico) man's faulting memory, and not the result of failing artistry as is often assumed. Or as David Roskies suggests in his essay "Jazz and Jewspeech," in *Mercy of a Rude Stream* Roth "is telling us that after he goes, there will be no one left to conjure this immigrant experience from within" (144).

Roth's career brackets all the major turning points of Jewish history in the twentieth century: the mass immigration and acculturation into American mores for the daughters and sons of the greenhorn immigrant generation; the almost complete annihilation of the European remnants of that immigrant culture in the European *shtetlach*; and the birth of the state of Israel fourteen years after *Call It Sleep* was published. This last event would eventually signal Roth's turn away from both Communism and Modernism, as he embraced Zionism and autobiographical memoir writing in repudiation of the Joycean lyricism that marked his first novel.

Cynthia Ozick has said that Henry Roth's *Call It Sleep* is surely "about discontinuity and rupture" (Kauver 385). Indeed modernist writers made rupture the very rubric of their distinct contribution to American culture. However, if many critics consider *Call It Sleep* to be the greatest Jewish American novel ever written, we must begin to ask in what way is *Call It Sleep* a Jewish novel? I would argue that *Call It Sleep*, far from being the quintessential Jewish American novel, as critics like Irving Howe and Leslie Fiedler maintained, Roth's first novel may be the prototypical anti-Jewish American novel; in fact, leaving the field of aesthetics for a moment, it might even be construed a downright anti-Semitic portrayal of Judaism. To those who are shocked by this suggestion I would ask whether there would even be a question of the obvious and blatant anti-Semitism in *Call It Sleep* had the novel been written by a non-Jew.

Roth did in fact write the quintessential Jewish American novel, but that was only after sixty long years of writer's block and the debilitating effects of both incest and rheumatoid arthritis. The resulting novel, *Mercy of a Rude Stream*, is Roth's attempt to finally write that long-awaited Jewish American novel, and although he was eighty-nine years old and near death when he finally got around to finishing it, in a limited way, he succeeded.

Before addressing *Mercy of a Rude Stream* more explicitly in this chapter, let us take a look at *Call It Sleep* and why it has been called the archetypal Jewish American novel of the first half of the twentieth-century, and see what this teaches us about what critics, until now, have generally regarded as Jewish. Roth himself gives us an idea of what an earlier generation of critics meant by Judaism:

> Being a Jew in the Diaspora is basically a state of mind, an attitude of not belonging. In that sense there are also Gentiles who are Jewish. Only two courses remain open to the Jew in America: he

assimilates and disappears completely, while giving the best elements of himself to his native culture—and God knows that he has a lot to give—or he goes to Israel and does the same thing there. . . . I do not think the Jew in America can exist much longer with a distinct identity. (*Shifting Landscape* 114)

Roth's anti-Jewish statement ignores the particularity of Jewish history and reduces Jews and Judaism to a neat symbol, a metaphor to be discarded when it loses its efficacy. As the quote above demonstrates, in the years between writing *Call It Sleep* and *Mercy of a Rude Stream* Roth made no attempt to hide his self-hating vindictiveness. Yet several generations of Jewish literary critics have called Roth's modernist novel *Call It Sleep* the greatest Jewish American novel ever written. While it is hard to deny Roth's brilliant contribution to high modernism, perhaps a reappraisal of just what kind of Judaism Roth represents in *Call It Sleep* is in order. Published in a time of increasing anti-Semitism worldwide and Hitler's rise to power in Germany, the novel is a ringing endorsement for doing away with Judaism and its followers. It reads, at times, as a fictionalized version of Roth's own ideas of wishing Jews would no longer be Jews: it shouts from nearly every page "Assimilate! Assimilate, and be done with it!" As a modernist artist and political communist, Roth does believe that as a people Jews do have much to give to the higher culture of America; they should then not be so stubborn as to remain Jews once their contributions have been given.

What can we learn about the state of Jewish culture and fiction in America from several generations of literary critics' amnesia to Roth's overriding hatred and fear of Judaism? Furthermore, did Roth modify his views over the years? In chapter 6 we will first look at Roth's modernist masterpiece *Call It Sleep* before turning to Roth's second career as a writer, this time as a Jewish American writer, one who begs for the mercy of his people. As we shall see, *Mercy of a Rude Stream* represents Roth's radical revision of his thinking, his repudiation of almost all he had written (both content and style) in the early part of his career.

YIDDISH AND *YIDDISHKEIT* IN *MERCY OF A RUDE STREAM*

In contrast to the *Call It Sleep* Yiddish that Roth translates into florid and elevated, almost Elizabethan, English, in his second novel *Mercy of a Rude Stream*, Roth uses a gutturally translated immigrant Yiddish to unstintingly conjure the horrific reality of Lower East Side immigrant culture. Other than Roth's second novel, currently the only place to experience even an echo of that culture is in the Lower East Side Tenement Museum,[1] a few blocks south of where young David Schearl was electrocuted. Not surprisingly, the museum tour does not approach the reality Roth inscribes on every page of *Mercy of a Rude Stream*. That reality experienced by millions of Jewish immigrants is now lost forever and may only be conjured through Roth's brilliant reimagining in his nonfictional (or fictionalized, depending on one's perspective) biography (novel) *Mercy of a Rude Stream*. But before delving deeper into *Mercy*, first let us return to Roth's first novel and his representation of Orthodoxy in the ungainly figure of Reb Yidel Pankower.

ORTHODOXY IN *CALL IT SLEEP*:
YIDEL PANKOWER

In *Call It Sleep* Roth's portrayal of Judaism is one of oppression and hardship. The two are nearly synonymous within the symbolic structure of the book. Indeed David's oppression by his overbearing and abusive father is most clearly seen in the scenes recounting religious instruction and during their talks concerning Judaism.

David's father wants his son to have religious instruction only because of self-concern and not for anything to do with young David's spirituality. While contemplating his own mortality, Albert worries that there will be nobody to say Kaddish on him after he dies. Consequently, Albert insists that his wife enroll David in a *cheder*: "The prayer. I was thinking should anything happen to me. . . . It would be a comfort to me to know that whatever else he becomes—and God only knows what he may become—at least he shan't be an utter pagan because I didn't try" (210).

The father's diction switches from lowbrow to highbrow *shan't* and *pagan*; Albert's language seems almost biblical toward the end of his speech. He continues: "I mean I'm little enough a Jew myself. But I want to make sure he'll become at least something of a Jew also. I want you to find a cheder for him and a rabbi who isn't too exorbitant" (210).

Wishing to keep her young boy by her side, firmly within the oedipal triangle and the Schearl family romance, Genya offers resistance; but the reader knows that, like Jonah running away from Yahweh, her resistance is superfluous. The inflated diction at the tail end of the father's speech signals his prophetic, even Old Testament godlike power over his wife and son. Once the word *cheder* is spoken there is no recalling the word: Genya knows David will be sent to *cheder*. Still she feebly protests: ". . . as for learning what it means to be a Jew, I think he knows how hard that is already" (210).

The godlike father nods curtly, according to the narrator, "in token that his decree had been passed" (210). Only two discussion points remain for the Schearl family: that the rabbi should be cheap, and that he should be harsh and unyielding. The father says: "You would do well to seek out a stern one—a rabbi I mean. He needs a little curbing since I don't do it. It might redeem him" (210).[2]

These overwhelmingly negative associations with Judaism continue unabated into the next chapter of *Call It Sleep*. While walking to the *cheder*, David's mother offers advice and blessings, hoping that he will prove a better *cheder* student than she had back in the old country *shtetl* of her youth. Reflecting on her lack of academic rigor, she recalls: "But I think the reason I was such a dunce was that I could never wrench my nose far enough away to escape his breath. Pray this one is not so fond of onions!" (211). The patently anti-Semitic quality of Roth's Orthodox Jewish characters, distinctly represented from either those assimilated or in the process of assimilation (although there has been a tremendous amount of scholarship devoted to *Call It Sleep* since its reissue in 1964), has remarkably not garnered any critical attention.

Similar to the dread with which Genya describes her Jewish training, Roth describes the *cheder* itself in ominous and foreboding, even dismal tones: "One edge shining in the vanishing sunlight, the little white-washed house of the cheder lay before them." The dismal structure of the *cheder* house is whitewashed; it catches the sun like a gleaming knife lying in wait, dangerous, ominous. Roth describes the structure as being penned in by the detritus of the Lower East Side: "Smoke curled from a little black chimney in the middle of its roof, and overhead myriads of wash-lines criss-crossed intricately, snaring the sky in a dark net" (211). In Roth's symbolic prose the Lower East Side *cheder* becomes transformed into an Old Testament *mishkan* (a base for sacrificial offerings to God). However much like Cain's tarnished, unclean offering, the smoke does not rise straight.

The medieval biblical commentator Rashi states on Genesis 4:4–5 that Abel's offering was accepted by God because the smoke rose straight up to heaven, whereas the smoke from Cain's offering went off to the side. Similarly, Pankower's offering of Torah learning, singing God's song in a strange land, seems to be overwhelmed by New York City and the pressures of the New World. The detritus overwhelms the *cheder*'s small offering, drumming laundry on its poor roof. The reader begins to believe that the downtrodden nature of the *cheder* is due to the polluted environment of the Lower East Side that has ensnared even the meager immigrant view of the sky between the tall tenement buildings. Yet even this somewhat mitigated portrait of the *cheder* is overwhelmed by the negativity of the next paragraph where Roth makes it clear that the *cheder* is not merely a victim of urban decay, but also a contributor to the polluted atmosphere. When David's mother opens the *cheder* door "A billow of drowsy air rolled out at them. It seemed dark inside" (211).

The violent image at the outset of this chapter, the *cheder* described as a knife in waiting, will be fulfilled in the violence of the last chapter, the Isaiah purification rite that David undergoes. It is as a result of his going to *cheder* that David begins to piece together a fanciful story of his origins that ineluctably leads to the immense violence at the end of the novel. While one could argue that the violent image that Roth uses to describe the *cheder* might contribute to the plot development of *Call It Sleep*, no similar argument can redeem Roth's anti-Semitic physical descriptions of Reb Pankower, which unlike the violent images of the *cheder*, serve no similar artistic function in the novel.

Roth describes Yidel (lit: little Jew) Pankower in classically anti-Semitic prose. He is smelly, ugly, cheap, and, as his name implies, is an all-around awful little Jew: "short and bulbous, oddly round beneath the square outline of the skull cap. . . . He ran large, hairy fingers through a glossy, crinkled beard" (211–12). Roth goes on to describe David's first impressions of Reb Pankower:

> He was old and certainly untidy. He wore soft leather shoes like house-slippers, that had no place for either laces or buttons. His trousers were baggy and stained, a great area of striped and crumpled shirt intervened between his belt and his bulging vest. The knot of his tie which was nearer one ear than the other, hung away from his soiled collar. What features were visible were large and had an oily gleam. Beneath his skull cap, his black hair was closely cropped. (212)

Roth's fictional rabbinic portrait might even surpass Dickens's description of Mr. Fagin from *Oliver Twist*:

The walls and ceiling were perfectly black with age and dirt . . . and standing over them, with a toasting fork in his hand, was a very old shrivelled Jew, whose villainous-looking and repulsive face was obscured by a quantity of matted red hair. He was dressed in a greasy flannel gown, with his throat bare. (105)

Whereas Fagin mostly only corrupts his young charges, Reb Pankower not only corrupts, but he beats and berates his students as well. When Dickens introduces his anti-Semitic stereotype, Fagin holds in his hand a large "toasting-fork" with which he prods his young charges to leave alone Oliver the new boy in the group: "These civilities would probably have extended much farther, but for a liberal exercise of the Jew's toasting-fork on the heads and shoulders of the affectionate youths who offered them" (105). Similarly, Roth places in Reb Pankower's hand a "cat-o'-nine tails" with which

he struck the table loudly with the butt-end and pronounced in a menacing voice: "Let there be a hush among you!" And a scared silence instantly locking all mouths, he seated himself. He then picked up a little stick lying on the table and pointed to the book, whereupon a boy sitting next to him began droning out sounds in a strange and secret tongue. (213)

Dickens was at least describing a pickpocket, a criminal and corrupter of youth; Roth's vile description is attached to a rabbi and *cheder* teacher. Even Pankower's language, likewise, is rather unrabbinic and is even worse than Roth's other tart-tongued character, Aunt Bertha, who curses her way through *Call It Sleep*. The life of Jews in the turn-of-the-century Lower East Side was not an easy one, but in *Call It Sleep* Roth (dis)places all the difficulties associated with immigrant life squarely on the shoulders of Orthodoxy and Judaism.

OEDIPUS COMPLEX?

Although *Call It Sleep* seems to be a perfect case history for Freud's "family romance," a reader armed with the knowledge of the factual Roth family romance understands how Roth was using Freud's family-romance theory to displace the true story of his sordid past. The real story of the Schearl family romance was not revealed until the publication of the second volume of *Mercy of a Rude Stream*, when *A Diving Rock on the Hudson* was published in 1995. In volume two Roth finally reveals the incestuous relationship between Ira (*Call It Sleep*'s David) and his sister Minny. Roth's earlier novel *Call It Sleep* begins with what (before volume two of *Mercy*) had appeared to be innocent "cold wet kisses" from Genya to David; in retrospect these kisses seem anything but innocent. Roth, living in Greenwich Village with his lover (and mother figure) Eda Lou Walton while writing *Call It Sleep*, appears to already be transmuting the horrific reality of his all-too-real family romance into sanitized fictional flirtation. Thus, ironically the Oedipus complex which was seen by Freud as an archetypical story of growth and maturation, a device used by all healthy psyches to assume adult sexualities and a normal love object, in Roth's troubled mind became a fictional mask, the instrument of Roth's hiding from reality.

AUTOBIOGRAPHY

In a letter dated July 3, 1994, Roth's sister, Rose Broder, chastises Roth for including in the second volume of *Mercy* information of the "revelation" of incest between the two. She threatens to sue him if he continues to make use of their incest in his book. Eventually a contract is signed and Rose is paid $10,000 in exchange for granting St. Martin's Press immunity from legal action. The second volume of *Mercy* appears with this warning: "This is a work of fiction. Although some characters were inspired by people whom the author knew, the narrative is not intended in any way to be a depiction of real events. This novel is certainly not an autobiography, nor should it be taken as such." The first volume makes no such warning. From Rose's letter as well as interviews given to his publisher Robert Weil, it seems apparent that much like the other violence depicted in *Mercy of Rude Stream*, the incest depicted in *Mercy* was not fiction at all, but all too real occurrences in the life of young Henry Roth.

NOT OLD ENOUGH TO SIN

In the midst of *Call It Sleep* a strange interlude, which defies the realism of the novel, appears. In placing the scene at the center of his novel, Roth, in a presciently postmodern moment seems to be drawing attention to the scene as artistic construction. This scene rips into the novelistic dream, almost becoming an analogue to the Brechtian theater of the absurd. Midway through "The Coal," the third section of the novel, young David has just recited the entire *Chad Gadyah* (the concluding song/prayer in the Passover Haggadah) in Yiddish for Reb Pankower. To the amazement of both David and his *cheder* friends, the notoriously cheap and abusive Reb Pankower is so overcome by generosity at David's virtuoso performance that he gives the young boy a shiny penny for his performance. On his walk home David thinks of ways to explain how he got his penny to his father. In *Call It Sleep*'s Lower East Side milieu, six-year-old boys do not ordinarily find themselves recipients of shiny pennies. David realizes that this occurrence is so unusual that Albert will never believe the true story, that he received it as reward in *cheder*. Consequently, if David tells the truth he would be in line for yet another vicious beating at the hands of his father.

Yet despite the rarity of this first happenstance, which Roth makes implicit in the text, as he's walking home on Friday evening David is accosted by an ancient-looking Jewish woman who, thinking David is not Jewish and thus eminently qualified for the age-old job of being a *shabbos goy*,[3] asks him to light the flame in her kitchen. When David replies that he is in fact Jewish, the woman says: "Well, it won't harm you anyway. You're not old enough to sin" (237). The elderly Jewish woman invokes the well-known *halachic* concept that a child's sins are the responsibilities of the father. Only when a boy becomes a man at his *bar mitzvah* (at age thirteen) does he assume the responsibilities of an adult Jewish male, only then is he held accountable for his sins.

As a reward for David's relighting the gas stove for the woman, he receives an additional shiny penny. The absurdity of this situation goes beyond mere questions of probabilities, which within the fictional world must conform more to the realities of the world than "real life." The old woman might tell herself that it would be legally permissible for the boy to light the stove since it is a *halachic* question of *kibbud shabbos* (honoring the Sabbath), but in such a situation she would certainly never give the boy a penny to bring home on *shabbos*, that would most certainly be *muktzah*,[4] and it would therefore compound the boy's sin.

In the first scene Roth equates receiving money in the recitation of the *chad gadyah* scene with Judaism, and in the very next scene identifies the same act of receiving money with the antithesis of Judaism, violating the Sabbath. Why did Roth insert this strange scene into the center of his novel, and what artistic purpose does it serve?[5]

LINCOLN VERSUS THE INDIANS
OR THE MYTH OF DUELING PENNIES

Roth's strange interlude might be understood in light of the heavy-handed symbolism of the two pennies: one is an Indian head, the other a Lincoln head. One penny, despite the old woman's protestations that he is not old enough to sin, represents David's "sin" of being a *shabbos goy*, while the other penny represents his performing a *mitzvah* (a good deed) in memorizing words of Torah in the *chad gadyah* song from the Haggadah. But which penny represents sin, and which represents a good deed? In a premulticultural moment, David contemplates them both: "So which is the sin penny? He looked at them. Indian this. Lincoln this. Lincoln just got" (238). So the mystery is solved; the Lincoln penny, redolent of the great American emancipator represents David's turning against Judaism, his being set free from Judaism, while the Indian head, representing a true "ethnic" identification or identification with an "other," represents the return to the traditional (represented by the Passover Haggadah and David's recitation), the un-American, that from which David will eventually rebel and leave completely as he becomes an artist at the conclusion of *Mercy of a Rude Stream*.

I would suggest this scene doesn't entirely work on a very basic level of fictional realism; therefore it is doubly doubtful that the scene will carry the symbolic import Roth has clumsily assigned to it. To say that Roth isn't entirely successful in this scene is in some small measure to suggest that he insinuates himself as artist into the scene heavy-handedly manipulating his signs and symbols. Where before Roth had characters speaking and acting, in these awkward scenes symbols interact beneath the artist's ponderous grasp upon his materials.

Let's momentarily return to Roth's initial conception of traditional Judaism, the scene where Genya brings David to the stifling *cheder* for the first time. In a "passive-aggressive" maneuver intended to short circuit David's ever making anything of himself as a *cheder* boy or future Yeshiva student, Genya tells her son a story which pokes fun at Judaism and rabbis. Knowing full well that David idealizes her, Genya tells David of her own miserable failure as a *cheder* student, and thus dismisses the importance of religious study to the young boy. She tells David: "When I went to cheder, my rabbi was always wagging his head at me. . . . But I think the reason I was such a dunce was that I could never wrench my nose far enough away to escape his breath. Pray this one is not so fond of onions" (211). When they finally arrive at the *cheder* and open the front door a "billow of drowsy air rolled out at them" (211).

Additionally, recall that the *cheder* is represented as being in the midst of crisscrossed wash lines "which snare the sky in a dark net" (211). There are numerous other similarities between the scene of David's first day at *cheder* and the old Orthodox woman asking David to sin as a *shabbos goy*. For example, when Genya seemed unwilling to enter the *cheder*, in a canine image Reb Pankower is described as repeatedly "wagging" his head at David's recalcitrant mother. Similarly, since the old woman would not touch money on *shabbos*, she instructs David to open her wallet and urges him to remove a penny for himself. Roth says the old woman "nodded as if she couldn't stop" (238). Strangely, the old Orthodox Jewish woman also can't seem to stop wagging her head.

Roth describes the air of the Orthodox woman's kitchen as "stagnant"; just like at the *cheder*, the atmosphere is oppressed by "a heaviness" and an overriding stench, but once David is out on the street his guilt is swept away. The street is the great equalizer for Roth; the street washes away all of Judaism in a universalizing sweep: "But the cool air of the outdoors as he entered the street whipped away remorse as it whipped the nostrils clear of kitchen odors" (238–39). Roth's conception of Judaism in *Call It Sleep* brings to mind the *Haskalah* slogan for the "emancipated" Jews of Europe: "Be a human being on the street and a Jew at home." As we have already seen in Roth's numerous interviews, he takes this already self-hating slogan one step further, advocating for the total removal of Judaism both at home and in public.

The old Orthodox Jewish woman who gives David the second penny is also described in terms as horrific as Reb Pankower and the Yeshiva:

> —a shriveled old woman with a face so lined with short, thin wrinkles, they slanted down the sere skin like a rain. She was stooped. A striped blue and white apron covered the front of her rusty black satin dress. The whites of her eyes were cloudy as an old tusk and caught in a net of red veins. Her nostrils were wet. Between her brow and the white kerchief on her head a stiff brown wig protruded like a ledge. (237)

Roth renders this traditionally Jewish woman in such horrific terms that David, seeing in her wizened face the description he recalls from fairy tales, momentarily believes she is a witch.[6] David recalls Grimm's fairy tale: "He stared at her. There was something terrifying and dreamlike about it all. The gingerbread boys the old witch baked. In two A one" (237).

What does Roth mean by "in two A one"? It makes almost no sense initially. On a first reading one imagines these words represent the inchoate half thoughts of six-year-old David, which Roth has sometimes let drift into the story to further solidify the young boy's perspective. But could this phrase be a cipher, could it mean something else entirely?

IN SEARCH OF LOST MERCY (IN TWO A ONE)

In two A one? Why the capitalized "A"? Is this some code only Roth (and his protagonist David) understands? The ethnic and the American as "A one"? Can this synthesis only be accomplished (or hoped for) in a fairy tale? Only after sixty years would Roth be able to reconcile the two broken halves of his fractured psyche: the American with the Jewish. To do so Roth would need to embrace the particularism of his Jewish heritage, without the mythmaking and universalizing role he assigns to the streets of New York in *Call It Sleep*.

Here, soon after the first *cheder* scene, when David finally makes it home, he overhears several boys arguing in the hallway before the open bathroom. One boy is squatting on the toilet; in need of toilet paper, he screams to his friends down the hall. It being *shabbos* the other boys will not allow him to tear the newspaper he desperately needs. Finally, the first boy disregards his friend's warnings and he tears the newspaper. His "sinful" action only leads to a vindictive cry from one of the onlookers: "Now yuh God it!"[7] The boy continues: "An id's a double sin too" (239). As David walks by the crowd of boys he overhears the sanctimonious *shabbos* observant boy explain to his indignant friend that the sin is double since it is *shabbos* and tearing is prohibited, and secondly since it "is a Jewish noospaper wid Jewish on id" (239).

In this scene Roth recalls the famous scene from *Ulysses* where Bloom also rips up the newspaper for his bathroom paper. Although the newspaper is presumably Yiddish, the lingua franca of European Jews, and not Hebrew (*lashon hakosdesh*), since both languages use the same alphabet it is sinful to rip the holy letters. This scene, appearing right after David has been told he is "too young to sin," shows Roth's true antipathy toward all things Jewish. It also begins to shed light on the previous scene of "two A one." Read in reverse (Yiddish and Hebrew are read from right to left) "two A one" becomes "one A two" meaning in one act, two sins are committed. Similarly, Roth is punning on his avowed belief that in 1934 it is patently impossible for one person to be in two cultures. Two cultures create a split psyche. There is no healing for Roth when he wrote *Call It Sleep*, no redemption in the Lurianic sense;[8] at least there is no mercy yet for the young Joycean modernist. One must step back from *Call It Sleep* and contemplate the long difficult arc of Roth's career to understand the two scenes of the pennies.

Roth was able to write *Call It Sleep* only as a result of David's pre-pubescence, and the author was unable to get beyond David's childhood for over sixty years. The old nameless Jewish mother institutionalizes David's innocence by *paskening* (a *halachic* or legal decision made by a rabbinical authority): "You're not old enough to sin." When the boy is old enough to sin, namely when he reaches adulthood and sexual maturity, Roth will be rendered incapable, not of sinning but of writing about his sinful behavior as a youth.

Roth spent over sixty years attempting to live by "holding gnashing memory at bay." Even *Call It Sleep*, despite its naturalistic view of the Lower East Side, was an evasion, albeit a beautifully artistic evasion, but one which Roth grew increasingly disenchanted with the older he got and the longer he worked at not remembering the truth of his past. In the opening pages of *Mercy* in one of his dialogues with his computer (whom Roth has nicknamed *Ecclesias*, and which symbolizes his split psyche: in one A two) Roth distances himself from the novel of his youth calling it an "evasion":

> —You'll sooner or later have to get over that hurdle.
> Yes.
> —I told you at the outset when you deliberately omitted that most crucial element in your account, that you would not be able to avoid reckoning with it.
> You did Ecclesias. Perhaps I wasn't ready for it.
> —And are you now?
> Yes. I became so.
> —When you had to. It finally became inescapable.
> Yes. Face-to-face with it as a consequence of continuing. Which is something, you notice, Ecclesias, I managed to evade in the only novel I ever wrote: coming to grips with it.

—It was adroit. You made a climax of evasion, an apocalypse out of your refusal to go on, an apocalyptic tour de force at the price of renouncing a literary future. As pyrotechnics, it was commendable, it found favor, at any rate. Proceed. (Volume I, 86)

In this dialogue between Roth and his computer, we see his renouncing his earlier evasion of the truth of his life in *Call It Sleep*. In the next section of chapter 6 we will see how in writing *Mercy of a Rude Stream*, Roth is finally able to become "in two A one." Through working through the difficult narrative structure of his second novel Roth is finally able to gain a measure of mercy and reconcile the split psyche that had pursued him since the evasive "pyrotechnics" of *Call It Sleep*.

THE RIDDLE OF "IN TWO A ONE"
ANSWERED IN *MERCY OF A RUDE STREAM*

In *The Image of Proust*, Walter Benjamin wrote: "all great works of literature either found a genre or dissolve one." Although Benjamin was speaking of Proust's great novel, he might just as easily have been describing Henry Roth's *Mercy of a Rude Stream*. Part novel, memoir, autobiography, confession, chronicle of old age, diary of a disease, Roth's masterpiece defies conventional generic boundaries. Racing against death, Roth strove to complete the work he should have written, but could not, sixty long years before. The more than thirteen hundred pages of *Mercy* document Roth's life from 1914 through 1927. At age eighty-nine, as he approaches death, Henry Roth, through the monumental act of giving testimony to his life, strives through his "holistic rendering of *his* lamentable past," to "reconcile one individual to himself" (Volume II, 285).

Call It Sleep began with Roth's immigration to America in 1907 and dealt with the years 1911 through 1913, and *Mercy of a Rude Stream* picks up Roth's story at the outset of World War I in the summer of 1914 in the Harlem apartment to which the Stigman family has moved from the Lower East Side. It documents with minute detail all the occurrences in the life of Ira Stigman (the David Schearl of *Call It Sleep*, and a clear stand-in for the young Henry Roth) until his decision to leave the suffocating Harlem family apartment in favor of bohemian Greenwich Village and Edith Wells (based on the real-life NYU English Professor and Roth's lover, Eda Lou Walton), on Thanksgiving 1927.

Roth dates the split in self that was to consume him all his life from the great move to non-Jewish Harlem. He says: "it was then and there the desolate breach opened between himself and himself that was never to close" (Volume I, 18). Roth's project in writing *Mercy* is an attempt in old age to confess and give testimony to the horrors of his formative years and, in so doing, reconcile with his own psyche. Although Roth maintains that the "void was never to close," it is through the writing of his narrative and the working through of his difficult narrative structure that he is finally, as he approaches death, reconciled and made whole.

Roth's split in self and identity leads to a crisis in witnessing and in giving testimony to his own life story. Perhaps we can date the genesis of that crisis and the deepening of the rift that began with his family's move to Harlem, to a scene midway through Volume II *A Diving Rock on the Hudson*. In so doing, we might also gain a glimpse of Roth's complicated reasons for breaking his sixty-year silence.

Ira's family, particularly his mother, sacrificed greatly so that he could receive an education and graduate from high school instead of going to work and bringing in some much-needed capital, thereby raising the family out of the squalor of their Harlem apartment. All his mother wishes in return is to actually see, witness firsthand, her son walk down the aisle and receive his diploma. Ira refuses her entreaties. The family recognizes Ira's reluctance to have his embarrassingly un-American Jewish parents present at the ceremony. Ira has done his best to root out any sign of Jewishness from his mien, a point not lost on his mother, who says:

> He shrinks from his Yiddish mother, that's the whole trouble, that's my curse. You're a Jew yourself, no? And there won't be other Jewish parents present? I'll find some niche, some crevice. I'll hide. No one will notice me, and you need not either. You don't know me. You don't have to present me to your friends. Just let me witness. (Volume II, 236–37)

This scene represents the spiritual nadir for Ira. Perhaps it is even more debasing than the many graphic scenes of incest conveyed with gleeful abandon by the octogenarian Roth. Ira's embarrassment at his own mother forces the reader to turn away in shame. His self-loathing behavior is even more shameful than the scenes of his bribing Minnie to allow him to continue sexually assaulting her. For in this scene, by refusing his mother's one request, Ira's hatred and fear of anything Jewish, his self-loathing can no longer remain hidden.

Ira's mother's flat statement, "Just let me witness," has haunted Roth all these years. Roth makes this explicit through one of his many metanarrative dialogues with Ecclesias. Roth says:

> Alas, my Mother. She breaks my heart sixty years too late, Ecclesias.
> —Indeed? Pity all mothers of such sons. The whelp treats its dam better than you did yours, my friend. But you're too late. The grave is a barrier to all amends, all redress. (Volume II, 237)

As usual, Ecclesias, part of Roth's split consciousness, is an exacting and truthful taskmaster. Leah's words "Let me witness" still haunt Roth years later. Through his evocation of this scene, Roth has literally reached back through the murky waters of time and allowed his mother to symbolically witness, if not the graduation ceremony, the crisis of confession that he has undergone.

The idea of hiding, of the pathetic figure of his mother finding some crevice, or niche, to hide in, her statement, an accusation really, "you don't know me," and the battle cry of "let me witness," all point to a global crime of conscience as well as to the private guilt and sin undergone by Ira Stigman. The scene brings together for the first time two main themes which course like a rude stream through all four volumes of the novel: the notion of giving testimony, and the act of that testimony, the actual witnessing being fraught with Holocaust imagery.

Much of the trauma of Roth's youth is conveyed through the many Holocaust images that are indelibly recognizable to Roth's late twentieth and early twenty-first century readers. This imagery appears in the narrative when Ira is denying his Judaism or is disparaging his connection to his past. In Volume II, we see Ira standing beneath the old Ninth Avenue El, trying to impress his new acquaintance Larry, whom Ira assumes is a non-Jew due to his upper-class demeanor. Ira tries to hide his own Jewishness from Larry as he stands talking to his friend "while thousands of people, vehicles, were making new configurations in tumultuous passing, and overhead too, rattle of the rolling coffins, the El trains" (Volume II, 195). Although this scene takes place in the 1920s, Roth's memory of his shattered, fragmented past is shadowed and suffused by the cataclysmic event of the Holocaust not known to Roth for twenty years after the occurrences of the scene he is narrating.

How has an innocuous New York City train passing overhead been terrifyingly transformed into a World War II cattle car transporting

Jews toward the crematoria? Furthermore, what does this transformation teach us about the difficulties of Roth's confession and testimony?

Roth prevents his mother from witnessing his graduation. This scene has taken on primal importance in Roth's imagination. Much of Roth's retelling of his story has been suffused with his guilt over withholding his mother's witnessing. One could argue that this guilt also arises from the further violation of his mother, or the sanctity of the family, through his avowed incest with his sister Minnie—a major theme from Volume II through the conclusion of Volume IV *Requiem for Harlem*. Over the years Roth's guilt over his misdeeds as a youth becomes entangled with Holocaust-survivor guilt. We can see this linking of guilt in Roth's choice of the name Genya as his fictional mother in *Call It Sleep*. Roth lost a cousin and an aunt named Genya in concentration camps. We see that the role of witnessing and giving testimony becomes for Roth suffused with guilt, shame, and a silence that must be overcome through the creation of fiction.

Thus the project of *Mercy* is the recovering of the witness. Roth does complete the story he set out to narrate. But concurrently *Mercy* is also a narrative of the forgetting to witness, the story of Roth's amnesia or forgetting of the truth of his past. Roth's sixty-year silence, his forsaking for so long his role as witness to the atrocities of his youth, might have much to do with the difficulty of testifying against one's own crimes, one's own self.

For Roth to witness he must also confess, and Roth's confession is nearly impossible because he occupies three separate roles at once. In their book *Testimony*, Shoshana Felman and Dori Laub locate three separate roles in the process of witnessing: victim, perpetrator, and bystander. Roth is paradoxically in all three positions at once. He is often seen as the victim while being savagely beaten by his father; as perpetrator during his incestuous assaults on both his sister Minnie and his cousin Stella; and through it all stands the old man Roth reporting and witnessing the tragedy while underscoring his witness of the past with present-day asides through his conversations with his computer Ecclesias.

How does Roth overcome this testimonial dilemma? He turns to a difficult and complex narrative structure at the outset of the novel. By *Mercy*'s completion Roth will have abandoned the complex split consciousness symbolized by "in one A two." As the internal rift heals and Roth is restored to himself, he may finally be able to embody the young boy's dream of becoming "in two A one" first heard in *Call It Sleep* sixty long years before.

Mercy begins with a third-person narrator closely following the consciousness of the young Ira Stigman. On page six, though, there is a short section in boldface type in which the narrator speaks directly to his computer, Ecclesias. This double narration continues almost until the end of the novel, while in a further wrinkle temporality also shifts from section to section.

Gerard Genette distinguishes between "Story," the actual telling of the events of the narration as they unfold, and "Text," which refers to any metanarrative statements made by the narrator, what Roland Barthes called "stage directions." The text role is reserved for the second narrator, the "I" in the boldface sections, or Roth himself. It is also important to note that this second narrator alternately refers to himself with the impersonal pronoun "I" or with the name of Ira, making clear that the two narrators of the different sections are understood to be one person, and furthermore that this one person is in fact Henry Roth because the events of the 1979 to 1995 time period correspond to known people and occurrences in Roth's life in New Mexico. *Mercy* slides between autobiography, memoir, and novel, obliterating these different genres and, as Benjamin suggests, creating its own genre.

The story time follows chronologically from 1914 through 1927. The text in boldface, however, has a more tortuous path to follow much like the rude stream within Roth's title. It is this second narrative within the first that will enable Roth to gain a measure of mercy before he dies, and not the actual events or "story" but the witnessing and giving testimony of the story itself, what Genette designates as "text." These sections of text refer at various times to 1979—when Roth began writing *Mercy*; 1985 when he substantially revised on computer (with Ecclesias) his handwritten manuscript; and lastly, his revision of this second manuscript right up until his death in October 1995. These sections of text often take on a deep confessional tone: "Shake your head in reproach, my friend; let your fingertips join in a cage and ponder" (Volume I, 14). Similarly, in Volume II Ecclesias upbraids Roth: "since you've chosen this mode of oblation, chosen to live, to scrive, then there's no undoing the done. There's only the outwearing it, the outwearying it, the attenuating of remorse, and guilt" (Volume II, 143).

What is the purpose of this dual narrative structure and why does Roth, in his late eighties, approaching death, suffering from debilitating rheumatoid arthritis, feel the need to turn to a public avowal of all his youthful sins? Roth's troubled relationship to his Jewishness will help us understand his confessional project, and his desperate need to testify to the story of his life.

Roth is both insider and outsider to the trauma of his youth. As a result of this split, being a witness to his own life story becomes difficult and an outside witness is needed to bridge this gap. That outsider is Mrs. Shapiro. In the overall scheme of the 1,355 pages of *Mercy*, Mrs. Shapiro is a character with a seemingly trivial role. Early in the novel when we meet her, she is simply described as the "new tenant in the 'back,' dumpy, shapeless Litvak Mrs. Shapiro" (Volume I, 32). Yet later in the novel she bravely interposes herself between Chaim and Ira who is being beaten with a stove poker. She says to Ira's father: "What, you'll destroy your own son for a goya's sake?" (Volume I, 33). Mrs. Shapiro is the witnessing agent that allows Roth to cross from the inside to the outside of his own life's story. She represents the reader or outsider who will give meaning to the testimony Roth has been shaping in the painful last years of his life.

When we see her again over thirteen hundred pages later, once again she is described as "dumpy and shapeless," almost like a mass of matter, a representation of the reader who will bear witness to the horror of Ira's upbringing. She is the outsider who gives validity to all of Ira's suffering as well as the suffering he visits on others. Mrs. Shapiro is the witness par excellence of *Mercy of a Rude Stream*; one might be tempted to call her the Jan Karski of Roth's project. Mrs. Shapiro's reason for first entering the Stigman apartment is obvious enough—to save Ira from literally being beaten to death with a stove poker; however, the question of why she returns at the end of the novel remains.

The pivotal moment in Claude Lanzmann's nine-and-a-half-hour documentary *Shoah* comes toward the end of the film when Lanzmann interviews Jan Karski, a retired professor of history from Georgetown University. As his *New York Times* obituary states: "Karski [was] a liaison officer of the Polish underground who infiltrated both the Warsaw Ghetto and a German concentration camp and then carried the first eyewitness accounts of the Holocaust to a mostly disbelieving West" (*New York Times* July 15, 2000 C15).

Jan Karski as a representative of the Polish Government-in-Exile and as a non-Jew from outside the Warsaw Ghetto was implored by Jewish leaders from within the Warsaw Ghetto to bear witness to the Nazi atrocities in Poland. After his first visit to the Warsaw Ghetto, he returns to the Ghetto a second time and walks down the streets as if in a trance. He says: "It was not a world. There was not humanity. . . . It was some . . . some hell" (Lanzmann, *Shoah: An Oral History of the Holocaust* 172–73). Throughout his ordeal of witnessing the horror of the Warsaw Ghetto, Jan Karski is told again and again by those on the inside, "remember this," and "Look at it, look at it" (173). Similarly, Mrs. Shapiro returns at the end of *Mercy* to frame the narrative of the horror of the *House of Stigman* and to replicate the return that is undergone by Roth himself.

Roth's central theme of reconciliation of self to self takes the reader from the inside of the horror that was his incestuous and exiled existence in Irish Harlem where he felt like "a stranger in a strange land," through the testimony of Mrs. Shapiro and Ira's leaving on a train on the last page of the novel "bound the hell out of Harlem" (Volume IV, 272), taking us back outside once again. Thus Mrs. Shapiro has saved Roth a second time, nearly sixty years after her first act of bravery.

Henry Roth is the voice speaking through Mrs. Shapiro that gives rise to the testimony that repels the silence that had engulfed and separated his psyche for sixty years. Indeed Roth's project is not really over. The last lines: "Ira boarded the train, his cold fingers still aching, and strait was the route, and strait the rails—the IRT swerved, squealing on the tracks of the long curve westward as it repaired downtown and the hell out of Harlem" (Volume IV, 272). The last image of *Mercy* is of an IRT train rolling out of the 116th Street station in Harlem on tracks that Roth calls "strait." Roth is clearly punning on the homophone "strait"/"straight"; "strait" is an archaic adjective meaning narrow or difficult, quite different from the common usage of the word "straight." Similarly, Roth's difficult personal journey of reconciliation, his ability to become "in two A one" was anything but simple or straight, resembling more the westward swing of the train due south. The train, earlier in *Mercy* described as a Holocaust-era cattle car, through the witnessing of Mrs. Shapiro and through Roth's overcoming his "split psyche," has once more been transformed, this time back into a regular IRT subway car. For Roth's readers, both images continue to roll through our imaginations and through the perilous and brave journey of reconciliation that Henry Roth successfully navigated during his last years.

CONCLUSION

The Future of Jewish Fiction in America

On the last page of Bernard Malamud's 1957 novel *The Assistant*, Frank Alpine endures a painful *brit mila*, a circumcision ceremony. In Malamud's symbolic system, Alpine's act is seen as a homecoming, as a sign of his finally belonging to the Jewish people. Frank's circumcision is also a marker of his complete transformation from selfish sinner into a selfless saint, a symbol of his becoming a true *mentsch*—on par with his suffering mentor, Morris Bober. Much like Malamud's conclusion to *The Assistant*, Philip Roth ends his 1986 novel *The Counterlife* with a discussion of circumcision. In a letter to his gentile wife, Maria, Nathan Zuckerman suggests that if their unborn child is a boy he would like the baby circumcised. Zuckerman writes: "Circumcision is everything that the pastoral is not and, to my mind, reinforces what the world is about, which isn't strifeless unity" (323). Yet here the comparison to Malamud ends, for in Roth's novel Zuckerman's circumcision represents a rejection of the pastoral sham of a life he had been living—it is in short an act of symbolic antipastoralism. Roth rejects the pursuit of perfection and purity[1] reaffirming the Jewish covenantal relationship with God signified by Abraham's *brit mila* (circumcision), the symbolic beginning of the Jewish people.

Roth's circumcision discussion, at the conclusion of *The Counterlife*, might also have inaugurated another resurgence: the reemergence, after a twenty-year hiatus, of serious critical attention by the literary establishment for Jewish American fiction. After years of neglect by the literary establishment, by 1997, for example, MELUS devoted an entire issue to the phenomenon of late twentieth-century Jewish American literature. Despite the increased critical exposure, perhaps the great prestige Jewish American literature held at the conclusion of the twentieth century might best be glimpsed in Roth's novel *The Human Stain* (2000), which uses Judaism as a metaphor for *inclusion* into American academic and literary society. Coleman Silk, Roth's light-skinned African American protagonist, passes as a Jew as a means of gaining acceptance at Athena College. Silk is a successful professor at Athena, a small liberal arts college, for many years before the political correct agenda of the day leads to his ruin. No matter what one thinks of Roth's book, the fact that in a realistic work of fiction (despite its improbable plot twists), the idea that Jewishness is seen as the ticket toward respectability represents a sea change in Jewish American fiction, and one which needs to be taken seriously in future appraisals of the Jewish American novel.

Stepping back from Coleman Silk for a moment, let us remember that in 1977, barely more than a quarter of a century ago, and only one year after Saul Bellow received the Nobel Prize for literature, Irving Howe edited an anthology called *Jewish-American Stories*. In his introductory remarks, Howe worried about the future of Jewish writing in America. Howe firmly believed that his introduction to the anthology would serve as the epitaph for the form. Howe wrote: "My own view is that American Jewish fiction has probably moved past its high point. Insofar as this body of writing draws heavily from the immigrant experience, it must suffer a depletion of resources, a thinning-out of materials and memories" (16). Howe, a socialist critic who upon entering "Alcove One" at City College left behind almost all vestiges of his Jewishness, could easily empathize with wanting to jettison a Judaism that in his mind was synonymous with the "streets and tenements of immigrant Jewish neighborhoods" (16). In Howe's conception, Judaism was a religion of oppression. Therefore, for Howe, any literature dealing with Jewishness would fade into memory with the passing of the immigrant generation; possibly, he reasoned, Jewish literature might survive in the memories of the next postimmigrant generation.

In hindsight, what Howe understood to be *Yiddishkeit* or Jewishness was actually the immigrant experience, an experience that had indeed been drunk to the lees within Jewish American fiction; had the next generation of Jewish writers attempted a continuation of writing concerned solely with the immigrant experience, no doubt Howe's remarks in 1977 would have been prophetic. Of course, as I have hopefully established in *American Talmud*, that has not proven to be the case.

Before we quickly dismiss Howe's conflation of immigration/Judaism, a nagging question persists: Was it ever really the case that Jewish writers were only dealing with issues of immigration? Or was Howe (and other like-minded critics, such as Fiedler, Kazin, etc.) merely using an expedient literary tool, tarring (so to speak) all of Jewish American writing with a broad brush? As we've seen in chapter 3 of *American Talmud,* by 1977 Saul Bellow had already begun publishing his very Jewish stories; indeed, "The Old System" had come out in *Playboy* in 1967. Cynthia Ozick had burst onto the literary scene with the publication of her novel *Trust* in 1966, and *The Pagan Rabbi and Other Stories* likewise had recently been published. By 1977 Mark Mirsky had already published four distinctively Jewish American novels. If his first work of fiction, *Thou Worm Jacob,* still had one indelicate foot in the world of his father and grandfather who had immigrated from Pinsk, his more recent fiction had become increasingly steeped in the contemporary Jewish American scene, be that of sixties Jewish radicals of *Blue Hill Avenue* or the bohemian lifestyles of the late 1960s Greenwich Village. In short, in the years prior to the publication of Howe's anthology, there was no shortage of significantly Jewish fiction of the highest literary and artistic merit being published in America. One might wonder then just why instead of proclaiming a revolution afoot, Howe pronounced the death (or imminent death) of the Jewish American novel? These developments did not just materialize with the 1989 publication of Allegra Goodman's *Total Immersion,* although that book certainly sped things along. Surely a critic of Howe's reputation would have noticed this obvious trend toward a more genuinely Jewish American literature taking shape all around him?

While Howe urged African American writers to return to their roots, which he believed to be protest literature; Howe famously dismissed Ralph Ellison's work on these grounds spurring a devastatingly eloquent response from Ellison. It would seem that Howe was concomitantly wishing for his fellow Jewish Americans to remain silent or perhaps to just disappear into the larger tapestry of American literature. Howe's ideas concerning the end of Jewish American literature are eerily reminiscent of Henry Roth's similar wish for Jewish assimilation.

Clearly, by no means was Howe alone in his beliefs. Howe's unease with things Jewish, his complete abandonment of his *descent* religion of Orthodox Judaism for his *consent* religion of Orthodox Socialism, led to his and other like-minded Jewish American critics, those who should have been championing its aesthetic and thematic achievements throughout the sixties, seventies, and eighties, to instead treat it like an embarrassing older uncle, someone to be ignored or wished out of sight.[2]

This attitude becomes even more obvious with just a quick perusal of the stories that Howe included in the anthology he was introducing.

A story by Henry Roth, "The Surveyor," which returns to Spain and the Spanish Inquisition while searching for the elements of the present Jewish *galut* in America, points to a distinctly new direction in Roth's writing; it is a story which would lead directly to the monumental *Mercy of Rude Stream*. Bellow's "The Old System" is also included in Howe's anthology, as are important stories by Ozick, Paley, and Olson, all of which dramatize generational conflicts, a decidedly American engagement, and which deal with immigration not as a substitute for Judaism, or other plot considerations, but for the obvious importance it had on the future generations and their engagement in the American *galut*. If the stories Howe chose for the anthology refute the major thrust of the argument put forward in his introduction, one must wonder if a different agenda, perhaps unbeknownst to Howe himself, was at work.

HEBREW IN AMERICA

That same year, 1977, while Howe was tolling the death knell for Jewish American literature, a brash young Mark Mirsky published a picaresque memoir. In *My Search for the Messiah*, Mirsky, who was raised on the tough streets of 1940s Roxbury and Dorchester in and around Blue Hill Avenue (Mirsky's Yaknapatawpha), travels the world in search of his Jewish roots. Having already published a handful of heavily Jewish novels in the late sixties and early seventies, Mirsky turns his sights toward Israel, and away from Jewish American practitioners of the novel. Mirsky writes:

> Critics like Irving Howe warn that even their favorites, Bellow, Roth, Malamud, may belong to no more than a minor genre. But I no longer find my kinship in those pages. I think there is another tradition, secret, bastard, like the Moabitess, Ruth, a foreign marriage that so enriches the native stock it begins to bring forth fruit of Eden. Hebrew has influenced America. (214–15)

With the idiosyncratic verve of a fiction writer, Mirsky goes on to list the ways in which Hebrew has influenced American writers William Bradford and Cotton Mather, before suggesting that "These rhythms reassert themselves in the middle of the nineteenth century, and the Bible, that Jewish Testament, haunts the decks of the *Pequod*, the maples of Walden Pond, the *House of Seven Gables*. These are Hebrew documents, a strong prophetic voice ringing in them" (215).

More than a quarter of a century ago, Mirsky's insight that the future of Jewish American literature in America lay in Hebrew sounds as prophetic as the American forebears he cites. The flowering of the Hebrew language in America, in conjunction with a rediscovery of Yiddish and its teaching at major American institutions has in fact proven Howe a Cassandra of Jewish American literature.

The reasons for Jewish American Literature's not just survival, but its late twentieth-century and early twenty-first century renaissance, has little to do with any one person, a savior who will singlehandedly rescue a genre, much like Faulkner did for Southern Literature. In the case of Jewish American Literature it is not a *whom*, but a *what*: Hebrew.

By Hebrew, I don't just mean the language that thousands of diaspora Jews learn to speak each year (certainly many more than did a quarter century ago). Although that is significant, the Hebrew language also signifies a far deeper engagement with things Jewish. In present-day America, Orthodoxy, the words of the Torah, the laws of *Halachah*, Jewish ritual praxis, are no longer exotic. This trend is powerfully reflected in the fiction that has been produced in the past thirty years in America, a fascinating development that has only gained momentum in the new millennium.

EMERGENT LITERATURE?
THE JEWISH AMERICAN BIND

In "Emergent Literatures," the concluding essay to the seventh volume of *The Cambridge History of American Literature*, Cyrus Patell describes Raymond Williams's formulation of the constant struggle between "residual and emergent cultural forms" (542). Patell suggests, "Both residual and emergent cultural forms can only be recognized and indeed conceived in relation to the dominant: each represents a form of negotiation between the margin and the center over the right to control meanings, values, and practices" (542).

In this book I have argued that Jewish American writers of the twentieth and twenty-first centuries, far from representing a radical departure from traditional Jewish culture, are yet one more chapter of postrabbinic literature produced in the diaspora. From *American Talmud*'s vantage point, I am uncertain whether Jewish American fiction would be considered "residual" or "emergent" in Patell's formulation. I am similarly undecided about the significance of the recent publication of *The Norton Anthology of Jewish American Literature* (2000). While I am hopeful that the anthology represents a nod of approval from the "hegemonic mainstream," I remain skeptical of a literary establishment that requires such approval in the first place. But if the *The Norton Anthology of Jewish American Literature* signals the beginning of a trend toward a higher regard for Jewish American literature and greater critical attention for deserving Jewish American writers then I am grateful for its publication.

I recall the astounded reviews that began appearing in the wake of the publication of Allegra Goodman's first novel *Kaaterskill Falls* in the summer of 1998. *The New York Times* raved, suggesting it offered a voyeuristic peek into the "religious rhythms of life in a cloistered Orthodox Jewish community" in America (Veale 28). Yet within a few short years, Orthodox characters have been appearing in the most unlikely places: Steve Stern has recreated the Orthodox world of the *shtetl* in his award-winning *The Wedding Jester*, and the lost world of Jewish Lower East Side in *The Angel of Forgetfulness*; in *The Ladies Auxiliary* and *The Outside World*, Tova Mirvis writes elegantly about a vibrant Orthodox community in, of all places, the deep south Bible-belt city of Memphis, Tennessee; Myla Goldberg memorably portrays the Naumann family in *Bee Season*; and with the publication of *The Golems of Gotham*, Thane Rosenbaum has recently completed his brilliant post-Holocaust trilogy. Lara Vapnyar has launched her career with an impressive story collection, *There Are Jews in My House*, and Gary Shteyngart has already published two brilliant novels: *The Russian Debutante's Handbook* (2002) and *Absurdistan* (2006). I do not mean to suggest that it is only these works of newcomers to Jewish American fiction, which fill bookstore shelves. Many of the established Jewish American writers I discuss in *American Talmud* have been quite productive recently as well. Philip Roth's *The Plot Against America* topped bestseller lists in 2004 and his most recent book *Everyman* was published in 2006. Cynthia Ozick's *Heir to the Glimmering World* appeared in 2004, and Rebecca Goldstein's latest book is a provocative work of non-fiction: *Betraying Spinoza: The Renegade Jew Who Gave Us Modernity* (2006), which argues, in part, that Baruch Spinoza cannot be fully understood without contemplating his relationship to Judaism. Allegra Goodman recently added to her already impressive list of works of fiction with her 2006 novel *Intuition*. The list of notable recent Jewish American fiction is quite extensive.

What unites many of these recent works of fiction is an abiding interest in representing Judaism and its traditions. In fact, this concept of representations of Orthodoxy in contemporary American culture has not only become a popular topic of fiction, it has also become, not surprisingly, fairly contentious as well.

Wendy Shalit, the author of the bestselling book *A Return to Modesty*, in her recent article, "The Observant Reader," paints a very unflattering portrait of contemporary Jewish American fiction writers' portrayal of Orthodoxy. In this feature article for the Sunday *New York Times Book Review*, Shalit writes: "Authors who have renounced Orthodox Judaism—or those who were never really exposed to it to begin with—have often portrayed deeply observant Jews in an unflattering or ridiculous light" (16). Shalit goes on to upbraid numerous contemporary Jewish American writers' portrayal of Orthodox (what Shalit terms "observant") characters. Although Shalit admits that some Jewish writers, notably Allegra Goodman, "have written sympathetically of the haredi," she wonders if other Jewish American writers are really writing from an "insider perspective." In framing her question in ideological rather than aesthetic terms, Shalit falls into the same trap that has ensnared many previous critics of Jewish writing in America. Rather than focusing on the aesthetics of Orthodox representation in Jewish American fiction, Shalit focuses on how observant particular characters seem to be.

I would agree with Shalit's contention that Jewish American writers have often portrayed Orthodoxy in "an unflattering and ridiculous light." However, this is where "The Observant Reader" and *American Talmud* part company. In both chapters 1 and 6 of *American Talmud*, I discuss the seemingly anti-Semitic and stereotyped caricature of Rabbi Pankower in Henry Roth's *Call It Sleep*. My discussion is concerned with Roth's representation of Judaism from an aesthetic perspective aimed at uncovering hidden themes in the novel and not in disclosing Roth's level of observance to the Torah and mitzvoth (which, needless to say, should be a nonissue in a serious literary discussion).

In calling contemporary Jewish American writers who do not conform to her standards of Orthodoxy or observance "outsider insiders," Shalit's remarks have ignited a firestorm of criticism. In her article Shalit goes so far as to suggest that Tova Mirvis "does not understand her orthodox characters" ("The Observant Reader"). Promising short-story writer Nathan Englander comes in for particular scorn for admitting in an interview to being a pork eater. Several weeks after Shalit's article appeared under the title "Orthodox Jews in Fiction," the *New York Times Book Review* devoted their entire letters-to-the-editor page to responses to Shalit's article. One of the writers Shalit chastises, Mirvis writes:

> The true sin seems to be portraying Orthodox Jews with any human failings, with having moments when they do not conform to the dictates of Jewish law. Shalit is not an observant reader but an ideological one. She's looking for public relations documents, kosher books by "insiders' insiders" that will "convert" even us "outsider insiders." I didn't realize that despite spending my life as an Orthodox Jew, I'm in need of conversion. But then, I also didn't realize that novels were in the business of proselytizing. ("Orthodox Jews in Fiction" 4)

On the same page Jonathan Rosen responds to Shalit by poignantly proclaiming that the authority of a literary work is not "a matter of birthright," but rather should lie in a writer's "imaginative power"—an idea, Rosen suggests, that is lost within Shalit's ideological reading of contemporary Jewish American fiction.

Although the discussion on Orthodox representation has only just begun, one idea seems underscored by this literary debate concerning Orthodox representation: Howe's conception that "American Jewish fiction has probably moved past its high point" could not be more wrong. Far from suffering from "a depletion of resources, a thinning-out of materials and memories" (16) as Howe opined over a quarter century ago, in the twenty-first century, Jewish American fiction seems to be breaking new ground. I believe that we are in the midst of a revolution in Jewish American literary production in America. I believe we have only seen the beginning. If the first century of sustained literary output of American Jews is any indication, I am confident we are on the cusp of what promises to be an adventurous and productive future for Jewish fiction in America.

In this book I have begun to codify an "American Talmud" and I have interpreted many of the Jewish elements of the postrabbinic literature produced by Jewish American writers. My hope is that through my aesthetic reading of the cultural heritage of Jewish American fiction, readers of *American Talmud* will be able to work their way toward a deeper understanding of the countless new Jewish American works of fiction that daily appear on the shelves of their local bookstores.

At the conclusion to his short story, "The Old System," Saul Bellow has his narrator ruminate on existential angst. Momentarily rejecting the certainty of scientific knowledge he settles for an "intimation of understanding" (*Mosby's Memoirs and Other Stories* 82). *American Talmud* has given its readers that intimation of understanding through its interpretation of the textual culture which Jewish American writers have inherited; if successful, it has also helped transmit that cultural and aesthetic heritage to a new generation of readers in America.

APPENDIX

An Interview with Rebecca Goldstein

Coinciding with the publication of her novel *Properties of Light*, Rebecca Goldstein was invited to participate in a panel discussion of writers who use math and science in their work. The symposium, titled *Proof*, took place at New York University on October 15, 2000; at the conclusion of the conference Goldstein graciously agreed to be interviewed by me. We met the following morning, October 16, in the library of the Hudson Hotel. In addition to Goldstein and myself, Natalie Stiene, a writer and former student of Goldstein's, was present for the interview.

EZRA CAPPELL: I was wondering if you could talk a little about your family history. My current research deals with Holocaust representations in contemporary Jewish American fiction.

REBECCA GOLDSTEIN: Well, I guess every Jewish person has some connection with the Holocaust. My father was born in a *shtetl* in Poland. He left before the war, he was one of the youngest in a large family, so they came over; his older sister is the only one who married and settled over there, so she and her four children, four of my first cousins of course, died. That was on the Polish side. On my mother's side, the Hungarian side, my grandmother had come over by herself from Hungary. She had a huge family, very artistic, very prominent, very wealthy; they almost all died. There were a few who managed to survive from this very large family. But when I was growing up, I was born in the fifties, some of our Hungarian relatives, the few remnants, came over and would pass through our house. They would stay in my family's house for a while, while they got on their feet. And there was one in particular who impressed me, Zanvilzer, who really impressed me because he was so arrogant. He would order my mother, and us girls around you know: "do this and do that." He was a shriveled-up, broken little man. And my mother did not like to be ordered around and she did it. She picked up after him. She did everything. And I said: "He's so obnoxious, why are you doing this?" And she would say: "You don't want to know. You don't want to know." And I was always hearing this: "You don't want to know." She'd say: "He was in the camps." I'd ask: "What does that mean?" She'd say: "You don't want to know." So I got the sense of these people that something incredibly horrible and mysterious had happened to them. I remember my mother saying of this guy: "He used to ride around on his white horse, he was a prince surveying his land, and now look at him."

So to my mind this was incredibly strange, romantic I guess. I was very young when this happened. Now my father was Polish and for some reason my younger sister and I, both throughout our childhood, somehow connected, we thought somehow that he was touched, that he had gone through the camps. There was something about him that made us really think that he had. He hadn't. My father had been studying German—

EC: Why do you think that was?

RG: Why was it?! My father carried an enormous amount of pain inside of him. In him. He didn't speak about the war. He didn't speak about his dead sister. He didn't speak about his nieces and nephews. I learned much later, after he died, that he had worked very, very hard to try to get them out and it fell through. This sister had married a very wealthy businessman and to get him out they had to say that he was a rabbi and that they had a position for him in America. And somebody in the town, one of his enemies, informed the authorities that this was a lie and then they lost total track of him. (Pause) I don't know, just imagine, you're trying to get your sister and her children out and then . . . he never. My father had studied, he was actually going for his doctorate in German Literature at City College, and then he would never speak German again. I had to take German of course for Philosophy and he wouldn't even help me with my homework; I mean he called it "faflcuhtah deutsche." I mean he was a very gentle man, he'd greet everyone with: "My Friend, my friend," but there was this implacable unforgiveness.

EC: Farfluchtah?

RG: Farfluchtah Deutshe—accursed German. It was sort of an ultimate denial—he wouldn't even speak the language. I came to understand that he had such a deep sense of betrayal. One of the things about Jews, I think European Jews, and I inherited this very strongly, is a love of German culture. I mean we love German culture, my father loved it, and we *loved* it. And it didn't love us back quite clearly. So there's a sense of betrayal on top of everything else that this culture had so let us down.

EC: Where was he from?

RG: He was from Poland; he was from a small *shtetl* in Galicia from what the Jews called Lemberg and the Poles called Lvov. It's called Borstchev, my family had been Rabbis there for many generations. My brother's a rabbi so the tradition continues (laughs).

Natalie Stiene: How old were you when you figured out that your father wasn't a survivor?

RG: It's so . . . I don't know . . . I was thirteen or fourteen when I put the pieces together, you know, because he was such a reticent person. He didn't speak, there was so much hurt, we never bought German products. I guess that's not unusual but I knew he was fluent in German, I knew he had been a Goethe lover, and now he wouldn't speak the language, and somehow I had thought he was a survivor; my younger sister had the same misconception. There was something . . . so if I am not a child of survivors, I think I have very much the sensibility, to a certain extent, of a child of survivors. There was such a sense of the hurt, of the betrayal, of the broken lives in our family.

EC: It's so interesting to hear you say that, because actual children of survivors often know no more than you did growing up in your house.

RG: Well, some survivors of course talk endlessly; you know the writer Melvin Bukiet, his father apparently talks about nothing else. Some of them talk very little. You're right, in some ways my father was characteristic: my house was characteristic of a sense of brokenness, of a great hurt that dare not speak its name, it was too large.

EC: How much of that influenced your writing, if you grew up believing into your teens that you were the child of survivors?

RG: Yeah. I grew up feeling a tremendous sense of protectiveness for my father, which I think is also very characteristic of children of survivors. How has it influenced me? It's hard to say. I know that it looms large in my psyche. In some sense it was something I actually wanted to get past, for example, in writing *Mazel*. I think that we have been scarred, all of us collectively, the world, not just Jews, although particularly Jews, scarred by the trauma, that we forget what their lives were like before. We see them in terms of their end and the tragedy and we forget about the fullness and the richness of that culture—and the joyfulness, the sort of life-embracing, vivid, intense celebration of life.

In one of Singer's very autobiographical stories—I actually lifted the music in *Mazel* because my character Sasha sees a young Singer walking down the street and overhears him saying something, something which he actually had said in a story—a woman asks him: "Why are we Jews so doomed?" And he answers: "Because we love life too much." (Laughs) And that to me somehow says so much about our history. You know not to see us only in terms of that tragedy, and not to feel the victim because that is not about us, that is about them. That is what they did to us, but that's not what we're about. We're not about being martyred, and we're not about suffering, and we're not about victimhood: we're about celebration.

EC: I see that very clearly in your fiction, that sense of embracing and celebrating the traditions, the rituals of the Torah as a way of rebelling against that victimhood, rejecting victimhood as the sole definer of what it means to be Jewish.

RG: Absolutely. Of course. The richness of the culture, a religious richness. Orthodoxy is a way of sanctifying every aspect of life. Every aspect of life, there is a way of doing it—

EC: Of hallowing the everyday.

RG: Exactly. You don't separate it out, everything is—although to outsiders it's sometimes—and you know (laughs) I'm not Orthodox. I don't actually believe this and do this, but I understand. I understand the rationale behind it and I respect this. I even revere it as a wonderful way of solving the twists in our personality of trying to reconcile all the different facets. You don't deny anything, you sort of sanctify everything. But yeah, it is a rebellion and to keep the traditions, if nothing else, has been an act of defiance. This is our identity. This is an identity that it is completely moveable. Another incredible genius. . . . The land was taken. You never knew when you were going to be kicked out so you create a culture that is completely moveable. It is an internal culture which has to do with learning, values, rituals—and you can take them anywhere: they're totally portable.

EC: Do you see your role as a writer as sanctifying the everyday, or as rebelling against victimhood?

RG: I think sometimes when I am writing specifically Jewish stories I think that my sense of our history of our culture, what it means, why we persist in it, which is one of the mysterious things, especially in our country (America), why we do persist in a Jewish sensibility—it is a great mystery. I think that when you write about Jewish things you can't help but be touched by that mystery.

EC: You mentioned that you had gone to Beis Yaakov—

RG: (laughs) Yeah . . .

EC: How did your family respond to your first becoming a philosopher, and then a writer? Was philosophy even a deeper movement, from their perspective, in the wrong direction?

RG: Absolutely, yeah, philosophy was pretty bad. Going to graduate school was—I was already married, I got married at nineteen and that gave me—

EC: That was good I'm sure—

RG: Yes, and that gave me a lot of freedom. My mother's attitude was: "You're his problem now; you're your husband's problem now." I don't think I could ever have done what I did, go to graduate school and become a philosopher if I hadn't been married. It's very funny, in my Bais Yaakov school we were told about Baruch Spinoza who after his excommunication became Benedictus Spinoza.[1] It was told as this cautionary tale. We were not supposed to go to college, but if we went to college we were not supposed to study the humanities right? It was supposed to be something technical, you know that's not about—

EC: To make a *parnussah*.

RG: Yeah, right, to make a *parnussah* until you got married.

EC: To help support your *kollel* husband—

RG: Exactly, that's right, if your parents were not rich enough to do it. Certainly not to study the humanities—those were seen as dangerous: And by all means not philosophy.

EC: Were they dangerous?

RG: (Laughs) From their point of view: yes, they were right. Philosophy teaches you to question everything; of course it's dangerous.

Even then I had such a sense that this must be so fragile, this belief system, if they are so afraid of anything that is going to challenge it. It must be so shaky; they must know it's so shaky. So even before I graduated from Beis Yaakov I used my summer vacation to take a course at Columbia in philosophy. That was my big rebellion. My contemporaries are rebelling by drugs, sex, and rock and roll, and I'm going off to take a course in philosophy feeling very wild, you know look at me . . .

EC: Benedictus Goldstein . . .

RG: That's right. And oh, I used to bring to Beis Yaakov books like *The Death of God*. I would sit in the back of the room with a little red cover on it—

EC: There's another four-letter word—

RG: Yes, very good. So was it dangerous? Of course it was dangerous.

EC: Back to your parents—

RG: Yes, so philosophy: bad move. Novels: terrible. You know sex and—

NS: How old were you when you started writing fiction?

RG: Well I was already an Assistant Professor of Philosophy—my father had already died. I don't think I would have done it, had he been alive. His dying had a lot to do with my writing my first novel. I was doing very technical philosophy of science, and in the grief of losing my father I got thrown into this other state. Sort of a metaphilosophical state thinking about "What has philosophy taught me?" Probably nothing. This sort of thinking. Philosophy had taught me to dismiss all those questions, about life, death, meaning. It was in that state that I wrote *The Mind-Body Problem*. His dying had a lot to do with my turning to fiction. The rest of my family, my mother, my siblings—mortified.

EC: You mentioned that your brother is a rabbi—

RG: Oh, he's mortified. . . . Maybe he read *The Mind-Body Problem*. I don't think he's read anything else.

EC: Is the mortification more a reaction to the sexual component to your novels or the fact that you're a writer who combines sexual scenes with a large amount of Orthodoxy within your work? People were so upset with Roth's early work, for example with his treatment of the Holocaust in "Eli the Fanatic." You might look at *The Mind-Body Problem* as sort of the "Eli the Fanatic" of Orthodox fiction.

RG: Yeah, it's true.

EC: Back in 1983, I don't think anyone was representing Orthodoxy . . . I mean there was Potok, but still it must have been quite a shock to the establishment.

RG: Yeah, I think so. I was seen as particularly pernicious because, you know, I know that world.

EC: Clearly, very well.

RG: I mean I also, I do love that world. All my characters move, gravitate toward it. How could I not love that world; it was the world of my father. Of course I love that world. But, it wasn't for me, and I see things about it that make it uncomfortable, especially for women of a certain sort. If I were a boy, chances are I would still be Orthodox. I chafed at being a girl. I was told that there are certain things I cannot study. You can't say that to a person like me!

EC: *Gemarah* (Talmud).

RG: Yeah, I mean, I can study math, I can study physics, and I can't study *Gemarah*?!

EC: What do you think of—I was going to bring it up later, but this seems like a pretty good segue—what do you think of what I term the neo-Orthodox feminist movement? Do you see this term as an oxymoron?

RG: No, I'm very excited about it. When I speak to these women—

EC: Blu Greenberg—

RG: Blu Greenberg, and this younger generation, all these young Orthodox women studying at Drisha (an Upper West Side Torah Institute), I think they are going to transform the religion. They are implanting it with this energy; the scholarship that's coming out is amazing. When you think that every interpretation in 2000 years has been given to Scripture, and they're coming up with new interpretations because they're women. They've been kept out for so long, there is such a greed, you know crashing down the gates, an enthusiasm and greed that they're bringing to it is amazing and I think that they have a lot to do with the revitalization of Judaism. It's funny, because to me Judaism still means Orthodoxy—this passionate engagement with the text, that's what Judaism is and that's what Orthodoxy has kept alive, so more power to them.

EC: Do you see that in terms of your own characters? I read a transcript of a symposium sponsored by *Tikkun* magazine in which you were quoted as saying that you consider yourself five-ninths a Jewish writer since five out of the nine stories in *Strange Attractors* dealt with Jewish characters and themes.

RG: Right.

EC: Can you talk about that a bit more, specifically in terms of your being considered a Jewish American writer. I know that a previous generation who were born before the war—I'm thinking of Malamud, Bellow, and Roth, those who did some of their best work in the aftermath of the Holocaust, although Bellow and Roth seem to be belying that—these writers would very certainly chafe at being considered a "Jewish" writer, feeling the label to be a hindrance. I'm interested in how you feel about this issue. Furthermore, I know I'm asking too much here at one time, but as a follow-up question to our discussion last evening (at the New York University symposium *Proof*), when we touched upon the issue of what constitutes a "genuine" Jewish fiction, if you do consider yourself a Jewish American writer, then what kind of Jewish American writer?

RG: These are big questions. There is not just a revitalization of Jewish life, but also of Jewish letters, going on. Young writers, younger than I, writing authentically Jewish pieces of fiction; not about assimilation, not about wanting out, but instead writing about a Jewish sensibility. Sometimes it's critical, you know Englander (Nathan Englander *For the Relief of Unbearable Urges*), but with an incredible knowledge, they are insiders—they know.

EC: As you are.

RG: Right. The way my imagination works, it's not exclusively involved with Jewish subjects and that five-ninths—yeah you're right it was partly in jest, but it's also kind of true—I never know the stories that are going to grab me. More often than I would expect they are Jewish stories: I respond very deeply, there is something very moving for me in this history. So quite often they are Jewish stories, but I guess for myself I don't want to be characterized as a Jewish writer because I do feel that then people are going to expect all my work to be Jewish and its hard enough to come up with a story that's going to sustain you for the years that it takes to write a novel, and a good character is hard to find, so I don't want to be limited in any way. I don't feel it diminishes a writer in any way, but for me it's constraining on my imagination. I don't want any expectations about what my next book will be. I'm also very moved by the life of intellectuals, women intellectuals, the doomed female genius, the life of the mind, mathematicians; this is another thing that really moves me.

EC: No one could ever say that your writing is only about one of these things.

RG: But my identity is very much Jewish. I see the world informed by my Jewish upbringing. I'll never leave that behind.

EC: What would you say about the term "Holocaust writer"?

RG: Well, Holocaust writing of course is very tricky, isn't it? We touched upon this earlier. How can it not dominate one's consciousness as a Jew, or with anybody as a citizen of a civilized world, what happened—and it does. How do we deal with that in fiction? The ethical problem seems to be it seems too large, too significant, and too important to be subverted in any way for aesthetic effect. And yet you want to. Part of what it means to be a Jew today is that the Holocaust lies in our path.

EC: So it is an ethical, but also an aesthetic, issue.

RG: Yes. It is an aesthetic problem: how do you do justice to this? I have always been very impressed with the way that Aharon Appelfeld deals with it: he will never, ever be in the Holocaust; it will always be before or after. And that is what I did in *Mazel*.

EC: I was going to ask you a question comparing you to Aharon Appelfeld, particularly parallels between *Badenheim 1939* and *Mazel*.

RG: Yes, I was directly influenced by him. It is the only way I feel to do justice. It is one thing to have a memoir, a firsthand account, but I will never, I wouldn't dare, dare to tread, to go in there, ever: It's holy ground. I wouldn't dare.

EC: It's what?

RG: It's holy ground. I wouldn't dare. They're martyrs. I wouldn't bring my, in comparison, trivial goals as a novelist onto that ground. But to somehow indicate how large, by skirting around it—I think it's very effective. Anyway, I think Appelfeld showed writers the way, how to do justice to the enormity of the Holocaust.

EC: Hearing you speak of this concept of "Holy Ground," I'm reminded of one of your short stories in *Strange Attractors*, "Mindel Gittel," which I consider to be narrated in what I would call perfect pitch Malamud—

RG: (clearly pleased) Thank you. He was such a *bubby*; he was such a wonderful guy to have in your head, that guy. He has this real Yiddish accent and the kids would come home from school and I'd say: "You want I should make you something to eat?" They'd say: "Finish the story Mom."

EC: For me that character, Uncle Sol, even one-ups Malamud. He's kind of like Morris Bober meets Bartleby the Scrivener, the way he narrates the tale after the fact, after the internal action of the story has taken place. Many of Malamud's *schlemieldik* characters wouldn't be able to narrate such a story. You've managed to create a character who is at once an old-world Malmudian suffering survivor, but at the same time you've imbued him with this linguistic ability, this knowledge to be able to narrate this type of story—something you don't always see in an earlier generation of writers.

RG: It's the legacy of my father. I could never have done that if I hadn't been brought up by my father. He (Uncle Sol) wasn't my father, but he was of that sort, the kind of *shtetl* Jew who doesn't exist anymore.

EC: Sol.

RG: Yah, the sort of person who has disappeared off the face of the earth for the most part. Big loss. Big loss for civilization.

EC: In talking about the concept of "hallowed ground," your narrator Sol constantly makes reference to that phrase, that euphemism—

RG: "Over there . . ."

EC: Right, "over there." That phrase, that euphemism: "over there." I thought that this was a fascinating element in your story. One way to think about that would be that this survivor is incapable of accessing his true feelings on the Holocaust, or to be able to verbalize his true feelings about the Holocaust. I think that this would be a valid reading of the story if it were in fact a survivor's tale, written by a survivor. However, you writing this story a generation removed from the Holocaust, the question aesthetically becomes how much of this is you—not necessarily the daughter of survivors, but the daughter of a generation of survivors—trying to represent the Holocaust in your fiction? Do you think that would be a valid reading of your story as well?

RG: Interesting. I was thinking from the point of view of this character. Just the enormity, the reticence. The reticence which I grew up with in my own family. It was: "You don't want to know. We can't say. We can't do justice. . . ." This is where language breaks down. It's where everything breaks down; it's the black hole of all values. There is no language adequate to it. It's either "Over there," or there's silence— which is what I had experienced. But as soon as he sees the *chazzan*, the cantor—

EC: The *schtickele chazzan*—

RG: Is that what they called him in the story? Is that what it was?

EC: I think you use that term in your story and also—

RG: Interesting, I had forgotten—

EC: I think you also use that term in *The Mind-Body Problem*—

RG: In *The Mind-Body Problem*, I remember; my father has been called a *schtickele chazzan*.

EC: Also some of the same names keep coming up. I was wondering about the name "Raizel," which appears in *Mind-Body* and the story "Raizel Kaidish"—

RG: My cousin who died was named Raizel.

EC: So that's a way of honoring her.

RG: Yes, I had toyed with calling my oldest daughter Raizel. I've always felt guilty that I hadn't—I didn't like the name and I didn't call her Raizel. When I had mentioned it to my father he was so happy, and then I didn't do it. So I name characters Raizel (laughs).

EC: And Renee—was that also, or is that Descartes?

RG: Well, Renee was Descartes, the mind part, the other side of me. (Pause). But the "over there," and that he (Sol) immediately recognizes the ashy color, which I remember of these people when I was a very little girl, these people who had a color which you didn't see; it was years later, but you didn't see the color of their skin was different. A grayness. I remember my cousin Zanvil, there was a grayness to them—

EC: Zanvil?

RG: Zanvil, who was ridden around on his white horse, the prince, it was a Hungarian name. You know where he used to work? When I was a student at Barnard there was a *Meal Mart* on the Upper West Side. You probably don't remember *Meal Mart* this Kosher take out—

EC: Sure, where I grew up in Cedarhurst of course we had a *Meal Mart*.

RG: (laughs) Okay. So there would be Zanvil who used to ride around on his white horse, and he worked there in white cap dishing out the stuffed cabbage. And I'd come see him all the time when I was at Barnard. And yet nobody dished out that stuffed cabbage with quite the flair.

EC: Well, you know that ladle was much like a riding crop . . .

RG: He'd make the customers feel as if he was deigning to serve them. It was very moving.

(Pause)

EC: Back to this issue of "over there" and the idea of a "hallowed ground" being such a part of you as an American Jew. I think it was Arthur Cohen who said that "American Jews are the Holocaust survivors who bear the scars without the wounds." I think it was his book *The Tremendum*. I'm wondering if you think this rings true in your own life's history, in your own writing. As you've said: how can you not try to represent the Holocaust, as a human being, let alone being an American writer acculturated in that world, being a Jewish American novelist. And yet realizing that writing about it is in some way to be treading on hallowed ground and to have to be so careful about that—

RG: Yes, it is a huge ethical problem, how you deal with it. There is a lot of Holocaust fiction, Holocaust literature which seems to identity with, that suggests that this is our identifying feature, that we are victims, that this is our history. And I'm not—

EC: Can you think of some that you're talking about?

RG: You don't want any particular names. Some of them are friends to tell you the truth, and I argue about this with them. I object to this. I don't agree with this. This is one aspect: it's not about our psyche, it's about them. It's not an essential defining feature of us that we're victims. We're something else. Perhaps it turns us into victims quite often. We are the perpetual outsiders, people who keep our own values and identities and refuse to merge. And also people who for whatever reason attract a lot of attention. I don't know why: there's an intensity, there's that life-lovingness of us that makes us very intense that makes us stand out quite often and attracts bad press, and worse . . . for whatever reason. You know it's a big issue why we attract the kind of attacks that we do. But you know what we are in ourselves: we need to do justice to that too. We do not love suffering. That's something we do not love. That is not a Jewish value at all—suffering. I don't want to celebrate our suffering.

EC: I feel often in Malamud's fiction, often you get the sense—although of course he has his non-Jewish character in *The Assistant*, Frank, suffering so damn much. He asks Morris: "Why do the Jews love suffering so much?"

RG: We don't want it, we're not going after it. Ask other people why we suffer so much, not us.

EC: Do you think that this aesthetic problem is one which is becoming less or more of a problem as we move further away from the Holocaust? In particular I'm thinking of writers who might be starting out today and not twenty years ago.

RG: It's hard to say.

EC: In the last twenty years that reticence which had overarched all of American culture has been exploded at this point. You can't open *The New York Times* without seeing three or four Holocaust-related stories every day. Does this make the aesthetic problems even more difficult?

RG: The Holocaust deniers which had come out had made people even more anxious to get the facts out and to do justice to the stories. Also, survivors are dying; our direct firsthand connection with the Holocaust will be gone. Some of the taboos and reticence have lifted . . . we have movies . . .

EC: Comedies—

RG: Comedies about the Holocaust. I don't know what to think about it all, part of me thinks that, well, good let all the world share in the experience. It shouldn't be just a Jewish experience. This is world history. This is a major, major event which showed us something extraordinary about human nature, and everybody should face up to it and try to deal with it. But I do feel that there's holy ground here and that we have to be careful and that we can't use this just as material. It's not just artistic material; it's too large. I mean suffering in general. This one is enormous. Maybe I feel it so keenly because I am Jewish, because there were these people passing through my life—cousin Zanvil and the others—so I feel it so strongly. But any large-scale human suffering: Can it be used toward artistic ends? Can you make what you will with it, do what you want, with your main priority being aesthetic? I don't think so. I'm very uneasy with that. It's a conflict. It's a huge conflict.

EC: And that comes through clearly in your writing, which does deal with the reticence, the hallowness upon which you do not want to tread. And yet these are qualities which I see throughout your fiction— the unresolvability of these conflicts: the mind-body problem. Light itself: is it particle or wave?

RG: Exactly, exactly.

EC: And these are issues which are basically irresolvable.

RG: Exactly. It's what it means to be human. There are things—you can shut yourself off from conflict by just shutting out the claims of various parts of life, and live an unconflicted life. But if you are open to everything, to the world, with claims coming at you from every part of life and the world, you are going to find irreconcilable conflict and you're going to be torn and that's what it means to be human.

EC: And you said, last evening, often times, that's what it means to be a Jew.

RG: (laughs) I think so. I believe—that's what I've come to—it's partly in self-justification because, you know, given my upbringing I can only say, as most of my family says about me, "I am a very bad Jew." (We all laugh). So part of this might be my way of dealing with this, self-justification, to try to understand what it means to be a Jew, and what it means to be a good Jew, to be open to life in such a way that none of the claims are shut out to be fully in love and engaged with life and therefore in conflict. And that's what I believe it means to be a good Jew.

EC: Your story "Mindel Gittel" ends on a note of irresolvability as well. One thing about your writing is that there are never any easy moral answers. You don't pick up a Rebecca Goldstein novel to be easily told: "What am I going to think now?" There's always a component where the reader must do that work, to try to think for one's self and perhaps to never come to a definitive conclusion.

In the end of "Mindel Gittel," as a result of the Zweigels not telling their daughter Melody (Mindel Gittel in Yiddish) about the Holocaust, either because of their inability to deal with it and talk about it or because of issues of Americanization and not wanting to burden her with that history, as a result she assimilates and marries a rather un-Lieberman-like Senator's son.

RG: Yes. Well put.

EC: So my reading of that story is that transmission of Holocaust history, or actual witnessing or testifying to the Holocaust, is very much— again you're the logician here, you're the philosopher, so please forgive me if I mess up the logic—so since they, the Zweigels, do not witness to the Holocaust and their daughter assimilates, therefore one may conclude that testifying to the Holocaust is an act of Jewish continuity.

RG: Well her father, Mindel Gittel's (Melody's) father, had been a scholar. So encased in that almost corpselike figure—he was the walking dead—all of Jewish culture, Jewish texts. That was what he didn't transmit. He couldn't transmit it through the fire. I mean he had been through the fire. He was a corpse basically. My feeling was that it was the culture, the continuity of what was created at Yavneh, when we were expelled. At Yavneh, where the first Yeshiva was created, we established a culture that we would be able to carry with us wherever we went. Wherever we got kicked out we could take that with us because it was internal. It was internal to him on the night of Chanukah that his daughter is born and survives and his wife survives. He quotes from the Zohar—that's what's not transmitted.

(Goldstein, overcome by emotion, asks to stop recording.)

RG: Think logic, think logic Rebecca.

EC: Is there a way that mathematics and philosophy itself—you mentioned "think logic"—is there a way that you went into philosophy as a way to get answers to these inconclusive questions, particularly Jewish questions, Holocaust issues?

RG: Yes. You've said that in my novels and short stories there's never any easy or real consolation. Iris Murdoch said somewhere that "False consolation is bad art." And that rang so true to me. Art is supposed to open you up to the world. It's not supposed to close you off with false easy answers: that's morally and aesthetically wrong. I've spent most of my life thinking about things that are irreconcilable, and if they're good questions there are no easy answers and you want to do justice to that. I do love to sit down and solve a math problem or a logic problem—I mean I do it for fun, to just solve a problem where there is an answer. Just that click of an answer locking into place; it's such a pleasure. I think I do. One of the great joys I get is the clarity of math and logic. It's clear, it's there, you don't argue with it when you've reached your conclusion. Objectivity. It's wonderful; it's a good balance.

EC: In another short story of yours, "The Legacy of Raizel Kaidish"—

RG: Yeah, it was the first piece of fiction I ever wrote.

EC: Really, how old were you?

RG: I was an assistant professor at Barnard (laughing), so I was I guess twenty-five.

EC: Had that appeared somewhere before it was published in *Strange Attractors* in 1992?

RG: It's very interesting, what happened when I was teaching a course on ethics, and I was making the claim to my students that rules often don't do justice to the ethical situation, that you often need to have the narrative, you have to have the story. A rule-oriented ethics is not fine-tuned enough.

EC: This was at Barnard?

RG: Yeah, this was at Barnard. I was trying to think of a situation that I could use to explain this to my students, and that's how that story came to me. I was trying to solve this pedagogical problem in a class of ethics. Of course the Holocaust preoccupation came out in that story. Was it published anywhere? Yes, I think it was *Commentary*. And this is interesting: the fiction editor at the time was going to publish it, and she said, "Of course the story's true?" And I said: "No. No, it's a story." And she said: "Well, I saw you're a Professor of Philosophy, and I thought this was true." And I said, "If it were true I wouldn't write it. It would be such a betrayal of my parents, because of the big secret of the mother. I would never write that if it were true. I would keep the family secret." And then she said, I remember this, she said: "It undermines the integrity of the story if it's not true." And they ended up not publishing it.

EC: She meant it had to be autobiographical?

RG: Yeah autobiographical, yeah.

EC: So it didn't really matter whether or not it had actually occurred; she needed it to be autobiographical?

RG: Yeah. So ultimately it wasn't published there. It was published in a now defunct journal called *New Traditions*. It was in its inaugural volume.

EC: Do you think that story would be rejected today on those grounds?

RG: I don't think so.

EC: Do you think the rules of the game have changed?

RG: Yes, I think the rules of the game have changed. I think that because it was a Holocaust topic, that's why Marianne Magid, she's now passed on, rejected it. And that story has been anthologized more than any of my stories, the *Oxford Book of Jewish Fiction*,[2] etc.

EC: Didn't you say that you were trying to write that story to teach your students an ethical dilemma? And of course you've taught your readers the same moral principle: you can't draw easy moral conclusions. It's one thing to be on the outside of a situation and quite another to be on the inside. When I finished reading that story, I was left feeling *My God I want to blame and*—

RG: Condemn her.

EC: —yes, and feel contempt for her and her actions. Instead I was left feeling how utterly, utterly impossible it is to do that after reading the last line of the story and you find out what has happened. Not only that but I felt somehow morally complicit in that crime itself in a way: that I, as a reader, have somehow been party to this betrayal in my own thinking.

RG: Exactly. No easy answers. I mean the last line is "She asks my forgiveness." I mean I felt incredible empathy for this mother who yes, if I had heard this tale of a betrayal of this sort, yes of course I would condemn this woman, and then—

EC: An interesting aesthetic question arises from this story: is the impossibility of condemning this mother a result of the subhuman conditions that the Nazi victims lived in during the Holocaust? Or perhaps another way to ask this is that could you imagine writing a story which could prove this ethical law, or prove this theory, without it having been a Holocaust story?

RG: That's a very good question: I think of course, yes one could. It says something about me, my history, my psyche that when I looked for a situation like that I went straight to the Holocaust. Sure. Sure. I think actually in my new novel (*Properties of Light*) I was playing around a lot with that idea, because things were done there that are terrible things, that seem to be acts of betrayal and yet I certainly was sympathetic to all the characters, and I hope the readers are too—

EC: Particularly the daughter?

RG: (Laughing) Particularly the daughter, but all of them Samuel, all of them, Justin, all of them.

EC: Your story "The Legacy of Raizel Kaidish" being rejected for its not being autobiographical brings up the question of just how much of your work is autobiographical, if any?

RG: None of it is straight autobiography. There's only one instance where I used a real person, and that was in *The Mind-Body Problem*; Renee's father is very much my father. You know I wrote it after he died. I wanted to get him down as a way of honoring him. And people say—just to explain—people often wonder how would a person like my father have a daughter like Renee? Unlikely. So I don't know if psychologically it makes all that much sense. I mean my father would have a daughter like me, or like my sisters, not a daughter like Renee.

EC: Yes.

RG: So that was the most autobiographical: I gave her my father; I sent her to Princeton; I sent her to Barnard—I mean she studies very different kinds of things at Princeton, her experience is different. When I was a student at Princeton, there was graduate student who studied the wrong things, for Princeton. You know she did that kind of mushy continental stuff, and she was given a horrible time. I did very technical stuff. You know I was a happy little graduate student there, and they loved me—until I wrote *The Mind-Body Problem* (laughs), but . . . it's kind of conditional thinking: What if? What if I was in that situation?

What if I studied the wrong things? What if I lost all my confidence? Etcetera, etcetera. So it is autobiographical in that sense, but also auto-biographical in that it deals with my preoccupations which come out of my history. (Pause) That's true for all writers.

EC: Going back to the issue of the impossibility of drawing easy moral conclusions from your stories. Can we talk for a moment about the ways in which, for example, "The Legacy of Raizel Kaidish," or much of your fiction for that matter, deals with the impossibility of knowing truth. There is much made within poststructural literary theory and continental philosophy that there is no such thing as an objective truth. I'm thinking of some of the excesses of Derrida's theory of Decon-struction, which posits the ultimate unknowability of objective truth. Deconstruction suggests that due to the subjective nature of language itself we must question and mistrust any notion of objective truth. Some of your fiction deals with this issue. I'm thinking of your satiric story in *Strange Attractors*, about an academic conference—

RG: "The Predicate of Existence," that one?

EC: Right. Where this philosopher is playing a joke on his colleagues and giving a false paper. It came out in 1995. You know Alan Sokal, the NYU Physicist?

RG: Yeah. Do you know that I'm actually footnoted in that paper?

EC: Really?

RG: As one of the jokes. My husband is a physicist, and he knows Alan, and we had actually read that paper[3] early on, and we were sworn to secrecy. I remember—I don't know how it got published—my husband gave it to me and after reading the first paragraph I said: "Well this is a joke, of course," and he said: "Well yeah, it's a joke!" I remember Alan say-ing, he had given it to us because he thought we would be amused. He was worried that some people wouldn't catch the joke so he put in the paper as a footnote: "As proved in Rebecca Goldstein's *The Mind-Body Problem*," thinking well they would know that this is a novel. And they still didn't get it! But you can look it up. I'm there; I'm very proud of that. (Pause).

I'm a big believer in objective truth, and I think that the argument that there is no objective truth collapses, because isn't that an objec-tive truth, that there is no truth? I mean, it's very hard to make out the case. You argue for the nonvalidity of argument? There's something inconsistent there. I think that it's real hard. I think that it keeps us honest. I think that it's a good thing there is objective truth. That's our standard; that's what we're matching our wits against. It's humbling because it's huge, it's hard to get to, it's inaccessible, it's so huge that we get conflicting information, we can't make sense of it, but that doesn't mean we give up on the idea of objectivity because otherwise we are the measure of all things, and I don't want us to be the measure. We're not up to that. We're not up to that.

EC: How important is that objective truth in your own work, in terms of your being a Jewish American writer, or in writing a story dealing with the Holocaust, in dealing with history, with a capital H. This is history; it can't just be pushed away.

RG: Exactly. You see it's so morally pernicious to think that we can mold the truth, we can fabricate it according to our social needs. No! I mean, things happened. They objectively happened. They happened in history. People suffered. People did good things. People did bad things. That's part of our reality and we have to be true to reality.

EC: What do you feel is your obligation as a writer?

RG: First thing, we do have to keep them interested. There are the tricks to the trade to keep people interested, and I have to keep myself interested. I see tremendous moral value in literature. The imagination, fiction, is really belittled in our day. People want "The Truth"—nonfiction. Even a novel that is based on the truth will have much more marketability, because people don't respect the truth of literature anymore, and the moral lessons of literature anymore, what there is to be gotten out of it. And I think this is *such* a danger; it is leading to a diminishment of our interior life, of our imagination. Our imagination is our way of understanding other people. We have to imagine our way into the lives of other people. We know our own interior, but to get a sense of other people takes a tremendous amount of imagination, and the imagination can be strengthened and trained, and literature is one of the major ways of doing that. I actually think it is a very high calling. I think true literature makes you understand others and have access to the psyches and souls of others, and cry for other beings. You cry for other people when you're involved in a book, and it gets you inside another, a character, in a way that film and plays, as much as I love them—and I am a total film and theater nut—can't do. They can't get you into the interior, so you actually are—it's an amazing thing—you are actually feeling the feelings of a character of another person.

EC: When does that break down in fiction, become an impossibility?

RG: I don't think it ever should be. I think that's the challenge of a writer, to bring your readers in with you into a different perspective, a different world, living a different life. It's an amazing source of moving people, informing them, it's a sort of prolegomena onto ethics. It's not ethics itself. Ethics is played out in the real world where your own self-interests are pitted against the interests of others. That's where ethics is played out, but there can be no ethics unless you have sense of the reality of other people, and that is one of the things that you get through literature. So I think it is a very high calling, and I think that the diminishment of literature, of the value of literature in our times, the diminishment of literature, the shrinking of it, the lack of ambition and lack of interiority and richness, I think it's not just a cultural problem. I think it's an ethical problem. I am deeply, deeply worried about it. I'm deeply worried that we have a generation of kids growing up who don't love literature, who are playing video games and don't love literature. I think this is a real diminishment of the psyche—

EC: The ability to empathize—

RG:—the ability to empathize, to imagine your way into another's life, to feel the reality of another's life as real as yours; that it's worthy, it's needing of respect. That their claims are real. And that is what literature does for you. It's a real problem. That's what I try to do in my work. That's my ultimate goal.

EC: This diminishment, do you think that this has to do with the history of the twentieth century, with the rupture at the center of the century just passed?

RG: No. It could be. It's been so tremendously traumatic, but it's a combination I think. The new technology, the preponderance of images, we live in an age of images and—

EC: Yes, the profusion of images in fiction I feel affects your own very careful use of images in your work, particularly in relation to something hallowed. I'm thinking of those stories of yours which do deal with the Holocaust. You're very careful to not use images in a hackneyed way. You often don't even use images at all. For example, in your story "Mindel Gittel" you use the phrase "over there." The only image you use, I think, might be in relation to the color of the survivor's skin which you refer to as parchment or ashen—

RG: That's right.

EC:—that's as close as you'll get. In actuality, as I'm reading your story, of course, that's all that you need, as the great masters knew. I'm reminded, in a very different context, I'm thinking of Chekhov's short stories, where he will lead his readers up to the bedroom door, and then silence, he stops.

RG: Exactly. The scariest story I've ever read is Henry James's "The Turn of the Screw." So scary because it's not said; he leaves it to the imagination. You know, credit your readers with having some imagination. Unfortunately, given our times, you worry about that, how much imagination your readers will have, because there's been a real diminishing of imagination. My kind of writer, I depend on the resources of my readers. I'm asking a lot of my readers. I'm not going to lay everything out for them. I'm asking them to do a lot of work. So it's chancy. (laughs) But why this is going on? I don't know. There's a new tribalism afoot in our world, primitive tribalism. Also a sign of tremendous lack of imagination and empathy for the other: just retreat back into your own kind, demonize the other. The world's blowing up with this stuff, and everyone should go sit down and read a good novel about the other, the ultimate other, and understand we're all human.

NOTES

INTRODUCTION

1. In addition to the two parts of the Talmud, there are two distinct versions of the Talmud that evolved over the centuries: The Babylonian Talmud (Talmud Bavli) and the Jerusalem Talmud (Talmud Yerushalmi). Although the Jerusalem Talmud is important for Jewish legal scholars, since the Middle Ages the Babylonian Talmud has almost exclusively taken precedence and it is to that work that I refer when I use the term "Talmud" in this study.

2. See Jeffrey L. Rubenstein's *Rabbinic Stories* for an illuminating discussion on this Talmudic passage.

3. The eleventh *Siyum HaShas*, which took place on March 1, 2005, might serve as inspiration for the perennially last-place New York Knicks and Madison Square Garden's management: if only the Knicks studied the Talmud, perhaps they too could sell out the Garden.

4. *American Talmud* will hopefully draw attention to this phenomenon.

5. In his preface to *Negative Liberties: Morrison, Pynchon, and the Problem of Liberal Ideology*, Cyrus Patell suggests that perhaps our notions of Emersonian individualism are misplaced to begin with: "The story told by Emersonian liberalism is an idealized narrative, an abstraction in which a great many variables are held constant" (xviii). In relation to Jewish American literature this further erodes Shechner's argument.

6. Actually, the *real* Sholom Aleichem (not the kitsch version familiar to an assimilated American audience) has had a vast influence over Jewish writers in America. "If I Were a Rich Man" is the subverted Broadway version of Sholom Aleichem, and does no justice to his caustic and deeply ironic Jewish humor; for example, Tevya, Shalom Aleichem's dairyman, can pun on scripture with the most learned rabbi.

7. Lurianic Kabbalah has influenced numerous Jewish American writers. See chapter 2 where I argue that Henry Roth's career follows a Lurianic trajectory.

8. Roth, on his deathbed at age 89, was reportedly still making revisions on the final manuscript of *Mercy of a Rude Stream*.

9. See chapter 6 for a complete discussion of Roth's *Mercy of a Rude Stream*.

10. Walter Benjamin, Gershom Scholem's close friend, makes a similar argument in his essay "The Task of the Translator" in *Illuminations* page 69.

11. Lit: the Hebrew Bible. An acronym standing for *Torah*, *Neviim*, and *Ketubim*: the Five Books of Moses, the Books of the Prophets, and the Sacred Scriptures.

12. At least two full-length studies have recently blamed multiculturalism for the marginalization of Jewish American fiction. See Andrew Furman's monograph *Contemporary Jewish American Writers and the Multicultural Dilemma: Return of the Exiled*. Syracuse University Press, 2000. See also, *Insider/Outsider: American Jews and Multiculturalism*. Eds. David Biale, Michael Galshinsky, and Susannah Heschel, University of California Press, 1998.

13. Steve Stern's most recent novel, published by Viking, is titled *The Angel of Forgetfulness* (2005). Soon after the novel garnered superlative reviews *The New York Times* published an article on the "obscure" Stern. The article was titled: "He's a Literary Darling Looking for Dear Readers." Stern has been publishing exceptional novels for over a quarter of a century, and Harold Bloom, after reading an advanced copy of *The Angel of Forgetfulness* had this to say about Stern: ". . . he has gusto, exuberance, panache; this is immensely readable and vibrant." However, during the same interview Bloom, genuinely surprised by the brilliance of the novel and that he had never before heard of Steve Stern, asked: "Who is he?"

14. Hirsch's concept is based upon a verse from *Pirke Avot* (*The Ethics of the Fathers*) 2:2 that is translated by Moshe Lieber as follows: "Torah study is good together with an occupation, for exertion of them both makes sin forgotten" (67). Although the *mishna* refers to an occupation or the earning of a living, Hirsch interprets this more widely to include Western culture as well.

15. This community is vividly portrayed in Henry Roth's second novel *Mercy of a Rude Stream*, discussed in chapters 1 and 6.

CHAPTER 1. HENRY ROTH'S FIRST NOVEL

1. Wisse's Jewish literary canon contains only a handful of novels written by American Jews.

2. As discussed in the previous chapter, *Tanach* is an acronym created by taking the first letter of the: *Torah* (the Pentateuch), *Neviim* (the Prophets), and *Ketubim* (the Writings), which collectively make up the 24 volumes of the Jewish Bible.

3. For example, see remarks by Ethan Place and Bernard Sherman quoted in *New Essays on Call It Sleep*. Ed. Hana Wirth-Nesher, page 54.

CHAPTER 2. REFLECTING THE WORLD

1. I mean to distinguish a set of circumstances within a fictional world that corresponds on a surface level to historical truth. An example would be a

novel that makes explicit use of historical data. Generally, Malamud side-stepped the narratological and representational problems associated with a historical novel through his use of allegory or symbolism, although a noted exception to this would be *The Fixer*, which could easily be read as a histori-cal novel since Yakov Bok's ordeal is largely based on the blood libel trial of Mendel Beiliss. *The Assistant* is a perfect example of Malamud's allegorical or symbolic use of history in a novel since Morris Bober's grocery store functions as a decaying tomb or pseudo death camp within which, at one point in the novel (see pp. 214–15), he is almost gassed to death.

2. Berger's thesis opens new approaches for analyzing Jewish American literature. In this chapter I follow Berger's lead in distinguishing genuine from spurious Holocaust literature. However, while analyzing Malamud's work, instead of judging the "authenticity" of his Holocaust witnessing I account for the relative "spurious" or "inauthentic" nature of his marginally Jewish characters and whether they can properly represent the historical real-ity of the Holocaust. Additionally, in regards to Malamud, I refer not only to Berger's use of *covenant*, but also to his use of the term *Orthodoxy*, allowing any manifestation of traditional Judaism to signify a nod toward a "covenan-tal" orientation.

3. In the context of Holocaust literature Malamud's statement has the unfortunate effect of diluting the impact of the Holocaust: clearly all men were not Jews in the context of the Final Solution. However, Malamud's uni-versalizing system might allow us, just for a moment, to view Malamud as a postmodern writer. Philip Brian Harper has observed that postmodern humanity feels the sense of alienation and despair that was historically an eth-nic identifier in modern American culture. Harper suggests "marginalized groups' experience of decenteredness is largely an unacknowledged factor in the 'general' postmodern condition" (4). Thus Malamud's appeal to a univer-salized Jewish identity resonates in today's alienated postmodern culture, and might help explain the renewed interest in Malamud's oeuvre. Of course, Malamud's brilliant prose might have more to do with the continued interest in his work than does any postmodern theory.

4. Along this theme, Earl Rovit has posited the theory that Malamud cre-ates his stories backward "beginning with his final climactic image and then manipulating his characters into the appropriate dramatic poses which will contribute to the total significance of that image" (6). If so, Malamud began "The Lady of the Lake" with an image of a scarred and tattooed breast of a Holocaust survivor and attempted to wring every bit of horror from Freeman's abandoning his Jewish identity.

5. Baudrillard considers this a natural progression of all images and high-lights the playfulness of the postmodern flexibility of images, indeed all lan-guage. However, within Holocaust literature, and its need for historical accu-racy, Baudrillard's theory acquires more serious consequences.

6. Malamud's misuse of this image while distorting the genuine Holo-caustal image hasn't yet reached the level of pure simulacrum. Malamud's writing, I would argue, corresponds to Baudrillard's second phase, where images have begun to become distorted on their way toward a new meaning and separate identity. A first stage in Baudrillard's system would be the non-fictional firsthand accounts by the survivors who witnessed the Holocaust. It should be noted that despite the veracity of first-generational eyewitness accounts of the Holocaust, due to its very nature, many of the images and rep-resentations of the Holocaust seem to defy understanding. Thus in his pref-ace to *Survival in Auschwitz*, Primo Levi felt the need to state: "It seems to me unnecessary to add that none of the facts are invented" (10).

7. Examples of Baudrillard's fourth stage, in which an image becomes a pure simulacrum, abound in contemporary Jewish American fiction. One example should suffice to illustrate this trend, which Baudrillard calls "nat-ural," but within the context of the Holocaust takes on a sinister, almost revi-sionist, quality. In Pearl Abraham's 1998 novel *Giving Up America*, on a Fri-day night with a yarmulke on his head, Daniel, an Orthodox Jewish male protagonist, debates whether to start an affair with his secretary, a non-Jewish Miss America contestant. He decides to have dinner with her and rips his yarmulke off his head as the omniscient narrator proclaims: "It was a stamp, a yellow star, marking him a Jew. . . . With the yarmulke off he was free" (207).

Once a Holocaust image has become a simulacrum, it can be used to rep-resent something antithetical to its original reality. In this case the image of the Yellow Star of David—a symbol of Nazi persecution—comes to represent a yarmulke, a covenantal symbol of Jewish Orthodoxy and tradition. By 1998, in Abraham's work, Baudrillard's simulacrum has become complete: Jewish American novelists have reached the point where the images used to describe the Holocaust and traditional Jewish rituals have become interchangeable.

I do not mean to imply a causal relationship between Malamud's misuse of a Holocaust tattoo in 1958 to Abraham's disturbing use of a Holocaust image (the Yellow Star of David) in 1998. However, Abraham's misuse of a Holocaust image would have been more difficult without the denaturing work accomplished by an earlier generation of Jewish American writers who repre-sented the Holocaust within their fiction.

8. Robert Alter has remarked on Malamud's misreading and misrepre-sentation of Jewish history within his short stories and novels. He argues: "European Jewry, even in the ghettos, often was, and felt itself to be, much more than a trapped group of 'half-starved, bearded prisoners'" (35). Yet despite this correct assessment of Malamud's distorted reading and represen-tation of Jewish history, Alter exonerates Malamud in his next sentence: "His-torical accuracy, however, is beside the point, for what is relevant to Mala-mud's literary achievement is that an aspect of Jewish experience, isolated and magnified, has afforded him the means of focusing in an image his own vision

of the human condition" (35). However, when dealing with the Holocaust, as Malamud does in "The Lady of the Lake," and "The German Refugee," historical accuracy should never be "beside the point."

9. If, as Robert Alter has argued, "Malamud's central metaphor for Jewishness is imprisonment" (33) it would appear that traditional, covenantal Judaism is the imprisoner—or in "The German Refugee" the executioner.

10. This loss of imagistic power may be the result of Malamud's attempt in "The German Refugee" to historicize his symbolic Jewish characters while universalizing their message. In so doing he oversteps the limits of his representative power. As Berel Lang suggests: "For many texts that involve the 'Final Solution,' the problem is not to determine *whether* that event is their subject but to assess it 'representation as' their subject—especially as they reach or pass its representative limits." Lang continues: "I would argue in respect to literary representation that the force of the historical limits that apply is compounded as the constraints (and so, risks) on historical representation are joined by constraints that hold specifically for artistic representation" (315).

CHAPTER 3. BELLOW'S SHORT FICTION

1. Although Bellow was approximately Joseph's age when he wrote *Dangling Man*, in his later work Bellow almost always writes from the perspective of an older man. For examples see: *Henderson the Rain King, Herzog,* and *Mr. Sammler's Planet* to name just a few.

2. See Lillian Kremer's article on this short story reprinted in *Small Planets*, Ed. Gloria Cronin.

3. Bellow's choosing to publish his first outwardly Orthodox short story in *Playboy* magazine is an irony that should not go unmentioned.

4. This "backlash" from the left, which may have begun with the publication of *Mr. Sammler's Planet*, perhaps reached it's high point in 1987 after Bellow wrote the forward to his friend Allan Bloom's bestseller *The Closing of the American Mind*, a book at the center of the late eighties culture wars which raged well into the 1990s.

5. An example of the leftist establishment who felt betrayed by Bellow's scathing critique of the excesses of the sixties counterculture revolution portrayed at the beginning of *Mr. Sammler's Planet*, when Sammler is heckled during a Columbia University lecture, would be John J. Clayton's postscript to *Saul Bellow: In Defense of Man*. Clayton writes: "Saul Bellow, like Spiro Agnew and George Wallace, is disgusted with the lack of law and order in America" (254). Clayton continues: "although Bellow and Sammler are not identical, Bellow's own politics are a flight from contamination, a flight from guilt associated with the desire for rebellion" (259).

Interestingly, numerous left-leaning critics similarly excoriated Philip Roth after his devastating portrayal of sixties counterculture radicalism in *American Pastoral*. Critics seemed particularly disturbed by the figure of Merry the suburban, teenage, Jewish bomb maker. Although a comparison of Bellow and Roth's political views would make for a lively, and important, literary essay in its own right, such a comparison is beyond the purview of this present chapter.

6. By "overlooked" I mean in comparison to his novels.

7. *Dangling Man* is almost universally thought of as Bellow's first novel; however in light of my study of Bellow's shorter works, it might be thought of as a novella.

8. I know several novelists who would be more than willing to debate Podhoretz on this issue.

9. In keeping with the genetic theme of the story, Bellow (and Dr. Braun) suggests that this emotional hyperbole is a genetic component of old-world Jews. Speaking of Isaac's sister, the narrator reports: "Hyperbole was Tina's greatest weakness. They were all like that. The mother had bred it in them" (62). Bellow exploits this "genetic disposition" of the Jewish character type in the plot of "The Old System" which, soon after Isaac's consummation of the business deal, takes an operatic turn.

10. Bellow's 1960s idea of material "rise" without a commensurate "loss" of spiritual values is in marked contrast to an earlier generation of Jewish American immigrant story. Perhaps most famously, Abraham Cahan's 1917 novel *The Rise of David Levinsky* is the classic example of a Jewish immigrant trading tradition and Orthodoxy for material wealth in the new world.

11. Tina's membership in the "old system way of doing things" is signified by her operatic "last stand" and her comical attraction to emotionally drenching scenes—the exact opposite of Bellow's WASPish businessman symbolized by Ilkington and his sterilized office.

12. Although containing important insights into Bellow's political ideas, this interview is almost laughable in its extreme cultural divide between interviewer and subject. On numerous occasions Bellow feels the need to explain ideas he would much rather assume a general knowledge of on the part of his interviewer. Bellow's attempt to explain basic concepts to his interviewer only leads to further misunderstandings and frustration. At one memorable moment the interviewer eavesdrops on Bellow's phone conversation with his son and speculates on the overheard conversation. The resulting interview, perhaps inadvertently, is an excellent, and humorous, introduction to Bellow's political and cultural thought concerning America and Israel in the early 1990s. Misspellings and grammatical errors are as they appear in the original publication of the interview.

13. The long cylindrical water tank also physically resembles a Torah scroll.

14. A famous section of the Haggadah, recited on Passover, called the "Arbah Banim," or four sons, presents a parable of four "types" of Jews sitting around the seder meal. The *rasha*, the evil son, is the one who asks: "What are these rituals which you Jews partake in this evening?" By separating himself from his people he is called evil. While I cannot say with certainty that Bellow was aware of this parallel, it would seem to be highly unlikely that this equivalency was merely coincidental.

15. Bellow has spoken about how much he enjoyed writing "The Old System." In addition to "The Old System" being the most "Jewish" of all Bellow's stories, it also has numerous biographical elements. One biographical example would be the parallels between Bellow's own birth story and the story told of Dr. Braun's birth in "The Old System." In his biography of Bellow, James Atlas, although he does not indicate where he gets this biographical information, retells Bellow's own birth story:

> On the morning of his birth—or so Bellow later claimed—one of the Gameroff boys was dispatched to find the bibulous obstetrician. "Sam made the rounds of the saloons until finally he found him, slumped over the bar counter, dead drunk. He dragged the doctor outside, cranked up his Model T, and drove him home to my poor mother, who'd been in Canada two years and couldn't speak a word of English or French. There she was, in the midst of labor, being tended to by a dead-drunk French-Canadian who could barely stand up. (8)

The almost identical birthing stories, Bellow's own and Dr. Braun's, draw attention to the parallels between Dr. Braun, who is used as a framing device for the story and as an obvious Bellow stand-in, and the elusive author himself.

16. Few people in attendance that day in 1987 could have foreseen Bellow's remarkable productivity (both personally as well as professionally) well into his eighties. In 2000, in addition to publishing a major novel, *Ravelstein*, at the age of eighty-five Bellow also fathered a daughter.

17. Most people referred to the Lubavitcher Rebbe, who died in 1994, simply as "The Rebbe." Not only has "The Rebbe" proved to be a figure revered by many of his followers as the messiah, but he has also lived quite a fruitful afterlife in fictional representations. As we will see in chapter 5, Allegra Goodman bases her *Paradise Park*'s Rabbi Bialystoker on "The Rebbe" as well.

18. Rashi (Rabbi Shlomo Yitzchaki) was born in Troyes, France, and lived from 1040 to 1105. Rashi was the most famous of the medieval commentators on both the Hebrew Bible and the Talmud. "Rashi's commentary on the Bible was unique. His concern was for every word in the text which needed elaboration or explanation. Moreover, he used the fewest words possi-

ble in his commentaries" (*http://www.jewishvirtuallibrary.org/jsource/biography/rashi.html*). Rashi would explain the etymology of numerous Hebrew words for his French-speaking students, and his comment on Gen. 32:33 is a paradigmatic example of his etymological and "close-reading," almost New Critical, mode of criticism and interpretation.

19. This is not unlike the great Yiddish writer Sholom Aleichem who has Tevya the dairyman almost constantly (and often incorrectly) alluding to biblical stories as he makes his meager living selling milk street to street. Much like Rashi before him, Sholom Aleichem could count on a shared knowledge between writer and reader and confidently assume that his readers would understand the biblical allusions as well as understand the humor that resulted when Tevya would mangle a scriptural phrase.

20. Many years ago, having grown weary of constantly being compared to Bernard Malamud and Philip Roth, Saul Bellow referred to "the big three" Jewish writers as "the Hart, Schaffner, and Marx" of Jewish American Literature. With the death of Malamud in 1986, most critics would agree that Cynthia Ozick has assumed the role of Schaffner (or is it Marx?) in this triumvirate; Bellow's death in 2005 has created a new vacancy.

21. Bellow is of course punning on the word "suffocation," an ironic reference to the gas chambers, referred to in the next passage, which killed by suffocating (and poisoning) its victims.

CHAPTER 4. REBECCA GOLDSTEIN

1. See Appendix for a complete transcription of this interview.

CHAPTER 5. FOUR QUESTIONS
FOR ALLEGRA GOODMAN

1. So have Jewish American filmmakers, i.e., Woody Allen in *Crimes and Misdemeanors*.

2. Indeed, Allen's biography reads like a bad Jewish joke; his face has become synonymous with a certain extremely un-American (read: unmasculine) type, not unlike Hemingway's Robert Cohen from *The Sun Also Rises*.

3. Goodman names her character Miriam, Ed's Orthodox feminist daughter, after Moses's sister in the Bible. The biblical Miriam has recently been "rediscovered" by Orthodox Jewish feminists who have named a ritual wine cup in her honor. However, Goodman may have had ironic intentions in naming Ed's newly Orthodox daughter Miriam since in "The Four Questions" she is mostly seen as an angry and selfish representative of Orthodoxy. Miriam does not share any insights or *divrei Torah* at the seder, all she brings to the table is bitterness and hostility.

4. Andrew Furman is the exception to this trend of Jewish American crit-
ics ignoring Israel. Furman devoted a full-length monograph to this topic:
*Israel through the Jewish-American Imagination: A Survey of Jewish-American
Literature on Israel, 1928–1995* (State University of New York Press), 1997.

5. Goodman has also previously satirized Lubavitcher Chasidim in her
first collection of stories, *Total Immersion.*

6. A book by David Berger, *The Rebbe, the Messiah, and the Scandal of
Orthodox Indifference*, is the first in-depth study of this fascinating (and
troubling) movement toward messianic fervor among the Lubavitcher
Chasidim.

7. See Goldstein's first novel (discussed in chapter 4) *The Mind-Body
Problem* and Englander's *For the Relief of Unbearable Urges.*

8. Goodman's means of differentiating between *goyish* Cloisters and
Jewish Washington Heights is highly ironic. Goodman names her Washington Heights characters as members of the Kirshner clan, a fictional name
that corresponds to the real-life Washington Heights Jewish community of
German refugees who followed the lead of Rabbi Breuer, their "Rav" who
left Frankfurt am Main soon after Kristallnacht and brought almost his
entire *kehillah* (community) to safety in New York where they settled in
Washington Heights. In the early 1950s the Breuer community began
spending their summers in Tannersville, a small town in upstate New York
and the fictional setting for most of *Kaaterskill Falls.* Although in her novel
Goodman changes the name Tannersville to Kaaterskill, in *Kaaterskill Falls*
there is no doubt about the attempt at verisimilitude; Goodman's details are
generally exact. For example, Goodman describes a character driving up to
Kaaterskill for *shabbos* as getting off the New York State Thruway (I-87) at
exit 20 before switching to route 23A, all roads that corresponds to actual
New York places.

Despite this exactitude in terms of setting in regards to her Orthodox
German Jewish characters, whom Goodman portrays as being anti-art, in my
own experience within many of the German Jewish homes of Tannersville
(Kaaterskill), far from there being a dearth of art, a visitor would find sculp-
tures and paintings as in any other community. In the case of the German
Jewish community perhaps even more so due to their intense love affair with
High German culture and art.

9. Numerous reviewers assumed *Chasidic* and *Orthodox* were synonymous,
a misnomer which no doubt would outrage Goodman's Orthodox (but decidedly un-Chasidic) German Jewish characters.

10. Ironically, this lack of verisimilitude was true back in 1998 when
Kaaterskill Falls was published. As *American Talmud* went to press in 2007,
Goodman's Orthodox characters might be able to eat a Hebrew National hot
dog while answering to a "higher *halachic* authority": Hebrew National is now
under the kosher supervision of Triangle K.

CHAPTER 6. HENRY ROTH'S SECOND NOVEL

1. Several editions of Roth's first novel *Call It Sleep* are for sale in the Tenement Museum gift shop, however, in fashion with the 'Disneyification" of twenty-first-century New York City, no copies of *Mercy* are for sale.

2. *Pidyon haben* is a redemption ceremony which is performed after a firstborn child is a son. This ceremony began as a response to the "special status" of the firstborn in biblical society. Rabbi Joseph Telushkin explains this tradition in the following manner: "In Jewish life, a firstborn son (one who is both male and the first child born to his mother) is supposed to be dedicated to God (Exodus 13:1–2), and to perform religious services for the priests (*Kohanim*). On the thirty-first day after the child's birth, however, the father can pay a priest five silver shekels (see Numbers 18:16; today five dollars in silver coins is generally used) to have the child released from this obligation" (*Jewish Literarcy* 672). In his curious use of the term "redeem" in the quoted passage from *Call It Sleep*, Albert might be referring to the *pidyon haben* ceremony since David is presumambly Genya's firstborn son. When we recognize this veiled reference to the *pidyon haben* ceremony, coming relatively early in the novel, we are in a better position to understand Roth's foreshadowing a major plot element of the later sections of *Call It Sleep*—David's obsession with his paternity. It is also interesting to note that this idea of redemption by coins (in *Call It Sleep* with pennies substituted for silver dollars or shekels) takes on major importance in the novel and it will be discussed extensively later in this chapter.

3. The role of *shabbos goy* is an old and noble job, one that has occupied many prominent non-Jews over the years. Pope John Paul II has written about his being used as a shabbos goy in the small Polish Village of his youth when his family rented an apartment from a Jewish family. Striking a slightly different note, the writer Steve Stern assures me with all confidences that when he grew up in Memphis, Tennessee, his neighbors, a prominent "Pinch" family, used a well-mannered youth named Elvis Presley as their *shabbos goy*. For those still interested in the subject, although there is no mention of Elvis, there has been an excellent and exhaustive study written on the topic: *The Shabbes Goy: A Study in Halakhic Flexibility*, by Jacob Katz, Jewish Publication Society, 1989.

4. *Muktzah* is a broad term which literally means "set apart." An object which is not fit for use on the Sabbath and Festivals is considered *muktzah* and it is forbidden to use or carry such an object. Since the Sabbath is a day of rest one must avoid doing work of any kind. The concept of *muktzah* bans the handling of objects that could lead someone to doing work on the Sabbath. Carrying money would be a prime example of *muktzah*—something that needs to be "set apart" during the Sabbath.

5. When one looks back on the strange arc of Roth's career an answer begins to emerge. Roth similarly inserts a strange and seemingly inconse-

quential scene into *Mercy of a Rude Stream* in the figure of Mrs. Shapiro, a scene to be explained later in chapter 6.

6. Grimm's fairy tales are filled with anti-Semitic rhetoric and descriptions. Roth borrows from the more abjectly anti-Semitic of these stories. Indeed, the "pennies episode" scenes of *Call It Sleep* would seem more appropriate in a fairy tale than in a realistic novel.

7. In the boy's humorous mispronunciation of *God* for *got*, Roth not only puns on the name "God," but he also continues his ongoing textual joke with the *chad gadyah* section of the Haggadah.

8. See chapter 1 for a more thorough discussion of the Lurianic structure of *Call It Sleep*.

CONCLUSION

1. Although in *American Pastoral*, Jewish themes take a back seat to the class warfare of the 1960s, readers can see Roth more fully developing this antipastoral idea of Judaism, first glimpsed in *The Counterlife*, in his 1997 Pulitzer Prize–winning novel. Furthermore, Roth's theme of the destructive and ultimately untenable pursuit of purity and perfection is seen even more explicitly in his novel *The Human Stain* published in 2000 and made into a major motion picture in 2003.

2. This shame of being seen as "too Jewish" is reminiscent of Henry Roth's loathing of his immigrant Jewish mother in *Mercy of a Rude Stream*. This shame and fear of being seen as un-American or as a "greener," leads to his banning his mother from witnessing his high school graduation, an event she is desperate to attend. See chapter 6 for a complete discussion of this section of Roth's novel.

APPENDIX

1. Ironically, the story of Baruch Spinoza, used as a cautionary tale in Goldstein's Bais Yaacov, continued to fascinate her. Instead of turning her away from philosophy, this story ultimately led to Goldstein's writing her book, *Betraying Spinoza: The Renegade Jew Who Gave Us Modernity*.

2. Actually, *The Oxford Book of Jewish Stories*, edited by Ilan Stavans, Oxford University Press, 1998. Perhaps unique among Jewish story collections, Stavans's collection is truly international in scope. Stavans covers not just North American, European, and Israeli Jewish writers, but he also includes a fair representation of Jewish Latin American writers.

3. Alan Sokal, a New York University physicist, wrote a parody essay which he submitted for publication. Sokal's essay, "Transgressing the Boundaries: Toward a Transformative Hermeneutics of Quantum Gravity," was published in *Social Text* #46/47, pp. 217–52 (spring/summer 1996).

WORKS CITED

Abraham, Pearl. *Giving Up America*. New York: Riverhead, 1998.

Alter, Robert. "Jewishness as Metaphor." *Bernard Malamud and the Critics*. Ed. Leslie A. Field and Joyce W. Field. New York: New York University Press, 1970. 29–42.

———. *The Art of Biblical Narrative*. New York: Basic, 1981.

———. *Canon and Creativity: Modern Writing and the Authority of Scripture*. New Haven: Yale University Press, 2000.

Appelfeld, Aharon. *Badenheim, 1939*. Trans. Dalya Bilu. Boston: David R. Godine, 1980.

Ariel, David S. *What Do Jews Believe? The Spiritual Foundations of Judaism*. New York: Schocken, 1995.

Atlas, James. *Bellow: A Biography*. New York: Random House, 2000.

Babel, Isaac. *The Complete Works of Isaac Babel*. Ed. Nathalie Babel. Trans. Peter Constantine. Intro. Cynthia Ozick. New York: Norton, 2002.

Bach, Gerhard, and Gloria L. Cronin, eds. *Small Planets: Saul Bellow and the Art of Short Fiction*. East Lansing: Michigan State University Press, 2000.

Baudrillard, Jean. *Simulacra and Simulation*. Ann Arbor: University of Michigan Press, 1994.

Bellow, Saul. *The Adventures of Augie March*. New York: Viking, 1953.

———. *Mosby's Memoirs and Other Stories*. New York: Viking, 1968.

———. *Him with His Foot in His Mouth and Other Stories*. New York: Harper & Row, 1984.

———. *The Bellarosa Connection*. New York: Penguin, 1989.

———. "Summations." *Saul Bellow a Mosaic*. Ed. L. H. Goldman, Gloria L. Cronin, and Ada Aharoni. New York: Peter Lang, 1992. 185–99.

———. *Dangling Man*. 1944. New York: Penguin, 1996.

———. *Seize the Day*. 1956. New York: Penguin, 2003.

Ben Isaiah, Rabbi Abraham, and Rabbi Benjamin Sharfman. *The Pentateuch and Rashi's Commentary: A Linear Translation into English*. New York: S.S. & R., 1949.

Benjamin, Walter. *Illuminations*. New York: Schocken, 1968.

———. *Reflections*. New York: Schocken, 1978.

Berger, Alan, L. *Crisis and Covenant: The Holocaust in American Jewish Fiction*. Albany: State University of New York Press, 1985.

———. "American Jewish Fiction." *Modern Judaism* 10 (1990): 221–41.

———. "The Logic of the Heart: Biblical Identity and American Culture in Saul Bellow's 'The Old System.'" *Small Planets.* Ed. Gerhard Bach and Gloria L. Cronin. East Lansing: Michigan State University Press, 2000. 93–102.

Berger, David. *The Rebbe, the Messiah, and the Scandal of Orthodox Indifference.* London: Littman Library of Jewish Civilization, 2001.

Bhabha, Homi K. *The Location of Culture.* New York: Routledge, 1994.

Bilik, Dorothy Seidman. *Immigrant Survivors: Post-Holocaust Consciousness in Recent Jewish American Fiction.* Connecticut: Wesleyan University Press, 1981.

Bilski, Emily. *Objects of the Spirit: Ritual and the Art of Tobi Kahn.* New York: Hudson Hills, 2004.

Bloom, Harold. *The Anxiety of Influence: A Theory of Poetry.* New York: Oxford University Press, 1973.

———. *Kabbalah and Criticism.* 1975. New York: Continuum, 1999.

———. Introduction. *Musical Variations on Jewish Thought.* By Olivier Revault D'Allonnes. New York: George Braziller, 1984. 5–32.

———. Forward. *Zakhor: Jewish History and Jewish Memory.* By Yosef Hayim Yerushalmi. Seattle: University of Washington Press, 1999. xiii–xxv.

Buber, Martin. *I and Thou.* Trans. Walter Kaufman. New York: Touchstone, 1996.

Bukiet, Melvin Jules. *Strange Fire.* New York: Norton, 2001.

Burch, C. Beth. "Allegra Goodman (1967–)." *Jewish American Women Writers: A Bio-Bibliographical and Critical Sourcebook.* Ed. Ann R. Shapiro. Westport: Greenwood, 1994. 88–94.

Cassill. R.V., ed. *The Norton Anthology of Short Fiction.* New York: Norton, 1990.

Chametzky, Jules, John Felstiner, Hilene Flanzbaum, Kathryn Hellerstein, eds. *Jewish American Literature: A Norton Anthology.* New York: Norton, 2001.

Cheuse, Alan, and Nicholas Delbanco, eds. *Talking Horse: Bernard Malamud on Life and Work.* New York: Columbia University Press, 1996.

Clayton, John. *Saul Bellow: In Defense of Man.* Bloomington: Indiana University Press, 1971.

———. "A Rich Reworking." *The Saul Bellow Journal* 6.2 (Summer 1987): 19–25.

Cohen, Arthur A. *The Tremendum: A Theological Interpretation of the Holocaust.* New York: Crossroads, 1981.

Cohen, Sarah Blacher. "Adaptation In and Of Saul Bellow's 'The Old System.'" *The Saul Bellow Journal* 12.1 (Winter 1993): 108–23.

———. *Saul Bellow's Enigmatic Laughter.* Chicago: University of Illinois Press, 1974.

Connelly, Sherryl. "The Divine Miss S." *New York Daily News,* March 4, 2001: Arts and Culture 1.

————. "The Other Side of Paradise." *New York Daily News*, April 1, 2001: Showtime 20.

Cronin, Gloria L., and Ben Siegel, eds. *Conversations with Saul Bellow.* Jackson: University Press of Mississippi, 1994.

————. "Immersions in the Postmodern: The Fiction of Allegra Goodman." *Daughters of Valor: Contemporary Jewish American Women Writers.* Ed. Jay L. Halio and Ben Siegel. Newark: University of Delaware Press, 1997. 247–67.

DeLillo, Don. *Underworld.* New York: Scribner, 1997.

Diaz, Junot. *Drown.* New York: Riverhead, 1996.

Dickens, Charles. *Oliver Twist.* 1839. New York: Penguin, 1985.

————. *Bleak House.* 1853. New York: Penguin, 1996.

Dickstein, Morris. *Double Agent: The Critic and Society.* New York: Oxford University Press, 1992.

————. "Fiction and Society, 1940–1970." *The Cambridge History of American Literature Volume Seven: Prose Writing, 1940–1970.* Ed. Sacvan Bercovitch. Cambridge: Cambridge University Press, 1999. 101–310.

————. "The Complex Fate of the Jewish American Writer." *Best Contemporary Jewish Writing.* Ed. Michael Lerner. San Francisco: Jossey-Bass, 2001. 375–91.

Edidin, Peter. "He's a Literary Darling Looking for Dear Readers." *New York Times*, 25 April 2005: C3.

Englander, Nathan. *For the Relief of Unbearable Urges.* New York: Knopf, 1999.

Epstein, Rabbi Dr. I., ed. and trans. *The Babylonian Talmud in 18 Volumes.* London: Soncino, 1961.

Faulkner, William, *Collected Stories of William Faulkner.* New York: Random House, 1950.

Felman, Shoshana, and Dori Laub. *Testimony: Crises of Witnessing in Literature, Psychoanalysis, and History.* New York: Routledge, 1992.

Ferraro, Thomas J. *Ethnic Passages: Literary Immigrants in Twentieth-Century America.* Chicago: University of Chicago Press, 1993.

Fiedler, Leslie A. *Waiting for the End.* New York: Stein and Day, 1964.

Finkelstein, Norman. *The Ritual of New Creation: Jewish Tradition and Contemporary Literature.* Albany: State University of New York Press, 1992.

Flanzbaum, Hilene, ed. *The Americanization of the Holocaust.* Baltimore: Johns Hopkins University Press, 1999.

Furman, Andrew. *Israel through the Jewish-American Imagination: A Survey of Jewish-American Literature on Israel, 1928–1995.* Albany: State University of New York Press, 1997.

————. *Contemporary Jewish American Writers and the Multicultural Dilemma: Return of the Exiled.* Syracuse: Syracuse University Press, 2000.

Genette, Gerard. *Narrative Discourse: An Essay in Method.* Trans. Jane E. Lewin. Forward by Jonathan Culler. Ithaca: Cornell University Press, 1980.

Giller, Pinchas. *Reading the Zohar: The Sacred Text of Kabbalah.* New York: Oxford University Press, 2001.

Goldberg, Myla. *Bee Season*. New York: Doubleday, 2000.

Goldstein, Rebecca. "Writing the Second Novel: A Symposium." *New York Times Book Review*, March 17, 1985.

———. *The Late Summer Passion of a Woman of Mind*. 1989. New York: Vintage, 1990.

———. *The Dark Sister*. New York: Viking, 1991.

———. "Looking Back at Lot's Wife." *Commentary*, September (1992): 37–41.

———. *The Mind-Body Problem*. 1983. New York: Penguin, 1993.

———. *Strange Attractors*. New York: Viking, 1993.

———. *Mazel*. New York: Viking, 1995.

———. Personal Interview by Ezra Cappell. Hudson Hotel, New York: 16 Oct. 2000.

———. *Properties of Light*. New York: Houghton Mifflin, 2000.

———. "Against Logic." *Best Contemporary Jewish Writing*. Ed. Michael Lerner. San Francisco: Jossey-Bass, 2001. 367–70.

———. *Betraying Spinoza: The Renegade Jew Who Gave Us Modernity*. New York: Shocken, 2006.

Goodman, Allegra. *The Family Markowitz*. New York: Farrar, Straus and Giroux, 1996.

———. "The Story of Rachel." *Genesis: As It Is Written: Contemporary Writers on Our First Stories*. Ed. David Rosenberg. New York: HarperCollins, 1996. 169–78.

———. "Writing Jewish Fiction In and Out of the Multicultural Context." *Daughters of Valor: Contemporary Jewish American Women Writers*. Ed. Jay L. Halio and Ben Siegel. Newark: University of Delaware Press, 1997. 268–74.

———. *Kaaterskill Falls*. New York: Dial, 1998.

———. *Total Immersion*. 1989. New York: Delta, 1998.

———. "O.K., You're Not Shakespeare. Now Get Back to Work." *New York Times*, March 12, 2001: E1.

———. *Paradise Park*. New York: Dial, 2001.

———. *Intuition*. New York: Dial, 2006.

Goodman, Walter. "The Return of the Schlemiel." Rev. of *The Complete Stories*, by Bernard Malamud. *New York Times*, 28 Sept. 1997, late ed.

Gurock, Jeffrey. *American Jewish Orthodoxy in Historical Perspective*. New Jersey: Ktav, 1996.

Guttmann, Allen. *The Jewish Writer in America: Assimilation and the Crisis of Identity*. New York: Oxford University Press, 1971.

Haidu, Peter. "The Dialectics of Unspeakability: Language, Silence, and the Narratives of Desubjectification." *Probing the Limits of Representation: Nazism and the "Final Solution."* Ed. Saul Friedlander. Cambridge: Harvard University Press, 1992. 277–99.

Hallamish, Moshe. *An Introduction to the Kabbalah*. New York: State University of New York Press, 1999.

Harper, Phillip Brian. *Framing the Margins: The Social Logic of Postmodern Culture.* New York: Oxford University Press, 1994.

Howe, Irving. *Jewish-American Stories.* Ed. and intro. by Irving Howe. New York: New American Library, 1977.

Jameson, Frederic. *Postmodernism; or, The Cultural Logic of Late Capitalism.* Durham: Duke University Press, 1991.

Johnson, Gregory. "Jewish Assimilation and Codes of Manners in Saul Bellow's 'The Old System.'" *Studies in American Jewish Literature* 9.1 (Spring 1990): 48–60.

Katz, Jacob. *The "Shabbes Goy": A Study in Halakhic Flexibility.* Trans. Yoel Lerner. Philadelphia: Jewish Publication Society, 1989.

Kaufman, Michael T. "Jan Karski Dies at 86; Warned West about Holocaust." *New York Times,* 15 July 2000: C15.

Kauver, Elaine M. "An Interview with Cynthia Ozick." *Contemporary Literature* xxxiv.3 (1993): 359–94.

Klingenstein, Susanne. "Destructive Intimacy: The Shoah between Mother and Daughter in Fictions by Cynthia Ozick, Norma Rosen, and Rebecca Goldstein." *Studies in American Jewish Literature* 11.2 (Fall 1992): 162–73.

———. "Visits to Germany in Recent Jewish-American Writing." *Contemporary Literature* 34.3 (1993): 538–70.

Kramer, Peter. "Interview of Allegra Goodman." *Forward,* May 11, 2001: 10–12.

Kreilkamp, Ivan. *Writing for Your Life #4,* Ed. Jonathan Bing. New York: *Publisher's Weekly,* 2000. 74–78.

Kremer, Lillian. *Witness Through the Imagination: Jewish American Holocaust Literature.* Detroit: Wayne State University Press, 1989.

Lang, Berel. "The Representation of Limits." *Probing the Limits of Representation.* Ed. Saul Friedlander. Cambridge, Mass.: Harvard University Press, 1992. 300–17.

———. *Holocaust Representation: Art within the Limits of History and Ethics.* Baltimore: Johns Hopkins University Press, 2000.

Lanzmann, Claude. *Shoah: An Oral History of the Holocaust.* New York: Pantheon, 1985.

Lasher, Lawrence. "Narrative Strategy in Malamud's 'The German Refugee.'" *Studies in American Jewish Literature* 9.1 (Spring 1990): 73–83.

Lerner, Michael, ed. and intro. *Best Contemporary Jewish Writing.* San Francisco: Jossey-Bass, 2001. xiii–xxvii.

Levi, Primo. *Survival in Auschwitz.* 1958. New York: Touchstone, 1996.

Levinas, Emmanuel. *Difficult Freedom: Essays on Judaism.* Trans. Sean Hand. Baltimore: Johns Hopkins University Press, 1990.

———. "Loving the Torah More Than God." Afterword. *Yosl Rakover Talks to God.* By Zvi Kolitz. New York: Pantheon, 1999. 79–87.

Lieber, Moshe. *The Pirkei Avos Treasury: Ethics of the Fathers: The Sages' Guide to Living with an Anthologized Commentary and Anecdotes.* New York: Mesorah, 1995.

Liptzin, Sol. *The Jew in American Literature.* New York: Bloch, 1966.

Lyons, Bonnie. *Henry Roth: The Man and His Work.* New York: Cooper Square, 1976.

Lyotard, Jean-Francois, and Eberhard Gruber. *The Hyphen: Between Judaism and Christianity.* Trans. Pacale-Anne Brault and Michael Nass. New York: Humanity, 1999.

Malamud, Bernard. *The Assistant.* New York: Avon, 1957.

——. *The Complete Stories.* New York: Farrar, Straus, & Giroux, 1997.

Materassi, Mario. "Shifting Urbanscape: Roth's 'Private' New York." *New Essays on Call It Sleep.* Ed. Hana Wirth-Nesher. Cambridge: Cambridge University Press, 1996. 29–59.

Mirsky, Mark. *Thou Worm Jacob.* New York: Macmillan, 1967.

——. *My Search for the Messiah: Studies and Wanderings in Israel and America.* New York: Macmillan, 1977.

Mirsky, Yehudah. "The Difficulty of Orthodox Fiction." *Response: A Contemporary Jewish Review* 65 (Winter/Spring 1996): 30–35.

Mirvis, Tova. *The Ladies Auxiliary.* New York: Norton, 1999.

——. *The Outside World.* New York: Knopf, 2004.

——. "Orthodox Jews in Fiction." *New York Times,* 27 Feb. 2005: Sec. 7, Col 3, p. 4.

Novick, Peter. *The Holocaust in American Life.* New York: Houghton Mifflin, 1999.

O'Connor, Flannery. *Collected Works.* New York: Library of America, 1988.

Ozick, Cynthia. "A Liberal's Auschwitz." *The Pushcart Prize: Best of the Small Presses.* Ed. Bill Henderson. Yonkers: Pushcart, 1976.

——. *The Cannibal Galaxy.* New York: Knopf, 1983.

——. *The Pagan Rabbi and Other Stories.* New York: Penguin, 1983.

——. "What's a Jewish Book? Promoting Virtue through Learning." *Forward,* Oct. 26, 2001: B1+.

——. *Heir to the Glimmering World.* New York: Houghton Mifflin, 2004.

Patell, Cyrus. "Emergent Literatures." *The Cambridge History of American Literature.* Ed. Sacvan Bercovitch. Cambridge: Cambridge University Press, 1999. 539–716.

——. *Negative Liberties: Morrison, Pynchon, and the Problem of Liberal Ideology.* Durham: Duke University Press, 2001.

Pelikan, Jaroslav, ed. *Sacred Writings Volume I Judaism: The Tanakh.* New York: Jewish Publication Society, 1985.

Pinsker, Sanford. "Satire, Social Realism, and Moral Seriousness: The Case of Allegra Goodman." *Studies in American Jewish Literature* 11.2 (1992): 182–94.

Podhoretz, Norman. "Bellow at 85, Roth at 67." *Commentary* 111.1 (July–August 2000): 35–43.

Posnock, Ross. "Purity and Danger: On Philip Roth." *Raritan* 21.2 (Fall 2001): 85–101.

Potok, Chaim. *The Chosen*. New York: Simon & Schuster, 1967.

Pynchon, Thomas. *The Crying of Lot 49*. 1966. New York: Harper & Row, 1986.

Rosen, Jonathan. *The Talmud and the Internet: A Journey Between Worlds*. New York: Farrar, Strauss, & Giroux, 2000.

———. "Orthodox Jews in Fiction." *New York Times*, 27 Feb. 2005: Sec. 7, Col. 3, p. 4.

Rosenbaum, Thane. *Elijah Visible*. New York: St. Martin's, 1996.

———. *Second Hand Smoke*. New York: St. Martin's Press, 1999.

———. The Golems of Gotham. New York: HarperCollins, 2002.

Roskies, David G. "Jazz and Jewspeech: The Anatomy of Yiddish in American Jewish Culture." *Ideology and Jewish Identity in Israeli and American Literature*. Ed. Emily Miller Budick. Albany: State University of New York Press, 2001. 131–46.

Roth, Henry. *Call It Sleep*. 1934. New York: Avon, 1991.

———. *Shifting Landscape*. New York: Jewish Publication Society, 1987.

———. *Mercy of a Rude Stream Volume I: A Star Shines over Mt. Morris Park*. New York: St. Martin's, 1994.

———. *Mercy of a Rude Stream Volume II: A Diving Rock on the Hudson*. New York: St. Martin's, 1995.

———. *Mercy of a Rude Stream Volume III: From Bondage*. New York: St. Martin's, 1996.

———. *Mercy of a Rude Stream Volume IV: Requiem for Harlem*. New York: St. Martin's, 1998.

Roth, Philip. *The Counterlife*. New York: Farrar, Straus, & Giroux, 1986.

———. *American Pastoral*. New York: Vintage, 1997.

———. *The Human Stain*. New York: Houghton Mifflin, 2000.

———. *The Plot Against America*. New York: Houghton Mifflin, 2004.

———. *Everyman*. New York: Houghton Mifflin, 2006.

Rothstein, Mervyn. "Bernard Malamud, Author Dies at 71." *New York Times*, 20 Mar. 1986, late ed., D26.

Rovit, Earl H. "The Jewish Literary Tradition." *Bernard Malamud and the Critics*. Ed. Leslie A. Field and Joyce W. Field. New York: New York University Press, 1970. 3–10.

Rubenstein, Jeffrey L. *Talmudic Stories: Narrative Art, Composition, and Culture*. Baltimore: Johns Hopkins University Press, 1999.

———. *Rabbinic Stories*. New York: Paulist, 2002.

Scholem, Gershom. *Major Trends in Jewish Mysticism*. 1941. New York: Schocken, 1995.

Shalit, Wendy. "The Observant Reader." *New York Times*, 30 Jan. 2005: Sec. 7, Col. 2, p. 16.

Shapiro, Gerald. *Bad Jews and Other Stories*. Cambridge: Zoland, 1999.

Shechner, Mark. "Literature in Search of a Center." *Divisions between Traditionalism and Liberalism in the American Jewish Community: Cleft or Chasm.* Ed. Michael Shapiro. Lewiston: Mellen, 1991. 79–105.

Shteyngart, Gary. *The Russian Debutante's Handbook*. New York: Riverhead, 2002.

——— . *Absurdistan*. New York: Random House, 2006.

Siegel, Lee. "Seize the Day Job: Sacrificing Saul Bellow on the Altar of One's Own Career." *Harper's Magazine* 302.1819 (March 2001): 75–83.

Sollors, Werner. *Beyond Ethnicity: Consent and Descent in American Culture.* New York: Oxford University Press, 1986.

——— , ed. *The Invention of Ethnicity*. New York: Oxford University Press, 1989.

Solomon, Deborah. "Designer Death Camp: Questions for Tom Sachs." *New York Times Magazine*, March 10, 2002: 19.

Solotaroff, Theodore. "Bernard Malamud's Fiction: The Old Life and the New." *Commentary* 33.3 (March 1962): 197–201.

Soloveitchik, Joseph B. *Halakhic Man*. Philadelphia: Jewish Publication Society, 1983.

——— . *Fate and Destiny: From Holocaust to the State of Israel*. New York: Ktav, 1992.

——— . *The Lonely Man of Faith*. New York: Doubleday, 1992.

Steinsaltz, Adin. *The Essential Talmud*. London: Weidenfeld & Nicolson, 1976.

Stern, Steve. *The Wedding Jester*. Minnesota: Graywolf, 1999.

——— . *The Angel of Forgetfulness*. New York: Viking, 2005.

Suggs, Jack M. et al., eds. *The Oxford Study Bible*. New York: Oxford University Press, 1992.

Telushkin, Rabbi Joseph. *Jewish Literacy*. New York: William Morrow, 1991.

Updike, John. *Rabbit Run*. 1960. New York: Knopf, 1995.

Vapnyar, Lara. *There Are Jews in My House*. New York: Pantheon, 2003.

Veale, Scott. "New and Noteworthy Paperbacks." *New York Times*, Aug. 22, 1999. Sec. 7, Col. 1, p. 28.

Venkateswarlu, D. *Jewish-American Writers and Intellectual Life in America.* New Delhi: Prestige, 1993.

Whitman, Walt. *Leaves of Grass*. 1892. New York: Signet Classic, 1980.

Wilde, Oscar. *The Picture of Dorian Gray*. 1891. New York: Penguin, 1985.

Wilson, Jonathan. *On Bellow's Planet: Readings from the Dark Side*. Teaneck: Fairleigh Dickinson University Press, 1985.

Wirth-Nesher, Hana, ed. *What is Jewish Literature?* Philadelphia: Jewish Publication Society, 1994.

————, ed. *New Essays on Call It Sleep*. New York: Cambridge University Press, 1996.

————. "Liturgy in Recent Jewish American Literature." *Ideology and Jewish Identity in Israeli and American Literature*. Ed. Emily Miller Budick. Albany: State University of New York Press, 2001. 115–30.

Wisse, Ruth. *The Modern Jewish Canon: A Journey through Language and Culture*. New York: The Free Press, 2000.

————. "What's a Jewish Book? Honest Reflections of Moral Collapse." *Forward*, Oct. 26, 2001: B1+.

Yeats, W. B. *The Collected Poems of W. B. Yeats*. 1956. New York: Macmillan, 1970.

Yerushalmi, Yosef Hayim. *Zakhor: Jewish History and Jewish Memory*. 1982. Seattle: University of Washington Press, 1996.

INDEX